DISTINCTION

TEACHER'S BOOK

ENGLISH
FOR ADVANCED
LEARNERS

MARK FOLEY ▪ DIANE HALL

Nelson

Longman Group Limited
Longman House, Burnt Mill, Harlow,
Essex CM20 2JE, England
and Associated Companies throughout the world.

© Mark Foley and Diane Hall 1993

First published by Thomas Nelson and Sons Ltd 1993

This impression Longman Group Ltd. 1995

ISBN 0-17-556396-9

Printed in China

Contents

Introduction   4

1   Playing the Game   11

2   Rogues' Gallery   17

3   The Risk Factor   22

4   All in the Mind   28

5   English Everywhere   35

6   A Question of Morals   41

7   Learning Experiences   47

8   Round the World   52

9   You are What You Eat   57

10   Talk to the Animals   62

11   Watching Brief   69

12   Fakes and Frauds   76

13   Weather or Not   82

14   The Secret of Life   90

15   Children's Language   96

16   The Written Word   101

17   Let the Good Times Roll   107

18   The Art of Selling   112

19   Personal Space   118

20   A Changing Language   122

What is *Distinction*?

Distinction is a comprehensive course for advanced learners of English as a foreign language. It is aimed at students who have reached the standard of the Cambridge First Certificate Examination and who have taken the exam, or who have followed a course at that level. It is a general course, concentrating on consolidating students' existing command of English and extending it into more advanced structures, but it covers the structures and skills necessary for the Cambridge Certificate in Advanced English and provides exam-specific exercises in the workbook, which will be useful for students intending to take that exam.

The Students' Book provides between 120 and 180 classroom hours with another 40 to 50 hours of self study in the Workbook. It is intended for adult (and young adult) learners.

One of the main aims of *Distinction* is to provide advanced learners with stimulating, accessible but challenging material and with interactive, communicative tasks which will broaden the students' general knowledge as well as extending their English, but without imposing upon them material or tasks which are too intellectual or too academic. Advanced learners are often frustrated because they feel that they are not progressing as fast as they would like to, because they assume that they should be communicating at a near-native speaker standard (which is often not the case), and because they are often faced with both materials and language that they assume they have 'already done'. Part of this is inevitable, but *Distinction* aims to reduce these feelings of frustration by combining interesting (and often 'new') input materials with a variety of realistic, communicative tasks which further the thematic development of the unit, and with a guided discovery approach to language which should help students to feel in control of their learning.

What does *Distinction* consist of?

The course comprises the Students' Book, Workbook, Teacher's Book and a set of two Cassettes.

Students' Book: full breakdown of the course, twenty theme-based units, a Grammar Reference section giving comprehensive information about the structures presented in the course and selected tapescripts.

Workbook: twenty units developing the themes of the units from the Students' Book, providing support in reading, vocabulary, grammar and writing. Many exercises follow the format of the CAE exam.

Teacher's Book: full introduction to the course, detailed teaching notes, especially for task types which teachers may not be familiar with, answers, tapescripts and suggestions for extra activities where appropriate.

Cassettes: all listening material, much of which is authentic (unscripted), in the form of monologues, dialogues, interviews, group conversations, panel discussions; and pronunciation models where necessary.

The Students' Book

The twenty units are based on topics as diverse as popular culture, fakes and forgeries, world travel, moral dilemmas and perceptions of reality. Four of the units are based on topics connected with language: language spread and language learning, animal communication, children's language and the development of English. Students who reach advanced level in a foreign language are generally interested in language itself, and these topics are intended both to provide areas within the students' sphere of experience for discussion and to extend students' understanding of the working of language in general.

Each unit contains at least one (usually two) major grammar points, often with the second extending the first (e.g. Unit 13 revises the three main conditionals and then goes on to present the common mixed conditional forms); development of each skill (reading, writing, speaking, listening) by focussing on particular elements of the skill; vocabulary extension and a number of communicative tasks. Most units contain pronunciation work, work on register, study skills and often language awareness exercises.

There is no particular format to a unit, but a typical unit contains the following sections (not necessarily in this order):

Introduction
The first activity in each unit is an interactive task which aims to get students thinking and speaking about the topic. This may be a quiz, a questionnaire, a problem-solving task, or simply a discussion-based exercise.

Language work
This is the section which concentrates on grammatical input. There are two Language work sections in most units. This usually consists of examples of the language drawn from the input material (or asks students to go back and analyse something in the input text), questions which lead students to thinking about the language and formulating rules, and one or two exercises to practise the language. (There are always further practice exercises in the Workbook.)

Reading
Each unit contains at least one section based specifically on developing the skills within reading: for example, reading for gist and detail, understanding text reference, or finding evidence to support statements about the text. There is usually more than one reading text in a unit, but they are not all vehicles for developing the reading skill. There is considerable further reading material with various forms of exploitation in the Workbook.

Listening
Each unit contains at least one section based specifically on developing the skills within listening: for example, listening to form judgements, identifying situations, speakers and functions, or listening for individual words. Again, there may be listening material within a unit that is not a vehicle for developing the listening skill, but presents language or develops the theme.

Speaking
Each unit contains one section based on developing aspects of speaking: for example, checking and clarifying, paraphrasing, expressing annoyance and regrets, or using fillers. These sections often deal with aspects of register. They are not the only section in each unit to deal with communication, as the majority of exercises in each unit has a communicative aim.

Pronunciation

This does not come under the heading of Speaking. Most units contain some work on pronunciation. For advanced students we feel that this should not be restricted to phoneme practice but should concentrate on connected speech. The phoneme work in the syllabus has, therefore, been limited to two sections which examine the relationship in English between the eighteen full vowel and dipthong sounds and their written representations. The other pronunciation work focusses on features such as assimilation, word stress, sentence stress and linking.

Writing

The organisation of the units in *Distinction* is partly based on a writing syllabus. There is, therefore, one writing section in each unit, which concentrates on a particular component skill within writing (e.g. punctuation or using text reference) or on a type of writing needed both in exams and in 'real-life' (e.g. personal and formal letters, narrative or summary writing). The three academic essay types – comparative, expository and discursive – are also covered. The Workbook contains further practice of the writing skills presented in the Students' Book.

Vocabulary

Each unit contains at least one section focussing on vocabulary. This may be: vocabulary extension, for example, word groups and mind maps; vocabulary organisation, for example, categorising; or methods of understanding new vocabulary, for example, understanding bias and guessing meaning from context.

Study skills/language awareness

Many units contain one of these sections.

Study skills sections concentrate on areas of language which will help students learn independently, such as understanding collocation, dictionary work and word formation.

Language awareness sections (often in the four language awareness units) concentrate on aspects of language which may be of interest to students, for example, words with multiple meanings; homonyms, homographs and homophones.

Clearly, in an integrated course, it is not always possible to separate each skill/section, and for this reason there is often an overlap between the sections, and the distinction between, for example, a vocabulary exercise and a language awareness exercise may sometimes be blurred.

Final task

Each unit ends with a final task, which is always communicative and multi-skill based. These tasks include activities such as reading jigsaws, debates, writing a children's story, devising a travel advert, and a board game.

In addition to these regular sections, there is systematic development of multi-word verbs, and a coverage of idioms. The idioms appear occasionally in the Students' Book, but more often in the Workbook, and are always grouped according to topic, for example, idioms concerned with the weather, with crime, with illusion and reality.

See page 29 of this book for information about the development of multi-word verbs.

Grammar reference section

This contains descriptions, examples and analysis of the structures presented in the course and should provide useful back-up for the students. When a structure is presented, the rules are always given or 'discovered' in the unit, but the grammar reference section gives more information and examples, which may be useful if students need to check anything or for revision purposes.

Tapescripts

The tapescripts are in the Teacher's Book, with a few exceptions. In most cases the listening exercises are purely for listening purposes, and the students do not need the scripts. However, in a few cases, it is useful for the students to refer to the script, for example, in Unit 11 when they have to compare a spoken and written review of the same film. These particular tapescripts have been included at the back of the book.

A note about examinations

Distinction is not intended to be a course specially designed to prepare students for any particular advanced examination. However, the Students' Book teaches and practises all the skill areas specified for the Cambridge Certificate in Advanced English and contains exploitation exercises similar to those found in the examination.

The Workbook

Each Workbook unit contains four sections:

Reading

This section incudes one or more passages linked to the topic of the Students' Book, with two or three exercises based on it. The exercises are often matching or multiple choice, as in the CAE exam, and are intended to help students get used to the idea of reading quickly and responding to fairly passive question types.

Vocabulary

This section develops the vocabulary of the unit and often takes it further, for example, providing idioms based on the theme of the unit, or revises it in an enjoyable way, for example as a crossword. It sometimes takes vocabulary from the reading passages in the Workbook.

English in use

This section provides practice in the structural points presented in the Students' Book, again often following exercise types in the CAE exam, such as finding errors and correcting sentences. It also provides some more traditional grammatical practice, such as sentence transformation and gap-filling.

Writing

This takes the writing skill/task of the unit and provides more practice in the form of both 'essay' writing and guided writing. There are usually three exercises, one of which will provide two or three options. Many of the writing exercises require responses to realistic input material and the tasks provide real reasons for writing. It is suggested that you choose which the students should do according to the needs of your course/ students. Most of the writing tasks require individual responses and should be taken in and marked. Many of the writing tasks reflect those found in the CAE Examination.

Key

A Key is provided in the book so that it can be used for self study. This contains all the answers to exercises in the first three sections, but not the writing exercises unless a very clear model is possible.

Methodology

Distinction uses a variety of different presentation and practice techniques and does not rely on any one methodology. The notes below are not intended to be a comprehensive guide to techniques in advanced teaching, but to provide a few ideas for the classroom which will be useful in teaching *Distinction*.

Classroom management

Distinction uses a number of configurations in the classroom. While most of the presentation and 'input' material can be approached with students working independently, much of the practice material is communicative, based on information gap, opinion gap or simulation and students will need to work in pairs or groups. It is useful to devise one or two very quick ways of dividing the class into pairs or groups, in order not to waste class time. This is dependent on whether your students can move around the class or not. If this is possible, then you can create pairs or groups by designating part of the class A, part B, part C etc, and then telling students to move around into A/B/C groups. This is more effective than allowing students to form groups around their seats, as it makes it possible for students to work with different partners. If your students have to remain in their seats, pairs can be formed by students working one day with the student on their right, the next day with the student on their left, the next day with the student in front, etc.

Several of the group exercises state a specific number of students per group, which may not always be possible. If the exercise states groups of three, for example, it is possible for some groups to be four students, with two students taking the role of C. If there is any reason for two students to take one role rather than another, it is stated in the teaching notes.

Many of the communicative tasks in *Distinction* involve material printed at the back of the Students' Book. Where students are directed to this material, ensure that each student reads only his/her role and does not look at the other roles. While students are working with this material, all communication should be oral and in English only; discourage students from showing each other their information and encourage them to explain, exemplify or demonstrate in order to make themselves understood.

Teaching grammar at advanced level

Advanced-level students of English generally have a very good passive command of the foundations of grammar, often combined with a reasonably good active command but a few 'fossilised' errors (i.e. habitual errors which they make consistently). What they need from an advanced course is practice in the major structures, analysis of those structures and comparison with other structures, as well as introduction to some of the more advanced structures and nuances of the English language. Students who have attained this level often get pleasure from thinking about the language as well as using it, and it is for this reason that *Distinction* presents and practises grammar to a great extent by the use of the guided discovery (or inductive) approach, i.e. presenting students with examples of the language and asking them to make hypotheses based on these. When you meet this type of exercise in your teaching, allow time for the students to think about the questions asked. The questions provided have been constructed in such a way that the students will generally be able to answer them and to understand the concepts quite easily. Allow them time to think about the questions, to ask you for help if necessary, and to form their own hypotheses, but steer them in the right direction if you see that they are

forming an incorrect hypothesis. Once you feel students have understood, refer them to the Grammar Reference section, which will confirm their ideas and give them more information. They can look at this either to help them while they are working on the exercises, or after doing them as a way of reinforcing what they have learnt.

Distinction provides a balance of 'old' and 'new' structures for the students. Most units will have some form of revision, often done in a way that might be new to the students. For example, Unit 1 examines the continuous tenses, looking at common meanings among the continuous tenses. This approach helps students to understand the relationships between different aspects of the language, and provides revision in a way which should be novel and challenging.

One of the aims of *Distinction* is to help students to be active in their learning. The approach to grammar embodies this, as can be seen from the approach to multi-word verbs. Unit 4 examines multi-word verbs both grammatically (looking at the position of nouns/pronouns in relation to the verbs) and semantically (looking at the meanings inherent in some particles). A chart is provided for students to register all the new multi-word verbs that they come across, in such a way that will help them understand the meanings of the words. Encourage students to use this chart, and to transfer it to their own books once the chart in the book is full.

Authentic input texts

The majority of the reading texts and about sixty per cent of the listening texts are 'authentic', i.e. they have been extracted from original sources and have not been adapted. The reading texts come from sources such as newspapers, magazines, novels, publicity materials, academic books, children's books and manuals. The listening texts are a mixture of interviews, monologues and group conversations. In all of these cases there will be some language that is unfamiliar to the students. Encourage students to read or listen for the global meaning when they first approach a reading text or listening passage (unless otherwise directed in the teaching notes), and discourage them from looking up new words in a dictionary. Explain to students that the exercises following the text will usually be constructed in such a way that they will be led to understanding the (key) new vocabulary and from there to understanding the text. Where some words or phrases may be particularly problematic, for example, where reference is made to items culturally specific to the English-speaking world, there are suggestions for pre-teaching in the teaching notes.

Recording vocabulary

One of the major ways of consolidating and extending language knowledge at advanced level is to present students with a lot of new vocabulary. However, this is only useful if students are encouraged to record the new vocabulary in a logical and helpful way (and shown how to do this if necessary). There is a lot of work in *Distinction* on meaning groups, word associations and definitions, which will help students to consider relationships between words. These exercises may also help them record their vocabulary logically. Encourage them to have a separate vocabulary book, which is divided into sections according to meaning (as opposed to alphabetical). Entries could be made across double pages under the headings listed below.

word	meaning	example	related words
innov'ation	something new	*The use of sound in the cinema was an innovation in the 1920s*	'innovate (verb), 'innovative (adjective)

Correction and marking

It is inevitable that students will make a number of errors while they are carrying out the linguistic/communicative tasks in the course. It is likely to demotivate them if you correct every single error that is made; it is, therefore, best to select what to correct when (and how). In exercises which are intended to practise a particular structure, concentrate on correcting errors in that structure. Likewise, in exercises that are generally practising accuracy, concentrate on any more wide-ranging errors in linguistic structure. It is best, however, to vary the method of correcting.

Often, especially at this level, a simple signal to indicate that something is wrong, for example, raising the eyebrows, is enough to make the student go back and correct him/herself. If he/she is unable to do so, encourage other students to supply the correction. If, however, time is short, then you may need to offer the correction yourself. If so, repeat the whole context of the error, correctly, so that students can hear exactly what the correct version is.

If you are concentrating on fluency, rather than accuracy-based work, such as information gaps, roleplays, discussions, it is often best not to interrupt too often and disturb the flow. Interrupt only if the errors are preventing communication. Otherwise monitor and make a list of the more serious/persistent errors for discussion at the end of the lesson/activity. A useful exercise is to write out and copy errors from a discussion, hand them out in the next lesson for students to discuss and correct or to correct for homework. If the facilities are available, recording communicative activities on audio- or videotape and playing this back later will allow the students to identify and correct their own or their colleagues' errors, a process which is more effective than simply telling students where their errors are.

Written work is a different matter. Ideally, all written work should be corrected. For written work done in the lesson, you will probably be able to circulate, read and correct while students are writing. As far as homework is concerned, you will probably have to take in and correct individual written work. Exercises from the Workbook can be checked by the students (using the Key), with discussion of any problems afterwards. If grammatical exercises from the Students' Book are given as homework, you could prepare a key on the board/OHP for checking, or take in a few of the students' answers for checking. Students then circulate the correct answers for all of them to check. Make sure that you use a consistent system for correcting written work, perhaps indicating the type of error by a code, for example, *sp* = spelling, *t* = tense, and allowing students to attempt the corrections themselves, checking with you only if they can't understand what they have done wrong.

An aspect of correcting written work that should be encouraged is editing and self-correction before the work is submitted to you. (It is particularly useful for students intending to take examinations.) This is taught formally in Unit 16 of *Distinction*, but you might find it useful to look at the guidelines in that unit and select some for the students to integrate into their writing from the beginning. For example, they should always make a draft copy of a written exercise, and read it through two or three times before writing it out, each time looking for different things, such as spelling mistakes in the first reading, tense/grammar errors in the second, and vocabulary/style improvements in the third. Once students are used to doing this, it can be extended by getting them to check each other's work, especially any writing done in the classroom. Applying the techniques above to another person's work is often easier than applying them to one's own, and can be very constructive. You should, however, judge with each class whether or not this is viable, depending on the atmosphere and relationships within the class, i.e. do not attempt this in a class where students are likely to be uncooperative, too competitive or over-critical of each other. You should also ensure that you take in any self- or peer-corrected written work for a final check.

Tackling the language skills

The four language skills are dealt with systematically in *Distinction* (See pages 4 – 5.) This section will not attempt to describe skills work in detail, as the teaching notes for individual exercises do that. It will instead provide a simple overview of a general skills approach at advanced level.

Reading

As a general rule, a reading text should be approached globally first (i.e. students read to understand the gist) and examined more thoroughly for detail later. This procedure is usually followed in *Distinction*, except in activities such as reading jigsaws (where each student in a group reads a different text in order to pool information orally and complete a task, such as filling in a chart or solving a problem) or where the text is considered easy enough not to present any difficulties whatsoever to students of this level.

At advanced level, reading texts are likely to be quite long and can be very time-consuming in class. It is worth assessing in advance which text(s) you are likely to be covering in any one lesson, and setting the initial reading as a homework task, accompanied by the first exercise or two.

Listening

Like reading, listening texts can be approached globally first and then repeated for more detailed comprehension. The teaching notes state the procedure to be used and say if the text needs only one or several listenings. This often depends on the complexity of the task. For example, where students are asked to analyse a spoken review (Units 11 and 17), they will probably need to listen to it several times before they are in a position to do so.

There are some ways of making the actual method of listening, as opposed to the passage or the task more 'authentic'. For example, with texts where one listening will be enough, refuse to replay it, as in real life the students are likely to be able only to listen once. Another possibility is to allow students to take control of the listening: one student takes control of the cassette recorder, and stops the tape/replays sections at the request of other students, or at the agreed request of the whole class.

Speaking

Most speaking exercises in *Distinction* are quite tightly controlled in order to provide practice in a specific skill or function. In these cases, the teaching notes provide the procedure. In free speaking/discussion exercises, it may be worth employing certain strategies to ensure that all students get a chance to speak. A simple way of doing this is the 'pyramid' technique: the students discuss the topic in pairs first, so that they can assemble some ideas; they then move into groups of four, where they repeat their opinions but maybe revise slightly what they are saying. Finally the topic is discussed as a class. By this time, even the most reticent students will have formulated the language to express their opinions and should feel happier about talking in front of the class.

You may wish to structure discussions more thoroughly sometimes. There are several ways of doing this. One way is to prepare beforehand a few slips of paper with statements on them about various aspects of the topic. You can provoke animated discussion by using controversial statements. These are then handed out to students in pairs, who discuss only their statements. This ensures that the discussion which follows will be broader and last longer, because the class has been given the chance to focus on a wide variety of aspects of the topic and every student has considered one in depth.

A couple of techniques for even more structured discussions are the shadow discussion and the 'shifting' roleplay. The shadow discussion involves arranging the classroom furniture in a circle (or two). Half the class (group) sits on the chairs in the circle. The other half stands behind those sitting down. The discussion commences. At various points in the discussion, clap your hands (or use a similar signal) and the standing students take the chairs, while those who were seated get up and stand behind them. The discussion has to continue from exactly the same point. This technique ensures that students listen to what is going on, as they may have to continue the conversation at any point.

The 'shifting' roleplay is an extension of this and can be done with a real roleplay or with a discussion. In this, the class configuration is the same, with a large circle (or two/three circles), but with all students sitting down. In this discussion, however, the role/opinion is assigned to the chair, not the student, i.e. the first student sitting on a chair 'gives' the chair its role. At a given signal, such as a handclap, the students all move one place to the left and then continue the discussion, but presenting the opinion of the 'chair'. This activity also involves very intensive listening. It can be combined with a shadow discussion if you have students standing behind the chairs as well. In this case you will need two signals – one to mean 'move to the left', one to mean 'swap with the person behind you'.

Writing

Some aspects of writing have been dealt with under correcting and marking. To minimise errors, writing tasks presented in the Students' Book of *Distinction* provide a model for the students to follow. It is wise for students, even at this level, to follow the model when they first tackle a new type of writing. They can then attempt a similar, but less controlled, example of the task from the questions in the Workbook.

Some of the activities in *Distinction* involve group writing. This is an activity that can be applied to all types of writing, and that can be very satisfying if done 'correctly', i.e. with true cooperation. In these activities, keep the groups fairly small (three/four), otherwise some students will get bored. The group should discuss the structure of the writing and its content together, before attempting the actual writing. For this, two techniques can be used: either each student in the group takes a different role, such as formulating the sentences, checking vocabulary/grammar, physically writing, editing the draft etc.; or each student can do part of the writing, such as one paragraph, which he/she then swaps with another student for editing/correction. In both cases, one student will have to write up the good copy. This is one activity where it is worth keeping the same groups for a number of tasks: students can then take turns in writing up the copy. If you have an overhead projector (OHP) in the classroom, it will be possible for groups to copy their written work onto OHP transparencies. These can then be shown to the whole class for feedback/discussion and peer-group correction.

Pronunciation

Distinction assumes that most students at this level will have more or less mastered the phonemic distinctions in English, and will not need a great deal of minimal pair practice. If this is not the case, refer to books which have minimal pair practice for ideas (for example *Ship or Sheep/Tree or Three*, or the Nelson *Skill of Speaking* series). The pronunciation work in *Distinction* is much more concerned with features of connected speech, such as contrastive stress, assimilation, intonation, etc. Models are provided on tape for all pronunciation work (unless it is totally receptive) and the teaching notes provide guidelines not only for teaching the features, but for describing them if necessary. The golden rule with pronunciation is always to present something receptively first, and never to try to get students to produce something they really can't hear, as it will be a demotivating, wasted exercise. If you are very unhappy about teaching pronunciation, for whatever reason, you will be able to omit the pronunciation exercises in *Distinction* without seriously disrupting the flow of the units, but we strongly advise you to use the notes here, and, if necessary, a good pronunciation guide and to teach the features presented.

Testing

At advanced level, progress is much less immediately apparent than at lower levels and students can find this very demotivating. Testing is a useful device for overcoming this problem, both by providing students with achievable goals and by confirming to them the progress they have made. Testing can also play a useful diagnostic role for the teacher in highlighting those areas which need more work and those areas which can be considered successfully completed. For students who are going on to take public examinations, testing will have an important role in preparing them for the exam itself.

The various components of *Distinction* can be used for testing in several ways. Many of the exercises in the Students' Book are in the form of tasks which can only be achieved through successful communication – thus many of the activities can be treated as a form of oral testing. The exercises in the English in Use section of the Workbook are largely designed to test understanding and the ability to manipulate the structures presented in the Students' Book. Similarly, homework can be treated as a kind of continuous, yet informal, method of testing. It is important to develop a consistent method of marking work if this is to succeed, especially in those areas which are more subjective (such as creative writing). It is a common convention, for example, to mark compositions out of 20, awarding half the marks for accuracy (grammar, spelling and range of vocabulary) and half the marks for content, organisation and style/appropriacy, etc. If you have a class which expects or enjoys a more formal approach to testing, it is possible to use the exercises in the Workbook as an achievement test. By using the Key, the students will have the additional satisfaction of being able to mark their own work and thus see their own progress.

 Before you begin the course ...

Finally, a few words about the lesson before you open *Distinction*. Teaching an advanced class is, for most teachers, a delightful (if sometimes extremely demanding) experience! It should be the same for students. The notes that follow are intended to help you foster the right kind of classroom atmosphere and spirit before getting embroiled in the inevitable problems of demotivation because the course is too difficult/is too easy/doesn't do enough grammar, etc. The notes here assume that the class you are starting to teach is not already familiar to you, but with minimal adaptation they can be used with a class you know.

One major difference between advanced classes and those of much lower levels is that the learners can communicate effectively: they can express their own needs and desires, and it is extremely demotivating for them if they find that their needs and desires are being ignored or rejected without explanation. It is therefore extremely useful to cross this potential barrier in the very first lesson with the class. As you are going though general introductions with (and of) the students, try to ask the following questions and elicit discussion, dealing with any queries as well as you can.

1 What has your previous language learning experience consisted of?
2 Which classroom methods and techniques have you found most useful for you?
3 What methods and techniques have you used outside the classroom to help you learn?
4 What is your ultimate reason for learning English?
5 Who do you feel should decide the content of your English course?

The students could work in pairs to discuss these questions, and then report back about their partners. The questionnaires relating to the final task in Unit 5 of *Distinction* may be a useful source of techniques to discuss if necessary. (Read them out/put them on the board if required.)

Discuss the questions as a class and take the opportunity to explain the following. Numbers relate to the questions above.

1 This is the most influential factor affecting the way each student regards your class. In some cases, the students will all have had the same experience (if this is the final year of a college course, for example); in others, they will all have had completely different experiences (if they are in a private language school in the UK for the first time). The important point here is for them to realise that there are several different ways of getting to the same point, and that they are all equally valid.

2 This question allows students to talk about aspects of classroom methodology they have found particularly useful. Discuss each method/technique as it is put forward. In most cases, you can say that they will be doing some work along those lines (be it grammar exercises, discussion, pronunciation techniques), but for some you will have to use your discretion. For example, if students think that translation is important (in a monolingual class), you will have to decide if you wish to incorporate that into your class. If you do, think of useful ways of doing so: for example, translating input texts is likely to be demotivating because they will be too difficult; however, translating model sentences which show grammar points will be very useful in pointing out differences between the structure of the two languages.

The students will almost certainly mention methods/ techniques they found difficult/not of any use. If the class opinion is almost unanimous here, you will have to consider cutting down on the kind of activity, or explaining why you feel it is useful and they should do it. One very important point in discussing this question is that you should elicit the differences in opinion which will inevitably arise (especially in a multilingual class), and point out that

different methods are more or less useful for different people, so a high level of tolerance is needed by the whole class.

3 This question will help you to understand the learning styles of the students, and also to see if any students are likely to be particularly 'good' or 'bad' learners. Any techniques which seem particularly good to you can be discussed further, and if possible, can be incorporated into the whole-class learning. For example, if one student has come up with a particularly good way of revising vocabulary, suggest regular vocabulary review sessions (or tests, if you prefer) and encourage all the students to try the method. Students learn in different ways and it is important for them to realise that they can learn from each other as well as from the teacher.

4 This question will help you work out whether you need to supplement the course with a particular kind of activity. For example, if all your students are taking the same exam, it is obvious that you will provide exam practice. However, if the ultimate aim of the majority of the students in the class is to use English at a high business level, then social strategies, register, polite conversation, etc. are important. (But business letters aren't, as these are in the realm of the secretary!) If the class has disparate aims, then they should realise that a general course is the only option.

5 This final question will help you to realise if the class 'spirit' is likely to be cooperative (with you), confrontational or disinterested. If some students basically say that the content of the lessons is up to you, they are likely to try to abdicate responsibility for their learning in every respect. It is important to make them realise now that *you* can teach them, but only *they* can learn, and that they will have to put effort into it. If some students feel that they should dictate the syllabus (because they are paying), point out again the fact that there are different needs, desires and learning styles in the class, and that you are the only person in the position to balance them. It is also worth discussing at this stage the limitations and the ethos of your school. For example, point out if there are video recording facilities and whether you intend to use them. Also point out if there are, for example, fixed break times, and why. (Canteen hours/staff meetings?) Point out where negotiation is possible, for example, if you are allowed to choose when to have breaks and how long to take, discussing as a group what to do, and where no negotiation is possible, for example, using the video recorder/language lab on a Friday (because there's a strict timetable) or the amount of homework expected from students.

A session such as the above should pave the way to open discussion and negotiation through the course. If you feel that the discussion didn't work because some students were too inhibited to speak, put aside a time after three or four weeks, preferably when the students are likely to be quite relaxed, and recap on it. It is a good idea to do this anyway, to find out how the students are feeling once they have got to know each other and you.

Unit summary

Themes	Sports and games; the history of two common games
Structures	Review of the continuous tenses; ways of giving instructions and descriptions
Vocabulary	Vocabulary connected with sports and games; idioms of sports and games
Skills	*Reading:* matching headings with texts; finding similarities and differences
	Listening: listening for individual words; completing a text
	Speaking: instructing and describing; contradicting; stress in contradictions
	Writing: describing rules; writing instructions
Language awareness/Study skills	Categorising

 ## Teaching notes

Introduction

1
- Focus students' attention on the photos. Get them to describe the sports and name them if possible. (See the answers below.)

Students match the names of sports and the definitions.

Answers

1	pot holing (photograph A)	6	stock-car racing
2	boxing	7	bungee jumping (photograph C)
3	speed skiing	8	tobogganing (photograph D)
4	hang-gliding (photograph B)	9	bullfighting
5	abseiling	10	parascending

- Make sure students understand the nature of all the sports.
- In pairs, students rank the sports 1–10 in order of danger.

Extension
- If you wish, you can get students brainstorming other sports at this stage and adding them into their ranking.
- Discuss the ranking in class. Does everyone agree?

Note: Exercise 4 asks students to discuss whether certain activities are sports or games. You could ask them at this stage whether they would classify all the activities above as sports and, if not, then what they would call them.

Reading skills

2 The six stories which the students read come from a collection of amusing anecdotes, and are therefore quite funny. Encourage students to read the texts for enjoyment before getting into the exercises. (The Workbook contains more of these.)

A
- Students read the texts on page 9 and match them with the appropriate headings.

Answers

1 E   2 B   3 A   4 F   5 C   6 D

B
- Students match the cartoons with the texts.

Answers

A 5   B 4   C 6   D 1   E 3   F 2

- Students work in pairs to choose the caption for cartoon A and to write captions for the other cartoons. Compare the captions as a class and take a vote to choose the best ones.

Suggested answers

A (The students choose.)
B I don't think anyone's listening to me.
C I think that's mine coming through there.
D Are you sure this is what they mean by 'lift-off'?
E You should have told me you weren't ready.
F I must have taken a wrong turning somewhere!

3 This exercise extracts some of the vocabulary from the texts. If students have found the texts difficult, this exercise should help them to understand better.

- Divide the class into groups of four and nominate A, B, C and D in each group. A takes Story 1, B Story 4, etc.
- Students work on the vocabulary individually, using a dictionary if necessary, and completing their part of the chart.
- Students complete the chart in their groups.

Note: This is an opportunity for students to help each other understand unfamiliar vocabulary. Encourage them to work together and not to ask you unless necessary.

Answers

story	activity	people involved	groups involved	equipment etc.	related verbs	related nouns
1	balloon-ing	balloonist	–	balloon, basket, hoop	rise, float	takeoff fire, ropes
4	football	goal-keeper	team	ball, goalmouth	pass, score	kick-off, goal, drive
5	rowing	cox, oarsman	crew	boat, oars	row, sink	water, race
6	horse racing	jockeys	–	horses	finish, cross, back	race, finishing line, course, judges, horse owners

Further practice: Workbook Unit 1, Exercise 2.

Study skills

4 Categorising

- Students list the activities discussed so far and decide individually whether they are games or sports. Introduce the concept of an activity for e.g. homing pigeons.
- Students work in pairs to compare their lists and to add the items from the list.
- Students complete the tree diagram. Tell them they might have to make more 'branches'.

Suggested answers

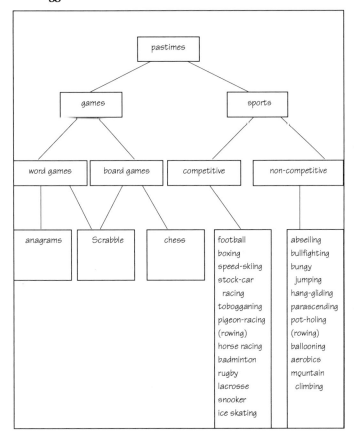

Listening skills

5 • Tell the students that they are going to hear a few people talking in a group. This might be quite difficult for them initially, but the exercises are constructed to encourage the students to listen for what they will be able to understand first.
- The first exercise will get students to listen carefully. If you want them to listen generally first, ask them to listen for how many people are speaking and to count the number of sports mentioned.
- Students look at the list of words and decide which ones are unlikely to appear in the conversation. They listen for this and make a note at the same time of the sports mentioned.

Answers

words not mentioned: football, swimming, fit
sports (and games) mentioned: golf, snooker, ice-skating, aerobics, body-building, weightlifting, tiddlywinks

Tapescript

JANET   That is very good, yes. Well, I always think of, when I think of golf, I don't quite think of it as a sport really, I must admit, you know, it's ... of course it has technique and skill and everything, but, like snooker does, but I can't think of it as a sort of real, physical ...
LOUISE   Yes, actually it's interesting you should say that

because someone said to me last weekend that they'd read somewhere that the definition of sport was that it involved a moving ball ...
JANET   Ah.
LOUISE   ... in other words, when you hit the ball, the ball was moving
ALL   Yeah.
TONY   So golf and snooker ...
LOUISE   So that didn't classify golf, or snooker, as a sport. That was a pastime.
JANET   That's interesting.
TONY   What about things that are in The Olympics, like ice-skating? Do you think those are sports? Because I always find those very difficult to ... because there isn't a definitive result. It always has to be judged by somebody.
LOUISE   Yes. That's more in the line of, sort of, dance.
TONY   Yes, but it is a sport.
STEVE   Isn't sport in that sense defined by its competitiveness? Can you have non-competitive sport?
LOUISE   Yes. Maybe that's the ... maybe that's the definition of sport.
TONY   That you compete ... (mmm) ... so that would include all sorts of games as well.
STEVE   Ah. There we are.
LOUISE   Ah. That's true. So that can't be right.
MARK   What about things like, em, say, aerobics, or body-building, or weightlifting?
LOUISE   Oh, I wouldn't call that sport.
MARK   They're not competitive, are they?
JANET   Yeah, it's strange. Yes, but I would consider some of those as sport, because if people say to me 'Do you do any sport?' then I say, 'Well, yes, twice a week I do aerobics,' so I view that as ...
TONY   But that's not really sport, that's exercise.
JANET   ... as a sporting activity, and yet ...
LOUISE   No, I wouldn't, I would call that exercise.
STEVE   Now, tiddlywinks can be competitive, but it's not a sport, is it?
TONY/MARK   No.
TONY   But I think that in a sport you have to be competing against somebody else, whereas in aerobics, or weightlifting, you're competing against yourself really, aren't you, to ... to improve yourself. You can't really have a competition in aerobics.
LOUISE   What about tiddlywinks though?
MARK   Because you're competing there but it's ...
STEVE   You're not, it's not making you very healthy, is it?
TONY   Perhaps that's why snooker isn't a sport?
LOUISE   So sport must be competitive and physical.

- Students listen again and make notes about the way each sport in their list is defined.

Answers

Snooker: not physical, player doesn't hit a moving ball, but it is competitive – a pastime?
Ice-skating: a kind of dance, but competitive, even though judged by someone else.
Aerobics: a kind of exercise, non-competitive.
Body-building: as *aerobics*.
Weight-lifting: as *aerobics*.
Tiddlywinks: competitive, but does not involve keeping fit or healthy.

- Students compare their lists in groups.
- If the discussion has changed their attitudes to what a sport is, they can go back and make changes to their tree diagram in Exercise 4.

Pronunciation

6   Stress in contradictions

This exercise looks at the way stress is used in contradictions: which elements of the contradiction are stressed, using the conversation as a starting point.

A   ● Play the extract for the students. They underline the stressed words in the contradictions.

Answers (stressed words)
LOUISE   *wouldn't, sport*
JANET   *I, sport*

● Discuss the elements which are stressed.

B   ● Students read the dialogues and mark the elements in the contradictions they think will be stressed.

Answers
1   don't, dangerous
2   think, wooden, Alan
3   can't, enjoy
4   not, seven, eight

● Students listen again and then practise the dialogues in pairs.

C   ● This is a very simple drill to practise the stresses. Monitor and insist on fairly exaggerated stress here.

D   ● This refers back to the work done in Exercise 5. Each student in the group of three is given an opinion regarding the definition of sport. They have to discuss the activities, using only their given opinions and contradicting as they discuss.

Further practice: Workbook Unit 1, Exercise 7.

Reading skills

7   Finding similarities and differences

A   This is a split reading exercise: the students have two texts on a similar subject. In pairs, they each read a different text and then compare the information. The two texts deal with the history of Scrabble and the history of Trivial Pursuit.

● Introduce the topic of games. What games do the students like playing? If they mention one of the above, ask if they know anything about its history. If they don't mention them, make sure you do so and find out how much they know about the two games.
● Preteach some key vocabulary:
Scrabble: *anagrams, percentage* (royalty)
Trivial Pursuit: *lucrative* (producing a lot of money)
Other items are dealt with in Exercise 8.
● Divide the class into pairs.
● Students skim their texts to find the answers to the pre-questions.

Answers
Scrabble, Trivial Pursuit.
Neither game was successful at first.
Scrabble: 1950s. Trivial Pursuit: early 1980s.

B   ● Students read their texts more carefully then work together to complete the chart. See the chart at the top of the next column.
● Students discuss how similar/different the stories of the two games are.

Answers

	Scrabble	Trivial Pursuit
inventor	Alfred Butts	Chris Haney and Scott Abbott
nationality	American	Canadian
reason for inventing it	to make him rich	to devise a game that could rival Scrabble
original name of game	Criss-crosswords	Trivia Pursuit
first rejected because	too highbrow, too serious	technical problems of printing, cost and appearance of game
first marketed in USA	1947	early 1980s
person/company to launch it	James Brunot	the partners themselves
american distributor	Selchow and Richter	Selchow and Richter
people who play it	Queen Mother, Sophia Loren, Dustin Hoffman	Ronald Reagan, British Royal Family

8   These exercises lead students to work on the vocabulary contained in the texts in more detail.

A   ● Students continue working in their pairs and help each other in this exercise. (The words are taken alternately from each text.)

Answers
1 i   2 g   3 d   4 c   5 f   6 e   7 j   8 b
9 a   10 h

B   ● Students work on the mind map in their pairs. This can be expanded on the board if you wish with students coming to the board and writing in words.

Suggested answers

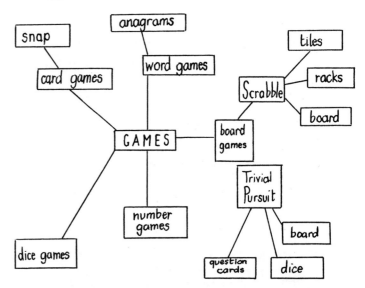

Language work

9 The continuous tenses

Students of this level should be familiar with the English tense system. As well as providing traditional revision in the tenses, we have chosen to look at aspect in this course: the continuous aspect in this unit and the perfective aspect in Unit 5.

A ● The examples are taken from the texts and illustrate most of the continuous tenses. Students read the examples and answer the questions.

Answers
present perfect continuous, future perfect continuous
1 Past simple, because it expresses an action that took place during the action expressed by the continuous.
2 It expresses a single action and therefore emphasises the relative continuity of the other activity.
3 It is a modal continuous.

● Students match the examples with the uses of the continuous.

Answers
a 1, 3, 4, 5
b 2

Note: A full explanation of continuous tenses is provided in the Grammar Reference section at the back of the Students' Book. The most common use is that of expressing an action starting before and possibly continuing after a certain point (and usually temporary). Here are some more examples:
He'd been cooking the dinner when she phoned/at 8.00 p.m.
He's been living in Cairo for three months.
I'm still working at the same place.
We were just talking about you when you walked in.
We'll be flying over the Atlantic this time tomorrow.
She'll have been living there for six years in March.

B ● Students look through the texts and find more examples.

Answers
Scrabble text
... while you are reading this text (a)
... a large proportion of them will be playing Scrabble (a)
Trivial Pursuit text
... were soon touring the games shops (a)
... the games were selling, money was coming in and thousands more sets were being produced. (a)
... were playing the game on the set between takes (a)

C ● This exercise contrasts the continuous and simple tenses.

Answers
1 *continuous:* expresses an action started before now and continuing after, for an unspecified but limited time
  simple: expresses routine
2 *continuous:* expresses a continuing action started before a certain time and continuing afterwards; likely to be used in this case as background information or interrupted by a past simple action
  simple: single action in the past
3 *continuous:* the match was still in progress but was very close to the end
  simple: the match finished at the same time or just after my arrival
4 *simple:* focusses on the number (every game)
  continuous: focusses on the duration (all season)
5 *continuous:* focusses on the duration (two hours)
  simple: focusses on the number of games (three)
6 *continuous:* statement of plans
  simple: offer

D ● Students complete the text.

Answers
1 was playing
2 was taking/studying
3 was studying/working with/using
4 had been playing/using
5 had been waiting
6 has been selling
7 will be receiving/getting
8 are designing/writing
9 will be sending/presenting
10 will be living
11 will be going to/attending
12 will be working

Further practice: Workbook Unit 1, Exercise 5.

Listening skills

10 Completing a text

● Refer the students to the photograph of lacrosse. Have they ever seen this sport? Would they like to play it?
● Play the tape once for students to get the general idea of the game. Ask them to listen for the rules only.
● Play the tape again while students try to complete the text.
● Students work in pairs to complete the text. Play the tape again to check if necessary.

Answers
1 public school sport (*i.e. a sport played by the more wealthy*)
2 a football pitch
3 twelve
4 net
5 is thrown
6 score goals
7 net and posts
8 higher than
9 head injuries
10 (try to) protect themselves
11 hard rubber
12 pads and helmets

Tapescript
TONY Lacrosse is another one which is quite an unusual sport, but apparently, is ... is quite aggressive.
JANET Have you ever played lacrosse? I've never played it.
LOUISE I used to ... I used to play for the Junior West of England ... lacrosse ...
TONY Did you? Wow, speak on!
JANET Yeah, I think ... because in England, obviously, perhaps it's more ... You know, in Wales we never had the opportunity to play lacrosse at all, but ...
LOUISE In fact, it's considered a bit of a public-school sport.
TONY Yes, it is.
LOUISE ... so the competition isn't that high, I mean, it's not as ...
STEVE What is it?
LOUISE ... impressive playing lacrosse as it is playing football or hockey.
JANET Good question. I couldn't tell you exactly what it is. Maybe ...
STEVE What is lacrosse?
LOUISE Well, it's played with a stick with a bag at the end, and you hold the stick and you throw and catch, em, you throw and catch the ball.
TONY The ball has to go into the net, doesn't it?
LOUISE No, it's similar, it's played on a large pitch, similar to a

football pitch ...

STEVE So, a grass pitch?

LOUISE ... with goals. Yes. And everyone has their positions, so it's quite similar to football but it's played with a stick, and rather than kicking the ball, or in rugby, throwing the ball, with your hands ...

JANET You pass it to each other.

LOUISE ... you pass it to each other with this stick and you catch it in the bag ...

JANET Yes.

LOUISE ... and throw it again and it's an incredibly fast game and ...

JANET What happens if the ball ...

LOUISE ... and it's quite aggressive because if you have ... you have the ball in your stick the person who is marking you, or in other words the person who you're, actually, who's kind of like ...

JANET Defending you?

LOUISE ... defending you, yes, will try and get the ball out of your stick by hitting your stick with their stick, and to try and protect yourself, to try and protect your stick, you have to keep the stick close to your head. So there are quite a few head injuries 'cos people come along and bash you over the head.

STEVE Is there much body contact?

LOUISE There's not much body contact but you get quite a few injuries by people bashing you over the head, and I remember playing in one game once when three people got knocked out and one girl lost two front teeth.

JANET So, it's as violent as rugby really.

STEVE Sounds more violent than football!

LOUISE It is, it is quite an aggressive sport.

JANET What happens when the ball actually hits the ground? Are you able to scoop it up ...?

LOUISE You scoop it up, yes

JANET ... with your stick?

LOUISE Yes, you scoop it up, so then there's a bit of a battle and you're trying to bash the other person's stick out of the way and, er, scoop it up into your stick.

STEVE What's the ball made of?

LOUISE Rubber.

TONY But I should think it's quite hard ...

LOUISE Hard rubber.

TONY ... if it hits you on the head.

STEVE Does it travel very fast?

LOUISE It travels very fast, yes, and you can throw it a long way.

JANET And do you score goals at the end, or ...

LOUISE Yes.

JANET Right. So, is there a goalpost, like in soccer?

LOUISE So, there's a ... a goal is very similar to a hockey goal in that there's a frame with a net behind it.

STEVE Same height as a hockey goal?

LOUISE A bit lower, a bit smaller than a hockey goal.

STEVE A bit smaller, yes, and, er, how big are the teams?

LOUISE There are twelve on each team. But it's interesting, because, I mean, obviously, at school we didn't have any protect ... protection when we played lacrosse.

STEVE So you all had sore heads?

LOUISE Yeah, but I've seen it played in London with people wearing pads and helmets with facemasks and things.

STEVE Yeah. Is it a good, is it a good spectator sport?

LOUISE Yes.

STEVE It sounds it.

LOUISE Yes. It's really exciting.

- Discuss whether students think it is a dangerous sport.

Language work

11 Instructions and descriptions

A • Students listen again, if necessary, to complete the sentences.

Answers
1 It's played with a stick ...
2 ... and you hold the stick and throw and catch the ball ...
3 ... it's played on a large pitch ...
4 ... rather than throwing the ball ... you pass it to each other ...
5 ... you have to keep the stick close to your head ...
1 and 3 describe the game.
2, 4 and 5 give instructions.
The passive (for description), impersonal *you* (for instructions).

B **Answers**
Left top to bottom: shuttlecock, service line, service court, baseline.
Right top to bottom: racket, net, tramlines.
Differences: In spoken instructions the impersonal *you* form is used; in written instructions *he/she* is used. The passive is used in both cases, but more in the written instructions.

Further practice: Workbook Unit 1, Exercise 6.

Writing skills

12 Describing rules and giving instructions

This exercise puts into practice the language of rules and instructions.

- Divide the students into pairs. They can use the pictures on this page and through the unit to choose a sport or game they both know. They should plan carefully how they would describe it to another person.
- Students work with a new partner and describe the game. The partners take notes.
- Each student writes a description of the sport/game he/she has taken notes about. Ensure they follow model given. They can then swap them in pairs for their partners to check.

Further practice: Workbook Unit 1, Exercise 9.

13 Discussion

- Present the proverb 'All work and no play makes Jack a dull boy'. It means that we all need to play as well as to work. Students discuss this theme in groups. If you need to give them some ideas, put on the board:
  More leisure time today.
  Need to have more exercise.
  Need to relax because of stressed environment – how?
  Is play or work more important?
  Can work also be play?

Vocabulary

14 Idioms: sports and games

Ensure that students realise that it is more important to be aware of idioms than to use them. In fact, using them could sound very strange.

Answers
1 ball   2 deep   3 game   4 skate   5 game
6 hand   7 swim   8 ball   9 sport   10 play

Number 1 refers to tennis, squash or badminton.
Number 2 refers to swimming, as does Number 7.
Number 4 refers to ice skating.

Further practice: Workbook Unit 1, Exercise 4.

Final task

15 Word games

- This final exercise consists of two simple word games that can be played at any time with the students.

A   Words within words

Answers
(These are just some of the words that can be formed from those given.)
examination: axe, tax, not, mate, time, tame, exit, mite, taxi, mint, mean, team, neat, note, meant, tonne, toxin, nation
universal: ran, run, sun, sale, save, sane, real, seal, veal, near, lean, saver, saner, learn, ruin, ruins, liver, sliver, raise, lives
institution: tin, ton, not, nut, son, in, inn, is, sun, stun, tint, stunt, stint, tuition, nouns, touts, snout

B   Anagrams

Answers
leap ➤ pale
melons ➤ solemn
praised ➤ despair
carthorse ➤ orchestra
excitation ➤ intoxicate

- The students can make anagrams of their own and write clues to give to other students.

Extension
Below are two more word games that your students could play.

Pyramids
The shape of a pyramid is built up, adding one letter at a time to form a complete word, until no more words can be formed:

A
AT
HAT
HATE
HEART
HEARTS
SHATTER
THEATRES

Two ways to start the students off are:

I	B
IT	BE

Rebus
A rebus uses words, numbers, symbols or pictures to represent words or syllables. This is likely to be too difficult for the students to do themselves, but you could give them these:

IOU = I owe you
T42 = tea for two
B4 = before
NE1 = anyone
NME = enemy
2 good 2B4 gotten = too good to be forgotten
YYUR YYUB ICUR YY4me = too wise you are, too wise you be, I see you are too wise for me

Unit summary

Theme	Famous criminals and detectives. Violent murder and the causes of crime. Prisons and forms of punishment.
Structures	Review of past tense forms. Linking words showing sequence.
Vocabulary	Murder and crime, imprisonment and punishment.
Skills	*Reading:* Comparing and contrasting *Listening:* Listening and inferring facts *Speaking:* Discussing and debating informally *Writing:* Writing a summary

Note: Please read the text in Exercise 2 and the follow up material in Exercises 3 and 4 carefully before deciding to use the material with students who may be particularly sensitive to the topic of violent crime.

 ## Teaching notes

Introduction

1
- Ask students to look at the leaflet. Explain that Madame Tussaud's is a famous waxwork museum which contains effigies (wax models) of famous people.

- Elicit answers to the questions.
  The leaflet is advertising the Chamber of Horrors at Madame Tussaud's.
  The Chamber of Horrors contains effigies of famous murderers and criminals from history.

- Read through the game introduction and instructions with the class.
- Divide the class into groups of three or four students and nominate students A, B, C (and D if necessary) and tell them to turn to the pages at the back of the book. Encourage them to work as quickly as possible.
- When the groups have completed the sentences ask them to read out their answers.

Answers
a The original 'Dracula' was a fifteenth century Romanian prince ... known as Vlad the Impaler ... who brutally tortured and killed over 20,000 Turkish prisoners.
b President John F. Kennedy ... was assassinated by ... Lee Harvey Oswald in Dallas, Texas in 1963.
c Gilles de Rais, known as 'Bluebeard', ... who fought alongside Joan of Arc, ... is believed to have tortured and killed 140 children.
d Five women prostitutes were severely mutilated and killed ... in the Whitechapel area of Victorian London ... by Jack the Ripper.
e Paul Getty III, grandson of the world's richest man ... was kidnapped by unknown criminals ... who cut off his ear and sent it with their ransom note.
F King Richard III of England ... imprisoned and strangled his two young nephews ... in the Tower of London in 1495.
g The actor John Wilkes Booth ... assassinated US president

Abraham Lincoln ... in a theatre in Washington in 1865.
h A fire which destroyed half of ancient Rome ... was started by the Emperor Nero ... who also murdered his mother, Agrippina, and his half-brother, Britannicus.
i Dr Josef Mengele, the 'Angel of Death' ... conducted medical experiments without anaesthetic ... on Jewish prisoners at Auschwitz (a concentration camp) during World War II.

2 Reading

- Discuss the questions with the class. Encourage students to discuss examples of famous crimes from their countries and to suggest why people find violent crime fascinating.
- Read through the introduction and elicit answers to the questions. Explain that the text is taken from a guide book written for people who wish to visit the scenes of famous crimes in London. *Vampires* are legendary creatures that drink human blood. From this the students might guess that the article is about someone who drank people's blood.

A
- Ask the students to read the text and complete the sequencing task.

Answers
1 Haigh's imprisonment for fraud
2 Haigh's separation from his wife
3 the murder of Donald McSwann
4 the murder of Mr and Mrs McSwann
5 the murder of the woman from Hammersmith Bridge
6 the murder of Mrs Durand-Deacon
7 the discovery of traces of a human body in the Crawley workroom
8 Haigh's arrest for murder

B
- Now ask the students to answer the comprehension questions, reading the text again if necessary.

Answers
1 No, we don't know exactly how many people he murdered.
2 He used the acid to destroy the bodies of his victims.
3 Haigh had worked for McSwann's father as a chauffeur (driver) and secretary.
4 The evidence of Mrs Durand-Deacon's remains and her handbag in Haigh's Crawley workroom connected him to the crimes.
5 Haigh claimed he was insane.
6 He was hanged.

- Questions 7 and 8 are more open. Use the questions to elicit a discussion. Let the students express their own ideas about how Haigh's childhood might have influenced him, and how we can define whether a person who can commit such crimes is sane or insane.

Note: The topic of insanity is explored in greater depth in Unit 4 *All in The Mind*, Exercise 7, page 30.

Vocabulary

3 Matching words with meanings

- Students can work individually to find the words and phrases and then compare their answers in pairs.

Answers

1	disintegrated	5	cauldron	9	manhole
2	effigy	6	petty theft	10	traces
3	sect	7	cosh	11	convicted
4	frowned upon	8	incision	12	gruesome

- Students can work in pairs to write definitions of the phrases.

Suggested answers

1 very controlled with severe punishments for bad behaviour
2 punishment administered by one's father
3 often repeated, happening again and again
4 did not successfully hide or destroy
5 told the court he was insane

Further practice: Workbook Unit 2, Exercises 4 and 5.

Extension

- You might like to discuss why Haigh 'pleaded insanity' with the class. Under English law, a person who is insane (mentally ill) cannot be found guilty of murder, only of manslaughter, a much less serious crime – which did not carry the death penalty in 1949. The moral dilemmas involved in this area of the law provide a good subject for class discussion.

Language work

4   Linking words showing sequence

A   Read through the introduction with the class and ask students to complete the chart with arrows.

Answer

He disposed of the bodies in the acid bath.   Haigh murdered four people.

time

Answer

The first event is the murder of the four people.

- Now ask the students to find and underline all the linking words showing sequence in the text. Elicit the answers and put the linking words on the board.

Answers

before (para 1, line 7)   *while* (para 2, line 19)   *after* (para 3, line 25; para 5, line 46)   *during* (para 3, line 26)   *when* (para 4, line 31)   *previously* (para 4, line 33)   *then* (para 4, lines 37 and 41)   *later* (para 4, line 42)   *subsequently* (para 4, line 44)   *following* (para 7, line 62)

- Ask students to look at the diagram and check that they understand the sequence. The students use the words they have underlined to complete the statements about the diagram.

Answers

1 before   2 Subsequently/Then   3 after   4 during
5 Following/After   6 Previously

- Some students may have problems using *during*, *subsequently*, *previously* and *following* as linking words. If so, put this grammar chart on the board.

+ noun phrase	+ verb clause
during	subsequently
following	previously

- Elicit one or two examples of each type and write these on the board. For example:
  (The student fell asleep during the test.)
  The student left following his failure in the test.
  He failed the test. Subsequently, he left.
  He left. Previously, he had failed the test.

- Point out that *during* and *following* cannot be followed by a subject and verb. We cannot say 'He left following he failed the test.' or 'He fell asleep during he took the test'. *Subsequently* and *previously* are usually placed at the beginning of a sentence.

- Point out to the students that *after* and *previously* are often used with the past perfect to highlight a sequence.

B   - Ask the students to complete the summary using some of the linking words above.

Answers

1 following/after   2 During   3 after
4 Then   5 Following/After   6 previously
7 then/subsequently   8 after   9 Then
10 during

Further practice: Workbook Unit 2, Exercise 6.

5   Review of past tenses

At this level students should be familiar with the past tenses. This exercise therefore does not present the tenses but is designed as a review.

A   - Ask the students to study the extracts and the definitions of use below and then complete the gaps in the chart. If the students are unable to complete the chart correctly they can refer to the Grammar Reference section at the back of the Students' Book.

Answer

REVIEW OF PAST TENSES		
verb form	example	use
past perfect	5	f
past perfect continuous	6	c
past simple	4	b
past continuous	2	d
would + infinitive	1	e
used to + infinitive	3	a

- Highlight the differences between *would* and *used to*. *Would* is used to describe repeated or habitual actions in the past. It cannot be used to describe situations and states. *Would* often expresses the idea that the action described was predictable or characteristic.

- Point out that in situations where the sequence of events is clear from the context it is not necessary to use the past perfect for the earlier event.

B   - Divide the students into pairs or small groups to work out the differences between the sentences. Explain that the differences are connected with the sequence of events. Allow students to compare their answers with other pairs/groups.

- If the students are struggling they might find it helpful to draw time line diagrams, as in Exercise 4.

- Elicit the answers.

Answers
1 and 2 The police went to the workroom. When they got there some remains were found.
3 Some human remains were found at the time when the police were on their way to the workroom.
4 Some human remains were found at the workroom. Later, the police went there.
5 The police went to the workroom and then left. Later, some remains were found.

6 This exercise gives the students oral and written practice in past tenses and linkers. (If you have access to an overhead projector you should use the method described in the introduction for the written part of this exercise.)

- Use the illustration to elicit information about Doctor Crippen.

Background information: He was one of Britain's most famous murderers. (He was an American, but lived in Britain.) His story has historical significance because it is the first known example of telecommunications (in this case the telegraph) being used by detectives to catch a criminal.

- Read through and explain the instructions to the class. Point out to the students that the information each of them will see is only part of the story, and is in note form.
- Form groups of three students and nominate an A, B and C in each group. If you have an odd number you can have two Cs in one or two of the groups.
- Allow students about ten minutes to write out their paragraphs. At this stage they should not talk to each other.
- Monitor the students, checking their understanding of the information and their use of past tenses and linking words.
- When the time limit is up ask students to join their paragraphs together to make a complete story.
- Ask one or two groups to read (or display) their completed story to the class and elicit corrections/comments from the rest of the students.

Further practice: Workbook Unit 2, Exercise 7.

7 Discussion

This discussion is on the topic of capital punishment and the suitability of different punishments. See the notes on organising discussions in class in the Introduction.

Background information: Until 1965 the punishment for murder in England and Wales was hanging. Now the punishment is imprisonment for life. (This is usually interpreted by judges as 20 to 30 years imprisonment.)
The saying 'an eye for an eye, a tooth for a tooth' originates from the Old Testament of the Christian Bible.

Note: The topic of capital punishment and its repercussions features in Unit 6 *A Question of Morals*, Exercise 3, page 41.

Listening skills

8 Listening and inferring facts

A
- Ask the students to describe the photograph. The class should be able to guess that it shows prisoners on the roof of an old prison. They should try to guess how and why the men are there. (The photo shows rioting prisoners on the roof of Strangeways Prison in Manchester, England.) Ask the students to suggest what is going on and what the possible causes might be. Write their ideas on the board.
- Play the tape for students to check if their ideas were correct.
- Explain that the recording is from a live news report and

that the reporter is not completely sure of all the facts. To answer questions 1 – 5, students will have to infer, making deductions based on the information they hear.
- Play the tape again and ask the students to answer the five questions.
- Students compare their answers in pairs. Elicit and check their answers.

Answers
1 According to one prison officer, the riot was caused by severe overcrowding and reductions in exercise and visiting hours.
2 It appears to have started at the Sunday morning service in the chapel.
3 There are unconfirmed reports of at least eleven dead and fifty wounded.
4 The fire in the gymnasium block is under control but we don't know if there are other fires still blazing.
5 Journalists have seen canisters of tear gas and rifles in the police vans. Therefore, the police might be planning to use these to control the riot.

Tapescript
ANNOUNCER (*fade in*)...which will be concluded at the meeting of the International Monetary Fund next month. In Britain reports have been coming in of further deaths in the Strangeways prison riot. Now in its second day, the riot seems to be escalating and the Home Office are refusing to comment on rumours that the riot is out of control. Renata Cohen has brought us this report from the scene:
RENATA COHEN I'm standing outside the main gate of Manchester's Strangeways prison. Smoke is billowing overhead and I can see a number of prisoners on the roof of the chapel. At the moment there appears to be a great deal of confusion over the situation inside the prison. This morning a squadron of riot police entered the prison followed by firemen who managed to control a blaze in the gymnasium block, but it is still not clear whether the smoke we can see is the result of this or if other parts of the complex are on fire. We have seen dozens of ambulances entering and leaving the building but the Home Office spokesman has refused to confirm reports of at least eleven dead and fifty wounded. It seems that at least half of the one thousand six hundred prisoners in Strangeways are loose in the prison, while an estimated seven hundred have surrendered and been transferred to other prisons.
Our latest information is that the remaining prisoners have barricaded themselves into several of the cellblocks and are resisting all attempts to remove them.
The riot appears to have started during the Sunday morning service in the chapel, one of the few times when the men are gathered together in one area. I spoke to one prison officer earlier today who claimed that trouble had been brewing for several months, mainly due to severe overcrowding and reductions in exercise and visiting hours. It seems that in some cases three prisoners have been forced to share cells designed for one person.
Some of the journalists here report that they have seen canisters of tear gas and rifles in the police vans, perhaps an indication of the extreme measures now deemed necessary to get this riot under control. This is Renata Cohen reporting for LCC news in Manchester.
ANNOUNCER This month's EC trade figures were announced today and show a distinct improvement on the second quarter.

B
- Divide the class into pairs. Explain the situation. They are the governors (the people in charge of the prison) and have to think of measures to prevent future riots. Ask each pair to think of two or three ideas for each of the items listed.

- Monitor and help with suggestions, such as:
  Increase time allowed for exercise and improve sports facilities.
  Make sure every prisoner has his own cell.
  Install a sprinkler system or provide fire extinguishers.
  Provide prison officers with guns. (Officers in British prisons are not allowed to carry guns at present.)
  Provide educational and leisure activities for prisoners.
  Limit gatherings to a maximum of 20 prisoners at any one time.
- When pairs have finished ask them to compare ideas with other pairs. In a small class this can be done as a whole class activity.
- Elicit and put some of their ideas on the board. Ask the class to choose the best suggestions.

Reading skills

9   Comparing and contrasting

- The two poems in this exercise contain some difficult vocabulary. You might want to pre-teach the following items:
  vilest worst, most evil or ugly
  withers decays, becomes old
  anguish feeling of despair, pain and depression
  warder prison officer or guard
  hermitage a quiet place where a person can be alone to meditate, literally a place where a hermit lives

Background information: The extracts are from well-known poems. The lines *'Stone walls do not a prison make/Nor iron bars a cage'* have become so well known over the centuries that they are now used as a proverb. The complete poems can be found in many anthologies of English poetry.

Note: The subject of poetry is dealt with in more depth in Unit 16 *The Written Word*, Exercises 11 and 12, page 105.

- Read through the introduction and ask the students to complete the matching exercise.

Answers

Oscar Wilde   b, c, e
Lovelace   a, d, f

- Play the poems on tape and ask students to answer questions 1-3.

Suggested answers

1 Wilde's poem concentrates on the negative influence of prison. Its message is that prison corrupts people, encourages evil and destroys 'goodness'.
   Lovelace's poem argues that mere physical imprisonment cannot imprison the soul or spirit. Those who are innocent will still be free in their own minds.
2 Both poems include the pronoun *I*, and the Wilde poem also includes the pronoun *we*, indicating that the authors speak from personal experience.
3 This is an open question. Use it to stimulate discussion of the contrasting messages of the poems and to encourage students to explain their own opinions, checking that they back them up with reasons.

10
- Elicit any alternative forms of punishment that students can think of.
- Students read the article and list the methods of reducing the prison population it describes.

A   Answers

1 The remission and parole system
2 Suspended sentences
3 Community Service Order
4 Fines
5 Electronic tagging/probation

B   Answers

1 The Home Office.
2 The rising prison population, overcrowding and increasing convictions for violent crime.
3 Courts impose longer sentences to compensate for the possibility of prisoners being released early.
4 The person will have to serve two sentences: the sentence for their current offence and the sentence for their previous offence.
5 It is pursuing two contradictory policies: building more prisons and encouraging alternative punishments. By building more prisons it may be encouraging more prison sentences.

- Introduce the discussion questions. With a mixed nationality class, start by eliciting different punishments from the students' countries. List these and any others the students know on the board. Some suggestions are:
  corporal punishment (infliction of physical pain)
  mutilation (marking the criminal's body in some way)
  paying compensation to victims
  manual labour (known as 'hard labour' in England)
  psychological therapy sessions
- Discuss the concept of 're-education' with the class. This can be tied-in with the earlier discussion (Exercise 2B) about the causes of John Haigh's crimes. Students with an interest in sociology might be interested in discussing the idea that crime has a social cause and that criminals can be 'cured' by educating them to fit in with society more successfully.

Writing skills

11   Writing a summary (1)

Summary writing is a skill which has many uses and is a requirement in several examinations. This exercise is an introduction to the skill.

Note: There is further practice of this in Unit 6 A *Question of Morals*, Exercise 17, page 45.

- Ask students what they know about summaries and whether they have written them before. If they want to see an example of a summary, they can turn back to the summary of *The Vampire of South Kensington* in Exercise 4B.
- Read through the five stages. The method described in the five steps is one of several possible methods. If your students haven't written summaries before, they should follow the steps as described, but if they have already been taught another method, they should be free to follow that. You should point out that 150 words is usually about 15 lines of handwriting.
- Point out that most original texts contain only one or two important points in each paragraph. Summaries, on the other hand, should have a key point in each sentence.
- If your students find it hard to distinguish between important and background information you can help them by eliciting examples of unimportant points from the class. The students can then cross these out in the text. The first paragraph, for example, is merely scene-setting, and needn't be included in the summary.
- When students have made their lists of important points they should form pairs or small groups and check they agree. They should then complete the summary individually.
- When the summaries are completed encourage the students to compare and evaluate each other's work.

Further practice: Workbook Unit 2, Exercise 9.

Speaking skills

12 Discussions and informal debates

This exercise is a structured but informal discussion and decision-making activity. Practice in taking part in a formal discussion or debate is provided in Unit 6 *A Question of Morals*, Exercise 9, page 52. This exercise can be used with classes of any size. You will need a minimum of 20 minutes to complete the exercise.

A
- Divide the students into pairs to add expressions to the lists.
- Ask the pairs to combine their ideas with other pairs. Elicit their suggestions and put them on the board.

Suggested answers

Interrupting: May I interrupt ...; Well ...; If I could say something ...
Giving an opinion: In my opinion ...; I think that ...
Agreeing: That's absolutely right; I go along with that; I agree with ...
Disagreeing: I'm afraid I can't agree with ...; I'm not so sure about ...

- Ask students to match the expressions with the situations. There are no correct answers to this task, the idea is simply to make students aware of levels of formality in discussion.

Suggested answers
a (*informal*) Sorry, but ... You must be joking!
b (*formal*) Can I come in here ...
c (*neutral*) If you ask me...; I feel that ...; You're quite right ... That's true ...; I can't go along with that ...

B
- Read through the introduction with the class and ask them to study the information about the four criminals. Check that they understand the situations.
- **Stage 1**   Divide the class into groups of about 3 to 5 students, the groups do not have to be the same size. Explain that they must reach a decision about suitable punishments as a group, in other words they must carry on discussing until everyone in the group agrees on the recommendations.
- **Stage 2**   Ask one person from each group to report their group's recommendations to the whole class. Put these on the board.
- **Stage 3**   Ask the whole class to respond to the different recommendations they have heard. Members of groups should defend their recommendations if they are criticised. After a suitable time bring the discussion to a close by asking the whole class to vote on the recommendations on the board.

Further practice: Workbook Unit 2, Exercise 10.

Final task

13 The Murder of Michael Roe

This is the first of several reading jigsaws in *Distinction*. See the notes on reading jigsaws in the Introduction. You should read the solution (on the right) before beginning the exercise in order to help students during the monitoring stage. You will need at least twenty minutes to half-an-hour for this task with an average class.

- As a warm-up, ask the students to describe the illustration and elicit everything they know about Sherlock Holmes.

Background information: Sherlock Holmes is a fictional detective created by the English writer, Sir Arthur Conan Doyle, in the late nineteenth century. The best-known books in which he appears are *A Study in Scarlet* (1887), *The Memoirs of Sherlock Holmes* (1894) and *The Hound of the Baskervilles* (1902). Sherlock Holmes is famous for his brilliant deductive abilities and has been the subject of many films and television series.

- Explain the task to the class. They are going to take the part of Sherlock Holmes. By combining the information they read and using their powers of logic and deduction, they will be able to solve a murder mystery.
- Divide the class into groups of 3, nominating students A, B and C in each group. If you have an odd number of students you can have four students in one or two groups, these will be student D.
- Ask each student to turn to the relevant page and study the information (in the form of letters to Sherlock Holmes and a newspaper report). They should then exchange their information orally with the other members of their group and try to solve the mystery. They must only use English and they must not show their information to their partners.

Note: If you have a weak group you should allow all the As, all the Bs and all the Cs to get together to discuss their information before they have to re-join their groups. This should iron out any difficulties in comprehension of the information. Another tip for weaker classes is to ask them to make a list of all the characters in the letters. This will prevent confusion later on. The characters are:
Inspector Tobias Gregson, Leonard Fud, Captain Hans Schweiger, the cloakroom attendant at the Moulin Rouge Club, Justin Milt, Michael Roe and Winifred Bun.

- Monitor the groups while they are discussing the mystery and help with clues and hints if necessary. Once a group thinks it has reached a solution, ask one of the members to explain it quietly to you. Insist on a complete solution with all the facts explained fully. If their solution is correct, ask them to prepare to explain it to the class.

Solution
Michael Roe, a filing clerk at the British Admiralty, stole or copied the plans of a torpedo boat engine to sell to Captain Schweiger for £1,000. The problem was that Captain Schweiger was being followed by British security agents. So they thought up a scheme whereby they could exchange the plans and the money without being seen.

The scheme was for Roe to put the secret plans in the inside of his rolled up umbrella and for Schweiger to put the cash in his. They would go to the Moulin Rouge Club on the same night and deposit their umbrellas at the cloakroom in exchange for tickets. Each would then go to the lavatory and leave his ticket for the other to collect. Each would then pick up the other's umbrella on their way out without having spoken to each other or in any way aroused the suspicion of the security agent watching Captain Schweiger.

The scheme went wrong because the cloakroom attendant at the club was drunk, and was giving out umbrellas at random. All the umbrellas, of course, looked exactly the same. When Roe picked up his umbrella and discovered it was empty, he assumed that Schweiger had tricked him, which is why he attacked Schweiger outside the German Embassy.

Luckily, the men who mistakenly picked up Roe's and Schweiger's umbrellas reported this to the authorities.

Extension
- As a written homework, students can write Sherlock Holmes' letter to Inspector Gregson explaining the solution.

Unit 3 The Risk Factor

 ## Unit summary

Themes	Degrees of risk; flying; graphs and charts; road safety; safety in the home; dealing with fires
Structures	Ellipsis and substitution; review of future forms
Vocabulary	Numbers, symbols and charts
Skills	*Reading:* taking notes from a text
	Listening: transcoding to a chart
	Speaking: advising
	Writing: writing a formal letter

 ## Teaching notes

Introduction

1
- Read through the introduction with the class and divide the students into groups of three or four to answer the questions.
- Once students have finished discussing and have agreed on their answers ask one person in each group to turn to page 158 of the Students' Book to check the answers.
- Elicit a brief discussion about the quiz. Did they find the results surprising? Why? Explain that they will be able to find out more about risks and dangers later in this unit.

Reading skills

2 Taking notes from a text

A
- Ask the class whether they suffer from fear of flying, eliciting any individual experiences they might have had.
- Students should read the text and answer the questions individually.

Answers
1 232.
2 Technical and regulatory improvements.
3 To check the crew are awake.

B
- Ask students to look at the notepad and the skeleton notes. Ask them why and when note-taking is used. Elicit some of the features of note-taking and write a checklist on the board.
  Only note the main points.
  Use graphic devices such as headings, underlining, highlighting, arrows etc.
  Use symbols such as:
  > greater than
  < less/smaller than
  ∴ therefore
  ∵ because
  → leads to/causes/results in
  = equals/is/are
  + and/plus
  ≏ about/approximately, roughly
  " ditto/the same as the line above
  Do not write full sentences. (Leave out articles, auxiliary verbs etc.)
- Ask students to read the text again if necessary and complete the notes. Allow them to compare their answers in pairs.

Answers

'FEAR OF FLYING'

Chances of fatal accidents
1950s: around 18 in a million
now: less than one in a million

Fatal accident statistics
1970s: 270
1980s: 232

The best airlines for safety:
1 Southwest Airlines   2 Ansett   3 KLM

The worst airline for safety:
Aeroflot

Technical improvements:
1   Introduction of turbofan engines
2   Autopilot systems
3   Ground Proximity Warning Systems
4   Wind Shear Alert Systems

Causes for concern:
1   Human error – pilots working longer shifts
2   Maintenance – may cut corners because of costs
3   Terrorist attacks

Note: The associated skill of taking notes from a listening input is covered in Unit 4 *All in the Mind*, Exercise 7, page 30.

Vocabulary

3 Numbers and symbols

A Students often get confused about the various ways of expressing numbers and statistics in English. This exercise covers the most common spoken and written forms.

- Elicit that the extracts all contain statistical information.
- Play Section A on the tape and ask the students to match the items a – f on the tape with the items in the Students' Book. Students should pay careful attention to the differences between the way figures are written and spoken.
- Now ask the students to match each item with its name.

Answers
a 1 in 25   b 125   c ⅟₂₅   d 0.125   e 1:25
f 125%
fraction: ⅟₂₅   ratio: 1:25   number: 125   decimal: 0.125
percentage: 125%   proportion: 1 in 25

Tapescript
a one in twenty-five   b one hundred and twenty five
c one twenty-fifth   d point one two five
e one to twenty-five   f one hundred and twenty five
                           percent

B ● Students should listen to section B and write down the figures they hear, using symbols wherever possible.

Answers

1 1/2/1999 *or* 1.2.99 *or* 01.02.99   2 1001   3 1.001
4 1:20   5 1 in 20   6 100.202   7 20%   8 ²⁄₂₀
9 100,202.022   10 20°

Tapescript

1 the first of the second of nineteen ninety nine
2 one thousand and one
3 one point oh oh one
4 one to twenty
5 one in twenty
6 one hundred point two oh two
7 twenty per cent
8 two twentieths
9 one hundred thousand, two hundred and two point oh two two
10 twenty degrees

● Divide students into pairs. Each student should write down ten figures at random, including at least one of each type from section A. He or she should then read these out to their partner, who must write them down using symbols and figures. They can then compare their lists.

4 Charts

In this exercise students study some of the standard types of chart used to present statistical information graphically. There are four examples in the Students' Book: a graph and a pie-chart on page 24, a bar chart (also known as a histogram) on page 25, and a pictogram on page 28. The ability to construct these charts and to explain them in writing is particularly useful for students using, or planning to use, English for business.

A ● Read through the introduction and elicit the answers (see above).
● Let students discuss the advantages of each of the types of chart and reach their own conclusions. (There is no fixed answer.)
● Students can work in pairs or small groups to decide on the best representation for 1, 2 and 3.

Suggested answers

1 a pie chart   2 a graph or bar chart   3 a pictogram

Extension

● If charts and diagrams are relevant to your students' needs, you could ask them to make up the figures and draw the charts they have decided on for 1, 2 and 3.

B ● Students should read the summary and use it as a model to write a summary of the sports injuries bar chart/histogram. Elicit the main features of the summary:
Begins with a description of the information contained.
Describes the information in rank order, starting with the most noticeable or important feature and ending with the least important or smallest.
Groups the statistics into manageable sections (most common..., less common...).
Uses phrases such as: *followed by...*, *respectively...* .

Model answer

The chart shows the injuries per 100,000 hours of play for seven sports. Football and rugby have the most injuries with about thirty-six and thirty injuries respectively. Women's hockey has about the average number of injuries at around fourteen. Sports which are less dangerous are cricket, cycling, boxing and swimming, with about seven, six, three and two

injuries per 100,000 hours respectively.

C **Note:** The best form of chart for the information given would be a pie chart, but allow students to suggest others if they can justify their decisions.

● Ask students to study the statistical information. They should notice that it is given in the form of percentages. They should then decide on the form of chart they prefer and make a sketch.
● Students should compare their charts in pairs or small groups.

Extension

● For homework students could make a neat copy of their chart, using colour etc., and write an accompanying summary describing the information it contains.

Language work

5 Substitution and ellipsis

Note: You may find it useful to read the section on substitution and ellipsis in the Grammar Reference section of the Students' Book on page 184 before beginning this section of the unit. Encourage students to refer to this if they experience problems with the concepts involved. Note that the connected subject of text reference is covered in Unit 20 on pages 151/2.

A ● With a weak class you should allow students to work in pairs for the three parts of Exercise 5.

Answers

In example 1 *do* refers back to *suffer*. In example 2 the word *taking* has been omitted.
Substitution: replacing a previously mentioned noun, verb or clause in order to avoid repetition.
Ellipsis: omitting a noun, verb or clause in order to avoid repetition.

B **Answers**

> In the early 1990s, airlines were required to introduce stricter safety regulations. Most of the larger airlines did <u>so</u> but some of the smaller <u>ones</u> were unable to follow suit for economic reasons.
> As a result, people came to the mistaken belief that travelling on the larger airlines was safer than * on the smaller*. In fact, most airlines are well within the agreed international safety limits – the American and European airlines certainly are*. If <u>not</u>, they are usually restricted to flying on domestic routes.

<u>so</u> (introduce stricter regulations)	1 substitution of a clause
<u>ones</u> (airlines)	2 substitution of a noun
than* (travelling)	3 omission of verb
smaller* (airlines)	4 omission of noun
are* (within the limits)	5 omission of a clause
<u>not</u> They are not within the limits	6 substitution of a clause

C ● Students should first underline the repeated or superfluous phrases and then compare their ideas in pairs before going on to rewrite the text.

Model answer

(Suggested improvements are in italics.)
<u>How safe is rail travel?</u>
Unlike air travel, which is regulated internationally, rail travel is in many cases controlled nationally. The degree of safety of rail travel is therefore highly variable from country to country, *depending on the degree and quality of regulation in the*

country concerned. In Britain and the United States rail passenger deaths work out at an average of less than *10 per year. Unfortunately, the statistics in the less developed parts of the world are considerably higher than in the western world.*

In the UK over the last 25 years there has been an average of one train accident for every million miles run. Because individual trains carry such a large number of passengers *compared with cars, buses and planes*, this actually means that the degree of risk is, comparatively, *almost non-existent.*

By far the greatest cause of railway accidents is human error, either in controlling or responding to signals. Recent improvements in accident statistics are in large measure due to the introduction of automatic and computerised signalling equipment. Radio communications systems between drivers and control centres have also proved influential in reducing accidents. With the continuing development of *these systems* we can look forward to further reductions in what are already impressively low accident rates.

Further practice: Workbook Unit 3, Exercise 6.

Listening skills

6   Listening and transcoding

*   Read through the introduction with the class and elicit their ideas. For example: provision of fire extinguishers and fire exits, fire doors and fire escapes, bans on smoking. Point out to students that statistics show the home as being the place where you are most at risk from fire.
*   Ask students to look at the illustration and elicit any fire risks they can spot.
*   Explain the task. Students must listen to the lecture and complete five more of the boxes on the drawing (as in the example), drawing in arrows connecting the boxes to the risks they describe.
*   After listening students should find four more risks and complete the remaining boxes.
*   Students should compare their answers in small groups.

Answers
(The first five dangers listed below are mentioned on the tape. The last four dangers (in italics) depend on the students' own observation.)
TELEVISIONS   Don't put televisions in front of curtains or soft furnishings.
ELECTRIC BLANKETS   Don't fold electric blankets.
OPEN FIRES   Don't dry wet clothes in front of an open fire.
SOFT FURNISHINGS   Cover them with flame retardant cloth.
AEROSOLS AND BOTTLES   Don't leave these on a window ledge in direct sunlight.
ASHTRAYS   *Don't put ashtrays on soft furnishings.*
ELECTRICAL SOCKETS   *Don't overload the sockets or let children play near them.*
SAUCEPANS   *Don't leave saucepans boiling with the handles pointing outwards.*
HAIRDRYER   *Don't use electrical equipment in a bathroom.*

Tapescript
FIRE OFFICER   Good evening ladies and gentlemen. I'd like to begin by quoting a few figures at you. 55,887... 8,500 ... and 1,000 degrees centigrade. That is the number of house fires reported last year, the number of people killed or injured in those fires, and the temperature of the flames given off by some items of furniture within 30 seconds of a fire starting.

All rather alarming, I think you'd agree. Well, what can we do to prevent these tragedies? In the fire prevention service we have three golden rules which we call 'awareness', 'precautions', and 'escape'. I'd like to start by dealing with the first of these – 'awareness'.

In the average home there are about half a dozen fire hazards or risk factors which we should all be aware of. Now the primary hazard is the electrical circuit. A lot of us live in older houses, and if your wiring is more than 15 years old, it may not be up to modern safety standards. Check that you have a functioning fuse-box, and if you're in any doubt, you really ought to get it looked at by a qualified electrician.

Electrical appliances come second on my list, and I'm thinking in particular of televisions and electric blankets. Some of you may not know that a colour television can generate over 20,000 volts, and this voltage can be retained for quite some time after a set has been switched off. So always switch off and disconnect from the mains when you finish watching. And don't put a TV in front of curtains or soft furnishings. The electric blanket is no longer the danger it was years ago, but it was the cause of 14 fatalities last year, so I think it is still important to remember not to fold them and certainly not to use one if it accidentally gets wet.

I just mentioned soft furnishings and this is a hazard which I want to emphasise. Many of you may have sofas and armchairs made before 1989 – when the new fire safety regulations came in. Now these may contain polyurethane foam fillings. You probably know that these fillings can give off extremely poisonous fumes in a fire, so if you do have this kind of furniture you should either get rid of it or have it recovered with flame-retardant cloth – which is now widely available and not expensive.

OK, I'd like to say a few words now about open fires. Recently we've noticed quite a fashion to return to open fires, especially in older houses. Obviously this is quite a hazard, and there are one or two fairly obvious things to be aware of. Firstly you should always use a fire guard in front of the fireplace, and make sure it's a fairly sturdy one. Secondly, never dry wet clothes in front of the fire. To be honest, if you have young children I think you're better off bricking the fire up and investing in central heating – it might not be so romantic on a winter evening but it's certainly a lot safer.

The final thing I want to draw your attention to is aerosols and bottles. Aerosols and bottles often contain flammable liquid or gas, so these should never be left in direct sunlight – on a window ledge for example. You'd be surprised at how quickly sunlight can heat up a pressurised container and lead to a fire.

So keep them in a cupboard or away from windows. Right, I'd like to go on now to the area of 'precautions'. Smoke detectors are perhaps the most common...

Speaking skills

7   Advising

A   Answers
All the examples have the function of advising. Forms with the imperative are stronger than the others.
The imperative: 1 *check ...* 2 *switch off and disconnect ...* 3 *Don't put ...*
modal verbs: 1 *you ought to ...*   4 *you should ...*
idioms: 5 *To be honest, ... you're better off ...*

*   Play the tape again for students to find further pieces of advice.

Answers
... risk factors which we should be aware of...
... the electric blanket ... it is still important to remember not to fold them and certainly not to use one if it accidentally gets wet.
... this kind of furniture ... you should either get rid of it or have it recovered ...

... fire guard...make sure it's a fairly sturdy one ...
... never dry wet clothes in front of the fire ...
... aerosols and bottles ... should never be left in direct sunlight ...

B ● Ask students to study the photograph and elicit any dangers it contains.

Suggested answers
No lifeguard on duty, no safety equipment visible, people swimming below chutes.

● Ask students about laws and regulations concerning swimming pools in their country. Elicit a short list, for example: quality of water, provision of lifeguards, edge markings indicating depth, supervision of children, etc.
● Divide the students into pairs and explain the role-play exercise. Point out that the Student Bs should use the notes to prepare some questions. Remind the student As to use the language of advice in their conversations.
● Monitor and check the correct use of advising language.

Extension
● Students could write up a list of safety requirements and then work out the reason for each of them. In a mixed nationality class you might like to discuss how regulations vary from country to country. The wearing of swimming caps, for example, is compulsory in some countries but not in Britain or the USA.

8 Ask the students to study the chart/pictogram and summarise its contents.

A ● Go through the list of questions eliciting answers from the class.

B **Note:** The underlined phrases in the poster and newspaper article are for use in Exercise 9. Tell your students to ignore them for the purposes of this exercise.

● You may wish to pre-teach the following:
kph (kilometres per hour)
anti-lock brakes (a device which prevents cars skidding when the brakes are applied)

● Give students a few moments to skim the poster and answer the questions.

Answers
The poster is concerned with the issue of improving road safety and reducing the number of cars on the road.
It was produced by the Transport Safety Campaign.

● Ask students if they agree with the aims of the poster and initiate a brief discussion of the issues involved.

C ● Read through the introduction to the newspaper report with the class and explain the reading task.

Answers
Measures accepted:
compulsory wearing of seat belts by all car passengers.
fitting all motor vehicles with anti-lock brakes.
Measures rejected:
the introduction of a 100kph speed limit.
compulsory wearing of seat belts by all bus passengers.
increasing the minimum age of drivers to 21.
transferring 50% of government investment in new roads to the rail system.

● When you have checked the answers, deal with any vocabulary problems which have arisen.

Language work

9 **Review of future forms**

Note: At this level students should be familiar with most of the future forms in English. This exercise, therefore, does not present them. Instead, it gives an overview of the forms used and concentrates on distinguishing between their various uses. Any students having difficulty should be referred to the Grammar Reference section at the back of the Students' Book. In addition to the work in this unit, *Distinction* contains work on the present and future continuous in Unit 1 (page 12) and on the future perfect in Unit 5 (pages 41–42).

● You may wish to point out to your students that the finer points of usage concerning future tenses are hard to define in English. Various uses overlap, which is why two forms are possible in some items of Exercise B, and why even linguistic experts can argue for hours on this subject. A practical approach, from a student's point of view, therefore, is to master the basic uses and then gradually build an awareness of and 'feel' for the finer points as they meet them.

A ● Ask students to read through both of the texts in Exercise 8 again, concentrating on the underlined forms.

Answers
1 g, h   2 c   3 d, g, h   4 e   5 f   6 a, b, g, h

● Students should work in pairs to explain the differences between the uses in questions 1, 3 and 6.

Suggested answers
1 g *is launching...* This has already been arranged for the future.
h *starts...* The date (March 22) is given, showing that there is an exact timetable for this event.
The two forms are more or less interchangeable.
3 All three forms indicate an arrangement for the future, see (g) and (h) above. The form in (d) is used for formal arrangements and is often used about parliamentary or official future arrangements.
6 a   refers to a date in the future (2025) at which time something will be in progress.
b   refers to a date in the future (2025) by which time something will already have happened.
g   refers to *next month*.
h   refers to a specific date (March 22).

● Ask students to complete the matching task.

Answers
future simple f
future continuous a
future perfect b   present simple h
present continuous g
be going to e
was/were going to (future in the past) c
is/are to d

B ● Divide the class into small groups to complete this task as they may wish to discuss their ideas together.
● When they have finished, elicit the answers and put some good example sentences on the board.

Answers

(Alternatives forms are in brackets. Suggested examples are given in italics below each form.)

1 *be going to* (future simple is also possible if the intention is a promise)
   I'm going to become a vegetarian one day.
2 *is/are to*
   The government is to introduce a new tax next year.
3 present simple (present continuous is also possible)
   The plane from New York arrives at midnight.
4 future simple (*Will be going to* is also possible if there is evidence for the prediction.)
   I think the Democrats will win the election.
5 present or future continuous
   I'm afraid I can't come, because I'm working on Friday /
   I'm afraid I can't make it, as I'll be working that evening.
6 present continuous
   I'm doing a tour of India next August.
7 future perfect
   I'll have bought a car by the time they arrive.

Note about Item 6: Students often confuse the present continuous form of *go*, *am/is/are going to* + place with the *be going to* + verb form. When speaking about travel, we often say e.g. *I'm going to Spain* – this is the present continuous form. We also tend to avoid the rather clumsy double use of *go*.

C Answers

hope   promise   expect   intend

D ● Students should work in pairs to complete the questions then form groups of four to compare their choices and reasons.

Suggested answers

1 b Use of present simple for timetables and schedules.
2 a Use of *be going to* for predictions with present evidence.
3 a Use of future simple for offers and decisions made at the time of speaking.
4 b Use of future perfect to indicate completion by a specified time in the future.
5 b Use of present continuous to indicate a future planned (or regularly occurring) action which will be in progress at a particular time.

Further practice: Workbook Unit 3, Exercises 7 and 8.

Writing skills

10 Writing a formal letter

A ● Give students a few moments to skim the letter and answer the questions.

Answers

1 The letter was written by Victor Grenville, Secretary of the South Kerstonleigh Residents' Association. It will be received by Councillor Pangbourne, Chairperson of Kerstonleigh District Council Planning Committee.
2 The letter is about the effect of the council's plan to build a shopping centre on road safety in the locality.
3 It is a formal letter. This is because it is addressed to a local government official from the representative of an official association.

● Students should go through the letter choosing the more formal of the options in brackets.

Answers

1 Further to   2 held   3 instructed   4 express
5 concerns   6 primary   7 schoolchildren

8 attending   9 a large volume   10 elderly
11 major   12 constantly   13 inform   14 outlined
15 reply

B ● At this level, students should be familiar with the conventions of formal letters (layout, salutations etc.). If necessary, quickly revise this by asking the class to analyse Victor Grenville's letter. They should note the position of the sender's and addressee's addresses, the inclusion of Councillor Pangbourne's name and job title above his address, the use of *Yours sincerely*, and the inclusion of Victor Grenville's job title under his signature. Note that the forms *Dear Sir/Madam*, and *Yours faithfully*, are used when we do not know the name of the person written to. Informal letters are covered in Unit 9, Exercise 13, page 74.
   ● Explain the task to the class. Point out that the notes contain three types of information: things which are unconfirmed, things which are confirmed, and things which have been scheduled. Students should reflect this in the future forms they use in their letter.
   ● Students can write the letter for homework.

Model answer

> **Kerstonleigh District Council**
> **The Town Hall**
> **High Street**
> **Kerstonleigh**
> **KE1 9LM**
>
> Mr V. Grenville,
> Secretary,
> South Kerstonleigh Residents Association,
> 87 Carlton Avenue,
> Kerstonleigh,
> KE6 89G
>
> Dear Mr Grenville,
>
> Thank you for your letter concerning the proposed shopping centre in South Kerstonleigh.
>
> In response to your queries about road safety, I can inform you that we are going to provide a new bus service for elderly people between Market Street and their social club. I can confirm that the council is building a new zebra crossing on Market Street and an underpass between the Market Street Estate and Mariton Road.
>
> As far as the timetable is concerned, construction of the shopping centre foundations begins on October 19 and in December we are commencing construction of the new access road. We will have completed the underpass and the zebra crossing by the end of March next year. The access roads are opening in May and the shopping centre itself opens on June 24.
>
> Yours sincerely,
>
> R. Pangbourne
>
> Councillor R. Pangbourne
> Chair of Planning Committee

Further practice: Workbook Unit 3, Exercise 9.

Final task

11 Surviving a fire

● Ask the students to study the leaflet cover and elicit suggestions as to its contents and purpose. (The leaflet is published by the London Fire Brigade and gives guidance to the public on what to do if they are caught in a fire at home.)

A • Divide the class into pairs. Ask pairs to predict the contents of the two sections illustrated. They should make brief written notes.

B • Divide the class into groups of 3 and nominate Students A, B and C in each group. (There can be two Student Cs in one or two groups if you have an odd number.)
 • Read through the instructions with the class and then let students turn to their respective pages. They must only use English and must not show their information to their partners. When they have worked out the order they should write the instructions for the spaces in the leaflets on page 31.
 • When groups have finished they can compare their ideas with other groups and with the notes they made earlier.
 • Elicit the answers from one or two groups and then tell them the 'correct' answer, that is to say the original instructions in the leaflet.

Model answers (from the original leaflet)

Fire Survival AT HOME – DAYTIME
1 Keep low, because smoke and heat rise to the ceiling.
2 Leave the room with the other occupants, closing windows if safe to do so.
3 Close the door of the room on the fire after everybody is out.
4 Leave the house, taking all the occupants with you.
5 Close the front door.
6 Alert your neighbours to the fire.
7 Call the fire brigade by the nearest available public or private telephone. Do not use a telephone in your home.
8 Wait outside in a safe position until the fire brigade arrives.

Fire Survival AT HOME – NIGHT
1 Roll out of bed on to the floor keeping low.
2 Crawl to the bedroom door and feel it with the back of your hand for heat.
3 If the door is cold, open it carefully and check for smoke. If there is no smoke wake the other occupants and follow the instructions for DAYTIME fire survival.
4 If the door is hot, do not open it, but act as follows:
5 Crawl back to the bed, remove the bedding and place it at the foot of the door, this helps to hold back the fire.
6 Crawl to the window, take a deep breath, stand up and open the window. If it will not open, break it with a chair.
7 Shout for a passer-by to call the fire brigade.
8 Wait at the window for the fire brigade to arrive.

C • Read through the instructions with the class and initiate a discussion on fire safety in the building you are teaching in.
 • Working in pairs, students can choose one of the two tasks. Allow time for them to complete their tasks. Then collect the leaflets/notices and distribute them around the class. Encourage students to comment on each other's work. If possible, display the work in the classroom at the end of the lesson.

Unit summary

Themes	Optical illusions, the psychological and visual qualities of colours; psychiatry and psychology, mental illness; *Jane Eyre*
Structures	The four types of multi-word verbs; the meanings of particles in multi-word verbs
Vocabulary	Colour adjectives, idioms of colour, science and medicine
Skills	*Reading*: transcribing to a chart; understanding and exchanging information
	Listening: listening and taking notes
	Speaking: exchanging information
	Writing: punctuation
Pronunciation	Stress in longer words

Note: Multi-word verbs often cause confusion. At earlier stages of learning students may have been introduced to over-simplified explanations which will not be sufficient preparation for accurate advanced work. We believe students need to understand the grammatical rules which govern the use of these verbs and they should be encouraged to develop a feel for the areas of meaning which are often associated with the various particles. In this unit, therefore, Exercise 6 introduces the standard terminology used to label the four types of verb and examines their syntactical rules. Exercise 12 introduces students to the 'areas of meaning' of various particles and concludes with a chart (on SB page 154) which students can add to as they meet more verbs during the course. Teachers may find it helpful to read the Grammar Reference section at the back of the Students' Book before teaching the unit.

 ## Teaching notes

Introduction

1
- Read the introduction with the class and elicit any experiences they may have had in which their eyes have deceived them, for example, mirages on hot days, special effects in films, seeing rainbows, or watching the tracks from a moving train.
- Divide the students into pairs to answer the questions about the optical illusions.
- Pairs should get together to compare their answers before turning to the solutions on page 158 of the Students' Book.
- Ask the students to react to the illusions and use this to initiate a brief discussion on the theme of perspective and colour as a lead-in to the next exercise.

Reading skills

2   Transcribing to a chart
- Ask the students if any of them have decorated their homes. Ask them to explain how they chose colour schemes and whether they looked at paint charts and thought about the effects of colour before they decided.
- Read through the introduction and allow students a few minutes to skim the paint leaflet and find the answers to the pre-questions.

Answers
1   Because few people can afford professional decorators, and it's more satisfying.
2   Green can make the observer feel relaxed and at harmony with his/her surroundings.
3   Blue.
4   Red and yellow.

- Ask the students to read the text again and use the information in the leaflet to complete the gaps in the summary chart.

Answers

colour	optical effect	psychological effect	reason for psychological effect
yellow	brings surfaces closer	bright, cheerful and welcoming	reminds us of sunlight and fields of corn
blue	recessive – appears distant	cool and tranquil	reminds us of sea and sky
white	reflective of other colours	can feel cold and clinical	reminds us of snow and ice
green	recessive – appears distant	soothing and restful	reminds us of nature
red	makes surfaces seem nearer	feeling of luxury vibrant/exciting	reminds us of blood

Vocabulary

3   Colour adjectives
- Elicit the answer to the introductory question.

Answer
e (7 million)

- Ask the students to look at the paint box and explain the matching task. Students can check their answers in pairs or small groups. Weak groups may need to use dictionaries.

Answers
1   mustard   2   lime green   3   maroon   4   navy blue
5   peach   6   khaki   7   purple   8   scarlet
9   chocolate   10   pink   11   turquoise   12   beige
13   cream   14   violet   15   bottle green   16   orange
17   aquamarine   18   lemon   19   royal blue   20   gold

- Ask students to work in pairs to answer a, b and c. There are no fixed answers.

Extension
- Ask the class to brainstorm the names of as many colours as they can. It can be very interesting to compare the way in which different languages describe colour. Students may find that their language has no exact equivalent for some of the colours in the paint box illustration.

Further practice: Workbook Unit 4, Exercise 5.

4   Students remain in their pairs to complete this exercise.

- Put the following categories on the board before students start.
  1 floor   2 walls   3 ceiling   4 curtains/blinds
- They should specify colours for each of these and make brief written notes.
- Ask students to compare their decisions in small groups. Elicit ideas from one or two groups for class discussion.

Further practice: Workbook Unit 4, Exercise 11.

5   Idioms of colour

- Ask the students to tell you about any idioms or expressions which use colours in their languages. Colours usually have different associations in different cultures and comparisons with English can often be amusing.
- Ask the students to complete the gap-filling and matching tasks.

Answers
1 a bit of a grey area
2 green with envy
3 showing a red rag to a bull
4 feel blue
5 through rose tinted spectacles
6 black and white

a 3   b 5   c 1   d 6   e 4   f 2

Extension
- There are a lot of idioms involving colour in English. You may wish to list some or all of the following and ask students to find out their meanings for homework.
a white elephant   as white as a sheet   a whitewash
a white lie   black humour   a black look   to see red
a red herring   to be in the pink   purple prose
a blue movie/joke   to be yellow(-bellied)   to feel green
to feel off-colour

Language work

6   Multi-word verbs

A   Ask the students to find the verbs in the text, circle them and study their contexts, before answering the questions.

Answers
Which type has no direct object? Type 1.
Which type has a meaning which can often be guessed from the meaning of the two parts? Type 3.
Which two types look basically the same here? Types 2 and 3.
Which type always has three parts? Type 4.

- In order to understand the rules of multi-word verbs, students should be familiar with the terminology involved. Ask the students to label the examples.

Answer

① verb   ② particle   ③ noun object
doing up a house
doing it up
④ verb   ⑤ pronoun object   ⑥ particle

- Ask students to study the chart before eliciting answers to the questions.

Answers
Type 2: The verb and particle can be split by a noun object or a pronoun object but the particle can only be followed by a noun object.

Types 3 and 4: The verb and particle cannot be split but the particle can be followed by a noun or pronoun object.

B   By studying the chart and the examples from the text, students should have enough knowledge to be able to complete the rules chart. They should compare their ideas in pairs or small groups before completing the chart.

Answers

MULTI-WORD VERBS: RULES
TYPE 1 Intransitive phrasal verbs *Has no direct object.*
TYPE 2 Transitive phrasal verbs *The stress is usually on the particle.* *The meaning is not usually obvious from the parts.* *A pronoun can be put between the verb and particle.*
TYPE 3 Prepositional verbs *The stress is usually on the verb, not the particle.* *A noun object cannot be put between the verb and particle.* *A pronoun object must not be put between the verb and particle.* *Meaning can usually be guessed from the meaning of the verb.*
TYPE 4 Phrasal/Prepositional verbs *An adverb can be placed between the first and second particles.* *Follows same rules as type 3 (prepositional verbs).*

- If students have had a lot of difficulty, they should refer to the Grammar Reference section at the back of the Students' Book.

C   Point out to students that they can work out which type a verb is by looking at the position of the example noun object in the dictionary. In other words, if there is no object given it must by Type 1, if the object is between the verb and particle it must be Type 2, if the object follows the particle it must be Type 3, and if it has two particles it must be Type 4.

Answers
fall down Type 1   *take off* Type 1   *take sb off* Type 2
take sth out Type 2   *take to sth* Type 3
see through sb Type 3   *see sth through* Type 2

- From the examples given, students should see that the same verb/particle combination can have several meanings. For example, *take off* and *see through*. Each meaning can be a different type. Put these examples on the board and elicit whether they are correct or not.
  1 I saw the task through. I finished it.
  2 I saw through the task. I finished it.
  3 I saw through the salesman. I wasn't deceived.
  4 I saw the salesman through. I wasn't deceived.

- The students should be able to work out that 2 and 4 are incorrect by looking at the dictionary extracts and the rules chart.

D   In order to correct the sentences the students will need to find the verbs and work out which rules apply to them. All the verbs are from the dictionary extract or are from the examples extracted from the paint leaflet.
- With a weak class, it is useful to ask students to work on the sentences in pairs and to write down the reason why they think there are mistakes. This will give you an idea of how much they have understood and help with correction.
- Remind the students that not all the sentences have mistakes in them.

Answers
(Reasons are given in brackets.)
1 Designers are always coming up with new colours (Type 4 verbs cannot have an object between the particles.)
2 The plane took off and headed south. (Type 1 verbs have no object.)
3 Decorators are expensive and people are reluctant to pay for them. (Type 3 verbs cannot have an object between the verb and particle.)
4 When I saw the young girl crossing the road in front of us, I told the driver to watch out. (Type 1 verbs have no object.)
5 CORRECT SENTENCE.
6 If you want extra leaflets you can pick them up at your local DIY shop. (Type 2 verbs cannot have a pronoun object following the particle.)
7 He fell down and hit his head. (Type 1 verbs have no object.)
8 CORRECT SENTENCE.

* Ask students to complete the re-writing sentences. Point out that they may have to adjust the word order.

Answers
1 Your house is very old, doing it up will take a long time.
2 By picking them up you have taken your first step to successful decorating.
3 The index is on page 89; if you turn to it you will find the reference you need.
4 Those chairs are rather valuable, I think I'll take them out when I repaint the walls.

Further practice: Workbook Unit 4, Exercises 5a, 5b, 6; Unit 20, Exercise 6 a – d.

Listening skills

7 Listening and taking notes

Background information: Dr Martin Lee is a consultant, that is a doctor who specialises in a particular area of medicine. Consultants are also known as 'specialists'. In his interview, he mentions the National Health Service (NHS). This is the system of public health care in Britain which is paid for by the government out of taxes and is free to all British citizens. In Britain private doctors and hospitals are comparatively rare.

* Refer students back to the optical illusions at the beginning of the unit and ask them if they remember which ones are used by psychologists (the information is on page 158 of the Students' Book). Elicit any knowledge which students have about psychology and ask them if they can explain the difference between psychology and psychiatry.
* Read through the introduction and explain the note-taking task. Although the interview contains a lot of complex vocabulary this should not be a problem for the students as it is explained by the interviewee as he talks.
* Allow students to read through the gapped notes before playing the tape.

Answers
See the notepad on the right.

Tapescript
INTERVIEWER Perhaps we could begin by defining the difference between psychology and psychiatry. I know it's something which a lot of people get confused about.
DOCTOR Yes, people often do confuse psychology and psychiatry, and, and equally psychologists and psychiatrists. Um, firstly, a psychologist will have a degree in psychology but will not have a medical training. A psychiatrist is always a fully trained doctor who also has additional specialist training

in the field of psychiatry. Psychiatry is the study essentially of mental illness. Psychology is really studying behaviour, including normal behaviour and mental processes: the way we think, behave and feel.
INTERVIEWER Right, so a psychiatrist is really more involved with people who are actually disturbed in some way rather than studying the sort of overall…
DOCTOR Psychiatrists' main work is in helping people that have a mental illness, uh, get better from their mental illness.
INTERVIEWER So how exactly do you define mental illness? How do you know when a person is mentally ill?
DOCTOR Its a difficult question actually to answer. Essentially, mental illness causes a disturbance in the way that people think, feel and behave. Um, most people think of mental illness in terms of a breakdown, um that the term 'a breakdown' is commonly used. Um, most often, people are thinking of someone who's become very depressed or anxious. But a breakdown may also describe someone who's had a major mental illness, um where their thinking, feelings and behaviour may become grossly disorganised.
INTERVIEWER Right. Um, I've heard of the ICD, the International Classification of Disorders, is that something which is used in Britain in psychiatry?
DOCTOR Yes, the, it's the International Classification of Diseases, um, which is the main classification used in England to classify all diseases; and all people admitted to

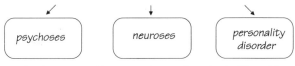

INTERVIEW WITH DR MARTIN LEE

psychiatrist – a fully trained doctor with additional training in psychiatry
psychologist – has a degree in psychology but no medical training
psychiatry – the study of mental illness
psychology – the study of behaviour and mental processes

International Classification of Diseases (ICD)

| psychoses | neuroses | personality disorder |

psychosis – the person loses all contact with reality
– thoughts, feelings and behaviour grossly disorganised
– behaviour will seem odd to the normal person

neurosis – the person remains in contact with reality
– behaviour is not outside socially acceptable norms

schizophrenia – a severe psychotic illness
– person may hear voices
– often have firm but abnormal beliefs
– treatment: anti-psychotic drugs and provide social and family support

Mental health statistics
– 26% of population consult family doctor each year with mental health problems
– 14% of days lost to work are results of mental health problems
– 20% of NHS expenditure is for treating mental health problems

Causes of mental illness
– genetic vulnerability
– stress
– physical illness

hospitals in England will have a diagnosis given within the International Classification of Diseases. This classification covers mental illnesses and really classifies mental illnesses under three main headings of psychoses, neuroses and personality disorders. Within each of those main areas of classification there are lots of other individual diagnoses.

INTERVIEWER Is, I mean, is it possible for you to give a brief description of those three categories?

DOCTOR Um, the main distinction is to be made between neuroses and psychoses; that distinction is not easy to make and describe but the essential difference is that with a psychosis the person loses contact with reality, whereas with a neurosis, although the person may suffer greatly, they remain in contact with reality – they know and understand what's happening around them. In a psychosis, again, people's thoughts, feelings and behaviours may be grossly disorganised: they may have very abnormal thoughts, very variable feelings, and behaviour that will seem very odd and unusual to the normal person. Um, with a person suffering from a neurosis, although thoughts, feeling and behaviour are all affected, their behaviour is not usually outside socially acceptable norms.

INTERVIEWER I'd like to ask you about schizophrenia because that's a word which people often associate with the most extreme kinds of insanity or lunacy or I'm sure you'd call mental disturbance of some kind. What exactly is that?

DOCTOR Schizophrenia is a severe psychotic illness. Psychiatrists term it a functional psychosis by which we mean that there's no clear cause that's been found within the brain – like a brain tumour, for example. Um, schizophrenia usually shows itself by the person perhaps hearing voices when there's nothing to account for the voice in the environment. They often have firm but abnormal beliefs: for example that they're being followed or persecuted, and their behaviour again may seem very odd.

INTERVIEWER Is there any effective treatment for this disorder?

DOCTOR Yes there is, there have been advances in the treatment of schizophrenia, particularly since really the 1950s when the major anti-psychotic drugs were introduced. The main line of treatment now includes drug treatments which can reduce or get rid of symptoms but we also these days very much provide social and family support and help to schizophrenic patients.

INTERVIEWER It has been argued, hasn't it, though, that these treatments often simply disguise the symptoms or treat the symptoms but don't actually cure the disease, is that true?

DOCTOR The drug treatments are essentially symptomatic, yes, they're treating and alleviating the symptoms. We're still not sure what the underlying disease process is.

INTERVIEWER Mm. There is a stigma, isn't there, attached to mental illness generally by society. But I believe it's actually a lot more common than people think. Is that true?

DOCTOR Mental illness is very common. I was reading a paper just today which was talking about mental health care and was pointing out some very staggering statistics: for example that 26 per cent of the population consult their family doctor each year with mental health problems, that 14 per cent of days lost to work are a result of mental health problems, that 20 percent of our total NHS expenditure is for treating mental health problems.

INTERVIEWER Well, how, how do we actually prevent mental illness? Is it preventable?

DOCTOR That's a really difficult question.

INTERVIEWER Isn't it true that, well at least one theory is that in many cases mental illnesses are hereditary, or people, you know, with parents or grandparents and so on, who are prone to this will get it themselves; and therefore presumably external factors aren't going to make any difference?

DOCTOR I think in terms of the cause or aetiology of mental illness there are often or most usually many factors operating; so the person may be genetically more vulnerable to that kind of illness. The vulnerability, though, is only one aspect. Stresses in their life, physical illnesses – which can cause mental illnesses – may be another factor bringing about mental ill-health. So there are a variety of factors interacting, which are leading to the, the mental illness.

INTERVIEWER So prevention really has to be tackled from a number of different fronts?

DOCTOR Yes.

Extension

● Students may like to discuss their reactions to the interview. Do they find any of the information surprising? Do they know of any alternative theories about mental illness and its treatment? How does Dr Lee's description of the British system compare with that in their own countries?

Vocabulary

8 Science and medicine

For some students many scientific terms can be 'false friends', appearing similar to words in their own languages but in fact having quite different meanings in English. This exercise looks at some of the most common sources of confusion.

A ● Ask students if they know any irregular plural forms in English. Elicit some of the following:
child – children   woman – women   mouse – mice
wife – wives   stratum – strata   criterion – criteria

Note: That the first four are survivors from Old English, the last two are Greek or Latin terms which have retained their original plural forms.

● If students cannot remember the special plural forms from the interview you can play the tape again.

Answers
psychosis – psychoses   neurosis – neursoses
diagnosis – diagnoses

● Ask students if they know any other examples which follow this rule. Elicit:
analysis – analyses, thesis – theses

B Students will need dictionaries for this exercise.
● Ask students to complete both parts of the exercise before you check their answers.

Answers
a *physics* the science of matter and energy
physical relating to the structure, shape and size of a thing, person or geographical feature
physician a general medical doctor
physicist an academic working in the field of physics
b *psychological* of the mind and mental processes
psychiatric relating to mental illness or its treatment
psychosomatic relating to a physical disorder or symptom caused by one's mental or emotional state
psychic relating to external phenomena or mental powers that cannot be explained
c *anaesthetic* drug or mixture of drugs causing temporary unconsciousness e.g. before an operation
analgesic drug which relieves pain
anaemia physical condition resulting from lack of red cells or haemoglobin in the blood
amnesia loss of memory

1 amnesia   2 psychic   3 anaesthetic   4 physicist
5 analgesic

Pronunciation

9 Stress in longer words

- Give students the clue that each column contains six words exactly. They should work in pairs or small groups, saying the words aloud to each other.
- Play the words on tape for students to check their answers.

Tapescript

See Students' Book, page 36.

Answers

O o o	o O o	o O o o	o o O o	o o O o o
physicist	physician	psychologist	schizophrenia	physicality
technical	psychotic	technology	schizophrenic	psychological
photograph	neurosis	photography	photographic	neurological
personal	technician	personify	anaesthetic	technicality
advertise	amnesia	advertisement	economic	personality
intellect	persona	intelligence	intellectual	economical

- Students should notice the following pattern: where words have the endings -icist, -cian, -ogist, -ical, -ity and -ical, the last syllable before this ending is the stressed one. This rule also applies to words ending in -tion.

Extension

- As a short game, ask students to work in pairs, adding three words from their own knowledge to each column. The first pair to finish is the winner.

Speaking skills

10 Exchanging information

This exercise is based on a reading jigsaw. (See the notes in the Introduction to this book on how to organise this in class.) You will need at least 30 minutes to complete the exercise. You may find it helpful to read the summaries of the extracts and the plot below before beginning the work in class.

Background information: Jane Eyre is the most famous novel by Charlotte Bronte (1816 – 1855). It was published in 1847 and is an example of the Gothic novel. It has been filmed many times and its plot has influenced many writers. Charlotte had two younger sisters who were also novelists: Emily, who wrote Wuthering Heights and was also a poet, and Anne, who wrote The Tenant of Wildfell Hall. The sisters were deeply influenced by their childhood in a remote Yorkshire parsonage.

- Introduce the exercise by asking students about their knowledge of attitudes to insanity in historical times. (This will be discussed further later in the exercise.)
- Introduce Jane Eyre and explain that the novel is written in the first person (like a diary). Read through the summary and check understanding. Explain that in Victorian times girls did not go to school. Wealthy parents usually employed a governess to educate their daughters at home. The governess would live in the same house as they did and was usually an unmarried woman from a middle-class family.

A
- Divide the class into five groups of more or less equal numbers and nominate each group A – E.
- Each group should sit and read their extract together, helping each other to understand it.
- With a weak class you can suggest that students make a list of the characters in their extract and a note of what happens.

B
- Re-organise the class into new groups of at least five students each, so that each new group has one representative from each of the former groups. It doesn't matter if one or two groups have six students.
- Students now tell their new partners about the extract they have read. Together the students must work out the story. The extracts are not in the same order as in the book so their first task is to try and work out the correct sequence.
- Go around and help the groups in their discussions, giving clues and hints if they are having difficulties.

Answer

The correct sequence is C D A E B.

- The following summaries of the extracts may assist you in helping the groups.

Extract C

One night Jane is woken from her sleep by strange noises in the corridor outside her bedroom. She hears someone walking along the corridor, laughing and moaning, and then going up the third floor staircase and closing a door.

Extract D

Jane tells Mr Rochester about a dream she has had. When she woke up someone was in her bedroom. It was not the maid Sophie or that strange woman Grace Poole. It was a tall woman with long dark hair and a contorted, savage face. The woman took Jane's wedding veil and ripped it in half.

Extract A

Jane is in church at the beginning of her wedding ceremony. A stranger comes into the church and announces that the marriage cannot proceed because Mr Rochester, her prospective husband, is already married, and his wife is still alive and living at Thornfield Hall. Mr Rochester admits that this is true. The strange woman living in his house is Bertha Mason, his wife, but she is mad. He invites everyone in the church to come to Thornfield Hall to see this for themselves.

Extract E

We are in a windowless room, where Grace Poole is cooking something over a fire. At the far end a mysterious female figure is grovelling on all fours. Mr Rochester starts to speak to Mrs Poole and the creature approaches and starts to attack him. Jane recognises her face. Mr Rochester struggles with the mad woman and eventually ties her to a chair. He points out to the other people in the room that this is his wife.

Extract B

Jane is talking to an innkeeper. He tells her that there has been a fire at Thornfield Hall. He believes a mad woman, Mr Rochester's wife, started the fire. He tells Jane that two months before the fire a young governess had left the house because she had fallen in love with Mr Rochester. Jane tells him to stop because she doesn't want to hear her own story. He goes on to say that the mad woman had jumped from the roof and died, but that nobody else had been killed.

- Once a group feels it has worked everything out, ask them to explain it quietly to you while the others continue their discussions. If they've got it right, they should then complete the written summary. However, if time is short, you might prefer to ask them to explain the plot to the whole class and then move all the students on to writing the summary.

Model summary

(The students will guess the ending.)

Jane hears strange noises at night. She falls in love with Mr Rochester and they decide to marry. On the night before the wedding, a mad woman comes into her room and tears Jane's wedding veil. She thinks this is a dream. At the church, the wedding ceremony is stopped by a stranger who says Mr Rochester cannot marry Jane because he is already married to Bertha Mason. Mr Rochester admits this is true but explains that his wife is mad. He takes the wedding guests to the house and shows them his wife, who is clearly completely insane, locked in a room at the top of the house and looked after by a servant, Grace Poole. Jane has to leave. Two months later she returns to the district and discovers from an innkeeper that Rochester's wife started a fire at Thornfield Hall and was killed, but that Mr Rochester is still alive. With his wife dead, Mr Rochester is at last free to marry Jane.

- In their groups the students should discuss the six questions.
- Elicit answers and open up to class discussion.

Suggested answers
1 She looks like a wild animal. She has long dark hair and a contorted face.
2 She grovels on the floor like an animal. She is physically violent and screams. Her behaviour is socially unacceptable and she seems to have lost contact with reality.
3 Her symptoms indicate that she could be suffering from schizophrenia, a severe psychotic illness.
4 According to Mr Rochester, her mental illness was inherited from her parents.
5 People can have a genetic vulnerability to mental illness, but it can also be caused by factors such as stress or physical illness. Psychiatrists believe there are usually a number of factors which interact to cause mental illness.
6 Nowadays schizophrenia is treated by anti-psychotic drugs and by giving social and domestic support to the sufferer, and his or her family.

Writing skills

11 Punctuation

A Even at this level students are often confused about many punctuation marks. This exercise will highlight those which need further explanation and practice.

Answers
1 ,   comma – separates parts of the same sentence
2 :   colon – introduces a list or further information
3 –   dash – usually informal, indicating a break
4 !   exclamation mark – usually informal, used after a command, an exclamation or something surprising
5 ;   semi-colon – divides two independent but related sentences
6 '   apostrophe – used in contractions and genitives
7 "   quotation marks – enclose words of direct speech
8 ( ) brackets or paratheses – enclose additional information, dates or references
9 .   full stop – shows the end of a sentence
10 - hyphen – joins the parts of compound words
11 ? question mark – used after a direct question

- Students can work in pairs to find the errors of punctuation and make the corrections.

Corrected sentences
1 She asked me if I could lend her my copy of the novel.
2 'I love you, Jane,' said Mr Rochester.
3 CORRECT
4 Charlotte had two sisters: Anne and Emily.
5 Charlotte's only brother, Branwell, was an amateur artist.

B **Note:** When reading out this dictation passage, you should not read the punctuation marks. Use pauses to represent commas

and full stops, use intonation to represent questions and exclamations, and use a different tone of voice (or accent) to represent the sections of direct speech. Listen to the actor reading the extract from *The Boys from Brazil* in Unit 14, Exercise 13, if you want to hear how this is done.

- Explain the task. Students should work individually.
- Read out the passage once without stopping to give students a feel for the situation. Then read the passage again slowly, repeating each section so as to give them time to write everything down. Finally read the whole passage again for students to check their transcription.

Dictation
  'Miss,' said the servant, who met me in the lobby, where I was wandering like a troubled spirit, 'A person below wishes to see you.'
  I ran downstairs without inquiry. I was passing the sitting-room to go to the kitchen, when someone ran out.
  'It's her, I am sure!' exclaimed the stranger, stopping my progress and taking my hand.
  I looked. I saw a woman attired like a servant: matronly, good-looking, black hair and eyes, and a lively complexion.
  'Well, who is it?' she asked.

- Ask students to compare their work in pairs and then allow them to turn to page 158 in the Students' Book to check their versions with the original.

Further practice: Workbook Unit 4, Exercise 9.

Language work

12 Meanings of particles in multi-word verbs

Note: There is some debate as to the origins and formation of multi-word verbs. It is clear that with phrasal verbs (verbs where the meaning cannot usually be understood from the meaning of the parts) the particle plays a key role in meaning. By studying the areas of meaning associated with particular particles, students will have a better chance of deducing the meaning of new verbs they come across. They should note two things, however. First, the areas of meaning are often rather metaphorical and not related to the literal meaning of the particle, requiring students to think laterally. Second, there are some exceptions which do not fit the areas of meaning that have been identified, making it necessary to point out to students that this approach will not cover all cases.

A Read through the introduction and ask students to study the underlined particles in the extracts.
- Students should know the meaning of the verbs in the extracts, thus they can work out the meanings of the particles and use them to complete the chart. Encourage students to discuss their answers in pairs or small groups, pointing out that some of the areas are metaphorical rather than literal.

Answers

particle	area of meaning	example
on	starting/continuing/ progressing	*Don't be hasty – carry on looking until you find the colour range (or ranges) you prefer.*
up	– completion/finality	*So don't give up if you have a room with low ceilings.*

	– growing/improving /increasing	Few of us can afford to pay for professional decorators when doing up a house.
	– movement in upward direction	By picking up this leaflet you have taken the first step.
off	departure/distance in time and space	The plane took off and headed south.
down	– collapse/movement downwards	He fell down and hit his head.
	– connected with writing	Note down your decisions.
through	endurance	Despite the difficulties, he saw the job through to the end.
out	– into the open	Those chairs are rather valuable. I think I'll take them out when I repaint the walls.
	– thoroughness	Using the information above, work out which of the following rules apply.

B Students must NOT use a dictionary for this exercise. They should use a combination of the context sentences and the areas of meaning given in the chart to work out the meanings of the verbs.
- Students should compare their ideas in small groups and try to reach definitions they can all agree on.

Suggested answers
1 *put sth off* delay until a later date
2 *take sth on* accept a new responsibility/task
3 *keep sth up* maintain performance
4 *jot sth down* write down in note form/write quickly
5 *get through sth* successfully complete a task
6 *see sb out* take/accompany somebody to the exit/to the outside

- Ask the students to turn to the multi-word verb chart on page 154 of the Students' Book. They should copy all the items from this unit into the chart.
- When students meet further multi-word verbs they can add them to the chart.

Further practice: There are a number of exercises on multi-word verbs and particles in *Distinction*.
Students' Book: + *in*, Unit 5; mixed, Unit 6; + *down*, Unit 13.
Workbook: + *up*, Unit 7; + *off*, Unit 9; + *through*, Unit 12; + *down*, Unit 15; + *on*, Unit 18; + *out*, Unit 19; revision, Unit 20.

Final task

13 Colour and personality quiz

- Read through the introduction and ask students if they agree with the idea that a person's favourite colour is an indicator of their personality.

A **Note:** With a weak class you might prefer the class to brainstorm a list of personality traits and put these on the board before asking the students to write down the ones they feel reflect their own personality. With a well-motivated and friendly class you can make the exercise more fun by getting the students to write down personality traits for each other rather than for themselves.

- When students have written down their five adjectives they should turn to the paint box on page 33 of the Students' Book and note down their three favourite colours in order of preference.

B
- Read through the list of groups of adjectives, checking understanding.
- Now students tick the group of adjectives closest to their own personality, they can only choose one group.
- Students write the three colours they have chosen next to their group.

C
- Divide the class into groups of five or six to compare their colour and personality group matches. By a process of elimination and comparison they should be able to link each group of characteristics with one or more colours.
- Re-divide the class so that new groups are formed, enabling students either to reinforce the matches they have already come up with or to add new colours to their lists.
- Once the groups have agreed (or agreed to disagree!) ask them to feed back to the whole class.

- Tell the students about the matches according to Dr Coleman.

Answers (from the psychology text book)
1 scarlet   2 orange   3 lemon   4 bottle green
5 royal blue   6 purple   7 violet

- Finally, ask the students to compare Dr Coleman's results with theirs, and take a vote on whether they believe there is any truth in the link between personality and favourite colours.

 ## Unit summary

Themes	Language awareness unit covering the international spread of English and ways of learning a language
Structures	The perfect tenses
Vocabulary	Multi-word verbs with particle *in*; vocabulary connected with methods of language learning (in WB)
Skills	*Reading:* understanding meaning from context
	Listening: predicting; identifying speakers; note-taking
	Speaking: using fillers; words with two stress patterns
	Writing: making written recommendations
Language awareness/Study skills	Words with two or more functions; words with multiple meanings

 ## Teaching notes

Introduction

1 This exercise consists of three puzzles about language, which will encourage students to think about the relationships between languages. Two of the puzzles have clues on page 158 of the Students' Book if the students have difficulty, and the answers to all of them are on page 159 .

A • Get the students to think about the appearance of the numbers and about where the languages are spoken.

Answers
English, French, German and Romanian are all from the Indo-European language family – English and German are from the Germanic branch and French and Romanian are from the Latin branch; Cantonese and Thai are both from the Sino-Tibetan language family; Arabic and Hebrew are both from the Afro-Asiatic family.

• Discuss the students' language(s) in relation to the chart: do they know, or can they guess from the chart, which language family their language comes from?

B • The students should be able to guess which are the most widely spoken languages. They can use the clues if necessary.

Answers

5	Arabic (*equal*)	4	Hindi
5	Bengali (*equal*)	9	Japanese
1	Chinese	8	Portuguese
2	English	5	Russian (*equal*)
10	German	3	Spanish

Note: See page 158 of the Students' Book for more information.

C • Students use their knowledge of other languages to work out this exercise.

Answers

b	*blitz*	h	*hurricane*	d	*shampoo*
d	*bungalow*	e	*influenza*	e	*studio*
a	*café*	a	*menu*	f	*tomato*
h	*canyon*	b	*poodle*	e	*violin*
c	*dollar*	h	*potato*	g	*vodka*
a	*garage*	d	*pyjamas*	c	*yacht*
c	*gin*	b	*quartz*		

Reading skills

This section encourages students to work out meanings from context in a fairly natural way, as the article contains a lot of 'corrupted' English words that are used in various countries across the world, but here their meanings are clear from the context. There is more analysis and practice of this in Unit 6.

2 Understanding meaning from context

A • Ask students if they are aware of any English words that are used widely in other countries. Discuss, then read the introduction to the exercise.

• Focus students' attention on the borrowed words in the first paragraph of the text. If you have a multilingual class, ask the (Swiss) Germans, Japanese and Russians (if any) to read aloud the relevant expressions. Students work out the meanings.

Answers
der TV television   *der talkmaster* host   *eine talkshow* a chat show   *das interview* interview   *der autor* author   *der bestseller* bestseller   *nekutai* necktie   *depato* department store   *hottu doggu* hot dog   *orenji juisi* orange juice   *veendserf* windsurf   *dzheenzi* jeans   *glidera* gliders   *mentolovky* menthol cigarettes   *importnaya* important

• Students now use the context to put the verbs in the correct gaps.

Answers
1 Turn on   2 conduct   3 buy   4 eat   5 drink   6 wear

B • Ask the students to read the text very quickly, without using a dictionary. Impose a time limit of three/four minutes for them to read and answer the questions.

Answers
Accepted: Russians, perhaps because they are accustomed to foreign influences. Japanese. No reason given.
Resisted: German, French.

3 • This exercise encourages careful reading of the text, as students must understand detail to be able to insert the missing sections.

• Ask students to read the text again, more slowly. Pre-teach the following if you feel it necessary.
blend mix
foreign correspondent reporter based overseas
I could swear I am sure
onslaught attack
fudge a statistika deliberately alter statistics
polyglot composed of many languages

• Students decide where to insert the texts.

Answers
1 B   2 E   3 D   4 A   5 C

4   ● Students can discuss these questions in pairs, before the discussion is opened to the whole class.

Answers
1 Remain intact: *TV, talkshow, interview, autor, bestseller, hotto doggu, glidera, telefon, viskey, computeri, budzhyet, statistika* (Many of these are slightly different from the original, but not enough to cause problems.)
Barely understandable: *talkmaster, nekutai, depato, orenji juisi, veendserf, dzheenzi, mentolovky, importnaya, dixie-go, travoltarse, dzhin-in-tonik, dzbazz saission, pepaa doraibaa, madamu kiraa, Kuraama-zoku, Makudonaru, pasokon*
2 He gives the example of foreign correspondents incorporating American terms in their reports. It's snobbish because the correspondents are trying to impress with their knowledge of a foreign language.
3 Because she uses so many English words.
4 It's come about from the fact that so much English has been absorbed into Japanese. It means a mixture of Japanese and English.
5 Students discuss their ideas – possibly the following: *sorilong* comes from 'to be sorry for a long time', *kisim ring* comes from 'kissing the ring' (perhaps once part of the marriage ceremony), *holim long ting ting* comes from 'to hold something for a long time'.
6 In the church, in the government and in newspapers.
7 Open answers.
8 Open answers. This can be made into a class discussion. See ideas on class discussions in the introduction to this book (page 8).

Vocabulary

5   Words with two or more functions

This exercise looks at words which can function as different parts of speech. (Exercise 7 looks at how their pronunciation may differ.)

● Students look back to the text and find the two words.

Answers
official = noun, import = verb

● Students complete the chart.

noun	verb	adjective
official		official
import	import	
blend	blend	
local (person or pub)		local
report	report	
influence	influence	
display	display	
trouble (uncountable)	trouble (bother)	
	complete	complete
comic (person or children's magazine)		comic
match (game, e.g. of tennis, good combination)	match	

● Students add any more words with different forms that they can think of.
● To provide practice in these words, ask students at random to put the words into context, making sure that they use the correct part of speech.

6   This exercise is the first of many which present a particle often used in multi-word verbs. Encourage students to think about its meaning and then to add it to the chart on page 154.

● Focus students' attention on the sentence in the text. *Caved in* here means *surrendered*. Discuss the two common meanings of the particle *in* (*collapse* and *make smaller*). *Cave in* here has the meaning of *collapse* (metaphorically).
● Students do the gap-fill.

Answers
1 caved in   2 take it in   3 falls in   4 give in
5 set in   6 turn in

● Refer students to the chart and check the examples they write in it.

Pronunciation

7   ● Read through the example with the students and ensure they can both hear and produce the two different stress patterns.
● Students work out the parts of speech of the words, using a dictionary if necessary, and mark the stress on them.
● Play the tape for students to check.

Tapescript and answers

'contrast noun	to con'trast verb
'frequent adjective	to fre'quent verb
'produce noun	to pro'duce verb
'suspect noun/adjective	to sus'pect verb
'desert noun	to de'sert verb

● Point out the following: The noun 'produce refers to fruit and vegetables. Students shouldn't confuse de'sert (abandon) with des sert (sweet course after a meal).

Divide class into pairs and read through the example with them.

Language awareness

8   Words with multiple meanings

In Exercises 2 and 4 the students looked at some of the borrowed words in the text and 'translated' them into English. The first part of this exercise asks students to look at the rest. You may have already done this, in which case, go straight to A.

● The only paragraph the students need to look at is *Resistance*– all the others have been dealt with, or are explained in the text.

Answers
viskey – whisky, *dzhin-in-tonik* – gin and tonic, *dzbazz saission* – jazz session, *computeri* – computers, *budzhyet* – budget, *statistika* – statistic
The words have been written in this way to illustrate the pronunciation (as those from Japanese and Russian would be written in a different script anyway).

A This exercise looks at homonyms – words which are spelt and pronounced in the same way but which have different meanings. This can be a problem in English for advanced students and the exercise is designed to raise awareness. (Unit 20 has a section on homonyms, homographs and homophones.)

- The meaning of *match* in the text is *compare, harmonise.* Other meanings and compounds of *match* that the students should know are: *game* (as in football, tennis), *match*(stick), fit together/be of the same colour (as in clothes).
- Read through the text with the students. Do not at this stage give them any meanings of the words mentioned.

B • Tell students they have to find meanings of the four words mentioned. They work in pairs and can choose either to search together for the meanings, or each student can take different words. They should really stick to meanings that they are aware of, and that they can explain.

Note: there is an exercise on this in the Workbook. Ensure that students are aware of the meanings given below so that they can do the exercise.

- Increase or decrease the time allowed according to the level of your class.

Answers
(These are only a few of the meanings – the ones that should be known, actively or passively, at this level.)
fine:
good, excellent;
delicate (e.g. workmanship);
very thin (e.g. fine hair, a fine blade);
fee paid for a crime or offence
sound:
noise; to make a noise (e.g. to sound the alarm);
free from damage, injury; financially safe (e.g. a sound investment)
round:
circular;
fully developed (e.g. of a character);
session (e.g. round of talks); series (e.g. a round in a tennis tournament or boxing match);
preposition meaning to follow the perimeter of something (go round the lake)
set:
put in position (set the table for dinner);
become solid (e.g. a jelly sets);
adjust (to set the timer);
locate (e.g. the novel is set in Albania);
of the sun – disappear beyond the horizon;
a group (e.g. a dinner set);
part of a match (e.g. in tennis and squash);
it is also used in many multi-word verbs, e.g. *set up* – establish

- Encourage students not only to explain the meanings but to put them in context.

Further practice: Workbook Unit 5, Exercise 3.

Language work

9 Perfect tenses

This section look at the perfect tenses in English. It assumes that students are familiar with the forms and uses of the perfect tenses and aims to revise the overall meaning of the perfective aspect, therefore it does not deal with each tense in detail.

- Ask students to give you the names and an example of each of the perfect tenses (present perfect, past perfect and

future perfect – simple and continuous for each tense).
- Tell students to find examples of the tenses in the text and to write them down.

Present perfect
English has become the prestige world language ...
Governments in both Bonn and Paris have tried to eliminate English words ...
In the Soviet Union there has been only some resistance ...
... so many words have been absorbed that the Japanese refer to them as Japlish.
Linguists have identified over a hundred varieties of these polyglot tongues worldwide.
... they certainly haven't become any more successful in the last decade or so.

Past perfect
Until recently the German post office ... had insisted on the word fernsprecher ...
... if attempts to prevent the mixing and matching of languages hadn't worked by then ...

Future perfect
... the language which remains untouched by English will have become extinct by the year 2000.

A • If your students are unaware of how time lines work, explain that each line represents a period of time and that actions and periods of action are 'plotted' on the line to show their relationship to each other.
- Students examine the lines and decide which tense each refers to.

Answers
1 past perfect
2 present perfect (past action with present result)
3 future perfect
4 present perfect (action still continuing, often the present perfect continuous)

Extension
- Ask students to make up a sentence to illustrate each time line, for example:
  1 When I got home he had cooked the dinner.
  2 I've walked for ten kilometres (and I'm very tired).
  3 I'll have finished my homework by 7.30. (It's now 6.30 and I started my homework at 6.00.)
  4 I've lived/been living in this house for three years.

B • Students use the time lines to match the tenses to the explanations.

Answers
1 present perfect
2 past perfect
3 future perfect

- If your students require a more detailed explanation of the perfect tenses, refer them to the Grammar Reference section of their books.

C For this exercise the students need to apply their knowledge of the tenses to a number of sentences, some of which may be incorrect.

- Students work in pairs or small groups and discuss the sentences.
- Warn the students that two of the incorrect sentences are correct in American English. Can they identify which ones?

Answers
1 INCORRECT. I hadn't learnt any French before I started that course.
2 INCORRECT. By the time my son leaves school, English will

have become the world language.

3 CORRECT.
4 CORRECT in American English but INCORRECT in British English. We have learnt ...
5 INCORRECT. I'll have finished all my work by then.
6 INCORRECT. We had already prepared your room before you phoned.
7 CORRECT.
8 CORRECT in American English but INCORRECT in British English. The course has already started.

● Point out to the students that American English often uses the past simple where British English uses the present perfect.

10 This exercise activates the use of the perfect tenses.

A The listening here is really only intended to contextualise the situation a bit for the students and to help them make their choice of tense.

● Ask students to listen to the tape and to write down the languages Suzanne speaks and the countries she has worked/studied in. They can check their answers by reading through the text.

Answers
Languages: French, English, German, Italian, Spanish, Portuguese, Czech, Japanese
Countries: Switzerland, the UK (England), Brazil, Czechoslovakia, Japan (Austria is also mentioned, but she does not say whether she lived there.)

● Students complete the text with the correct tenses.

Answers
1 had learnt   2 had become   3 had gained   4 had lived   5 had taught   6 had perfected   7 had spent
8 has worked   9 has already been   10 has been interpreting   11 will have received   12 will have learnt

Tapescript
INTERVIEWER ... so perhaps you could tell us how exactly you became so proficient at language learning, Suzanne.
SUZANNE MARTEAU Well, I think it all started with a really fortunate accident of birth. You know I was born in Lausanne, Switzerland; my father was Swiss – French Swiss and my mother was American, so, of course, we spoke both languages at home and I grew up bilingual. Then, of course, I learnt German at school – in Switzerland that's normal. And because I was already fluent in English my second language at school was Italian. So I had a real head start!
INTERVIEWER So that's ... one, two, three, four – you had learnt four languages by the time you left school? How fluent were you?
SUZANNE MARTEAU Erm, I was native speaker standard in French and English, but I'd become a bit rusty in German and my Italian was only school standard. I decided the best option was to study in the UK, and I did Hispanic Studies at university, studying Spanish and Portuguese, with some Italian, and living in Manchester. Then I went to live in Brazil for two years, teaching English.
INTERVIEWER So by this time you must have been fluent in six languages?
SUZANNE MARTEAU Nearly. My italian wasn't perfect, but I had a boyfriend from Uruguay while I was there, so my Spanish also became pretty good!
INTERVIEWER And then what did you do?
SUZANNE MARTEAU When I was 25 I came back to Switzerland, went to interpreters' school and then got a job in the United Nations when I was 28.

INTERVIEWER And you've been there ever since?
SUZANNE MARTEAU Not quite. In the first few months I met Jan, a Czech interpreter, who became my husband. We went to live in Prague in 1987 and that was where I learnt Czech.
INTERVIEWER And the eighth language?
SUZANNE MARTEAU Well, unfortunately the marriage didn't last; I was very upset and I decided to take a long break. I went to Japan on holiday, got a job and stayed for two years, which was when I learnt Japanese.
INTERVIEWER That's amazing! And now you're back at the United Nations?
SUZANNE MARTEAU Yes. Well, I never really left. I carried on doing work for them when I was in Prague – some in Prague, some in Austria and Switzerland, and I took a 'sabbatical' to work in Japan. They need people who can understand Japanese. But, yes, I've been back with them full-time for two years now.
INTERVIEWER And your plans for the future?
SUZANNE MARTEAU I'm going to learn more Oriental languages. It was such a challenge learning Japanese – it's so different from all the others. So I'll spend another two or three years here with the the UN full-time, during which time I hope to get a substantial promotion, then I think I'll go back and learn Korean, or perhaps Chinese, and Thai – I'd love to learn Thai. And then, perhaps an Indian language. Whatever, I want to be fluent in another three or four languages before I'm 45.

B This exercise aims to get students using the perfect tenses in a communicative way.

● Students read the three *find someone who ...* statements, and write three of their own.
● Students ask around the class to find at least one person to fit each of their statements.
● If you wish, students can use the statements given instead of writing their own, or they can work in groups to write a few statements and then circulate to ask other students.

Extension
● Students report their findings, either in an oral discussion at the end of the activity (encourage students to report only interesting findings) or in writing as homework.

Further practice: Workbook Unit 5, Exercises 6 and 7.

Listening skills

11 Predicting, identifying and note-taking

This exercise introduces the topic of personal experiences of language learning.

● Encourage the class to discuss what the differences might be between traditional and modern methods of langauge learning, and what the unorthodox method might be.
● Students predict which words they will hear on the tape, in connection with which method of learning.

Answers
On tape: grammar, reading, translation, writing, communication, dictionary.
One would normally associate grammar, translation, tests/exams and drills with traditional learning and communication, speaking, functions with more modern learning methods.

● Students listen and say which speaker describes which experience and which of the words they use.

Answers
1 *Louise:* the 'unorthodox' experience; dictionary, grammar
2 *Tony:* the traditional experience and a modern method – direct method; reading, writing, translation, communication, grammar
3 *Mark:* the modern experience; grammar, translation

● Students listen again and note down the methods mentioned.

Answers
Louise learnt Japanese simply by looking up words in a dictionary and then experimenting with them.
Tony learnt languages at school by rote (by heart), reading, writing, learning grammar and translating. He learnt Spanish at college by the direct method.
Mark learnt Spanish at evening class by a communicative method, using photographs etc and playing games.

● Students discuss the methods in groups. Play the monologues again if necessary.

Tapescript
1 *Louise*
INTERVIEWER Right, Louise, have you had any interesting experiences in learning a language?
LOUISE Well, I did learn Japanese on my own, em, purely through, with a dictionary, which was probably not the best way of learning Japanese, em, but it worked incredibly well.
INTERVIEWER It's very unorthodox.
LOUISE It is unorthodox. Em, but, I mean, from Day one I had to speak Japanese because the people around me couldn't speak any English. So, I literally learnt it through learning words and, er, in fact, it worked incredibly well, I mean, my grammar was probably appalling – well, it obviously was appalling – but just learning one word after another, em, in the end I managed to make myself understood, and I could chatter away about various different subjects, just through these words. So I think that's unorthodox, but it worked.
INTERVIEWER But what about pronunciation? [Mm, I was going to say that.] How did you know how to pronounce the words?
LOUISE Through, ... I used to test them out, saying them in different ways and when people understood me I'd know that I'd got the right pronunciation. But also people would, would, ... people tended to repeat them ...

2 *Tony*
TONY ... The way I learnt languages was rather boring in fact, because at school we learnt most things by rote, or by heart, and so a lot of the language was just written down – it was reading and writing, translation, there was very little in the way of real communication. And so I just remember learning long tables, in Latin and – *amo, amas, amat* – and in French the, you know, the same. So learning a lot of grammar, a lot of writing, a lot of reading and a lot of translation. But in fact when we went to college we had to learn – I did modern languages – and we had to learn one language which we'd never done before and I did Spanish, and the first day it was in fact direct method – and so it was the first time I was exposed to somebody speaking in a foreign language in a natural way and we had to respond to it.
INTERVIEWER And how did you react to it?
TONY Well, it was quite a shock at first, I suppose, but in fact it, the system worked very well, and that converted me to direct method language learning.

3 *Mark*
MARK ... I was, em, I went to Spanish evening classes recently and it was interesting because I actually felt, you know, the most communicative things where we were all playing games, or, we used a lot of photographs and cards; that was really exciting and interesting but at the same time I

sort of felt guilty because I felt we should be learning grammar, we should be learning irregular verbs. That's the way you should learn a language. Even though I was enjoying doing it the other way, there was something inside me saying, you know, you're not really learning anything, you're just enjoying yourself. And it's very different when you've had a traditional sort of, you know, the type Tony was describing – translation, learning grammar by heart, to go to another where it's more enjoyable, relaxing and you talk a lot; you enjoy it but at the same time you think, am I really learning? It's very difficult.
INTERVIEWER Were you there long enough to decide whether you were really learning?
MARK I did two terms and, em, I felt that if you already knew something it was a very good way of sort of practising it and making it stick, you know, but if you didn't know anything at the beginning you felt even worse at the end because you couldn't play the games or talk to the other students. So it was quite difficult.

Speaking skills

12 'Fillers'

● Read through the explanation of 'fillers' with the students.
● Discuss with the students what words and phrases carry this function in their language(s) to ensure that they understand the nature of the words.
● Students match the 'fillers' with their uses. (Ensure that students realise that the primary use of 'fillers' is to create time when speaking; the 'meanings' here are rough guides to the use of each one.)

Answers
a I mean   b sort of   c in fact   d well   e you know

● Students read the dialogue and put suitable fillers in the gaps. Then play the tape for them to check.

Answers
1 sort of   2 you know   3 Well,   4 well
5 sort of   6 I mean   7 Well,   8 you know
9 in fact   10 I mean

● Discuss the usefulness of these phrases with students: they allow time for thought, they give a real impression of 'Englishness' (if that is the aim of some of your students).

13 Discussing a text

A ● Students work in pairs to discuss the statements about language learning. Monitor and encourage the use of fillers as they discuss.
   ● Open the discussion to the class. Find out if they all agree with the statements or not. (This will be useful in future for planning lessons and deciding on the balance of grammar/analysis/skills work etc.)

B ● The texts describe five approaches to language learning. Tell the students just to skim the texts at first to see if any 'match' the statements they have discussed.

Answers
You have to learn about the language ...:
Grammar Translation
Everything ... should be conducted in the target language:
Direct Method
Language learning should involve real tasks ...:
Communicative Approach
People retain things better if they learn them actively ...:
Discovery Approach

C
- Students read the texts again and discuss the approaches in groups. Open out to a class discussion if you wish.
- It may be useful to teach the following vocabulary before the students reread the texts: *input* (texts), *facilitator* (someone who helps to make things run smoothly – from discovery approach), *emulates* (copies from communicative approach).

D
- Still in their groups, students read the profiles of the people and decide which method would suit each one best. Encourage students to give reasons for their choices.

Suggested answers
Mats: Community Language Learning, because he is nervous about speaking and would have to feel secure; and because he wants to speak the language.
Elena: probably a mixture of the discovery approach because she is analytical and the communicative approach, because she needs to be able to use the langauge socially.
Karel: Direct Method because he needs total immersion for a short while, and because a child is more likely to learn by demonstration than by analysis.
Fatima: Communicative Approach, because she mainly wants to speak the language and to be able to function in real situations.

- Open the discussion to the class. Does everyone agree?

Writing skills

14 Making recommendations

- Students read through the paragraph about Elena. Do they agree with the recommendations?
- In groups, the students discuss their recommendations for the other three people, then they choose one person to write about.
- As a group, the students write recommendations for one of the other people. (See notes on group writing in the Introduction to this book, page 8.)
- Students can write a further recommendation for one of the others, for homework.

Extension
- Hold a class discussion on the best way to learn the students' language. (If you have a multilingual class, this can be done in groups of students sharing the same language as far as possible.) Is there anything about their language(s) that would lend itself to a particular method? How would they recommend that an adult beginner learn their language?
- Students can write another paragraph of recommendation, about their language, or do this instead of the suggested homework above.

Further practice: Workbook Unit 5, Exercises 8 and 9.

15 Final task

A
- Divide the class into groups of three or four students, A, B, C and D. A turns to page 164 and reads the questionnaire for Student A, B turns to page 171 etc.
- Students complete the questionnaires for themselves individually.

Note: If necessary, all the A students can read their questions together and help each other understand, all the B students can read their questions together, etc.

B
- Practise the intonation of questions. Students read through the questions and decide whether the voice is likely to rise or fall on each one.
- Play the tape for the students to check their answers.

Tapescript and answers
1 Have you had any interesting experiences in learning a language?
2 But what about pronunciation?
3 How did you know how to pronounce the words?
4 And how did you react to it?
5 ... am I really learning?

- Discuss the usual rule for intonation in questions. (Voice rises in *yes/no* questions – 1 and 5; it falls in questions starting with a question word. Discuss exceptions, e.g. surprise will make the voice rise, as in question 2.)
- Students repeat the questions after the tape.

C   Students now work in groups of three or four and ask each other questions to complete their questionnaires.
- The groups try to work out what their needs as a group are and the best techniques for them.
- Discuss the results as a class. If you wish, this can be opened out into a discussion as to the best methods and techniques for the class as a whole, although students must be aware of the restrictions imposed on the teaching/learning method by the time available, the type of school, and so on.)

Unit summary

Themes	Moral dilemmas in the personal, professional and political fields; crime
Structures	Review of passives; connectives of contrast; review of multi-word verb patterns from Unit 4 (in WB)
Vocabulary	Lexical fields connected with crime, law, religion; prefixes *in-, im-, un-, contra-*; guessing meaning through context; idiomatic language (in WB)
Skills	*Reading*: reading for gist and for detail; finding evidence to support or refute a statement *Listening*: listening for detail and to infer *Speaking*: expressing opinions formally *Writing*: writing a summary (2)
Study skills	Semantic categorisation

 ## Teaching notes

Introduction

1
- Students look at the photograph in pairs and answer the questions/decide what they would do in the situation.
- Clarify the dilemma for them if there are any problems: the woman has found a letter to her daughter while tidying her daughter's bedroom, and she is trying to decide whether or not to read it.
- Elicit opinions around the class, ensuring use of *It depends on*, as this will be needed in Exercise 2.
- Ask students briefly if they have been in that or any other situation where they have faced a moral choice.

2
- Explain the steps in the exercise and divide the class into threes, each three comprising A, B and C. (If some groups have four students, two students take the role of B, which is the most complex of the three quiz pages.)
- Students look individually at the relevant pages. Ensure they check the meanings of the words in italics in their questions, and ask you or use a dictionary if they are not sure of anything. This is useful preparation for the exercise, as they will find they are asked the meanings of these words in the group work.
- Students read through the questions, make a note of their own answers and then ask the others in their group the questions. Ensure that they do not show each other the questions but that they ask and answer orally.
- Give them a few minutes to work out the scores at the end then do a quick class survey to see 'how moral they are'.

Note: It is worth monitoring the groups to ensure that they are all working at approximately the same pace.

- Students categorise the dilemmas. The ambiguity is intentional in order to provoke discussion. B7, for example, relates to both personal and professional life.

Suggested answers
personal: A1, A3, A4, B6, B7, B8, C9, C10, C12
professional: B5, B7, C11
political/official: A2

- Open class discussion of the questions.

Reading skills

3 ## Reading for gist

A This dilemma is a true one. The article was written as a summary of the situation, given in a television documentary. The photograph shows Death Row in the United States.

- Students read the article quickly and find out the dilemma.

Answer
The British Government is in contravention of a treaty, whichever route they take.

Note: It is best to avoid pre-teaching or explaining any vocabulary in this text; the unfamiliar vocabulary will be dealt with in Exercise 5. If you wish to deal with the vocabulary at this stage, do Exercise 5 at this point.

B ## Reading for detail

- Students go back over the article to find answers to the questions.

Answers
1 They were stabbed to death.
2 In August 1985, for cheque fraud.
3 She is in prison in the US.
4 He is in Brixton Prison, London, fighting extradition.
5 Because he would face the electric chair in the States, whereas he would be imprisoned for life in Europe.
6 Treatment of prisoners facing the death penalty in the US.

4
- Ensure that all students understand the dilemma.
- Discuss the questions either in groups or as a class, but summarise as a class in order to do the class vote.

Vocabulary

5 ## Guessing meaning from context

It is easy for students to worry about unfamiliar vocabulary when they read a text. However, it is often possible to guess the meanings of a new lexical item by understanding its relationship to the words around it and its function in the sentence. The following tasks will help students formulate a way of guessing the meanings of new words.

A
- Students read through and complete the first part of the exercise with the verb *upholds*. (There is help on page 159 if they need it.)

Answers
It's a verb.
It is in the context of treaties and conventions, therefore quite legal.
The prefix up conveys the idea of support.
It means *maintain, defend*.

B
- Students do the same analysis with the words given. Check their understanding of the words, then allow them to match the words with the definitions.

Answers
1 fraud
2 severed from
3 extradition
4 brutal
5 unenviable

6 accessory
7 trace
8 eradicate
9 fateful
10 contravenes
11 ruling

6 Prefixes

A Establishing meanings of prefixes.

Only four prefixes are examined in this exercise, two of them sharing the same meaning.

- Students match the prefixes with meanings.

Answers
1 in-, un-
2 contra-
3 im-

- Check that students have correctly underlined and matched the prefixes. Make sure that they are aware of the root word in each case.

Note: *in-* becomes *im-* before *b, m* and *p, il-* before *l* and *ir-* before *r*.

B Discriminating between prefixes and root words.

- The purpose of this part of the exercise is to show the students that the letter combinations above are not always prefixes, but sometimes part of the root word. For example, in *understand*, *un* is not a prefix.
- Students look through the words and decide if any do not contain prefixes. One way to help students do this is to get them to underline the root word in each case. They cross out any which do not contain prefixes and divide the words into the three categories.

Answers
opposite/negative: *inanimate, untidy, impatient, unimaginable, undeniable, uncertain, incapable, imperfect*
against/preventing something: *contradict*
in/towards/within: *immigrant, imbibe, implant*
words not containing a prefix: *contraption, understand, imagine, contribute, insistent, universal, contraction*

C • Students match some of the words from B (only those containing prefixes) with the definitions.

Answers
1 imbibe   2 inanimate   3 unimaginable
4 undeniable   5 incapable   6 immigrant
7 untidy   8 implant

Further practice: Workbook Unit 6, Exercise 2.

Language work

7 The passive

A This exercise focusses on the form of the passive.

- Students skim through the text again and find examples of the passive, which they enter in their chart. Tell the students to write only the first example of each type of passive (which contains a subject of the passive verb) that they find.

Answers
present simple   *the sentence is carried out ...*
present continuous   *extradition ... is being fought*
past simple   *Derek Heyson and his wife were stabbed to death*
present perfect   *She has since been sentenced ...*
past perfect   *Such force had been used ...*

modal   *Elizabeth and her boyfriend ... might be involved*
infinitive   *Zuring is hoping to be tried in the UK ...*

- Make sure students are familiar with the structure of the passive and that they have no problems with the word order.

B • Students rewrite the verbs in the text in the correct tense of the passive.

Answers
1 be broken into   2 to be burgled   3 have been burgled
4 has been taken   5 is/will be made   6 is being checked   7 had a window been left open?   8 was made
9 had been left ajar   10 have been carried out

8 This exercise checks that students understand the reasons for the use of the passive.

A • Ask students to match up the reasons for using the passive with the sentences given, using the text if necessary.

Answers
1 a   2 c   3 b   4 d

- If any explanation is necessary, tell the students:
In **a** we don't know who did the action, only that an action has been carried out.
In **b** we know who the agent of the action is (*the murderers*), but the emphasis has been placed on the force used. The fact that no agent is mentioned tells us that this information is not important. However, the passive can be used to emphasise the agent of the action, e.g. *This room was done by the man who decorated your house.*
In **c** the subject is known (*the UK police*), but we do not need to state that.
In **d** *It was thought ...* tells us that there was a general rumour that the daughter may be involved. This is an impersonal passive.

B This exercise is intended to make the students think about the passive as well as just transforming passive/active sentences.

- First, ask students to decide whether or not to transform the sentences, according to the criteria above, then to do the transformations.

Answers
1 Probably better transformed as the jury is unimportant here.
  At the end of the trial the offender was found guilty.
2 Better transformed as *someone* is too vague.
  The murder was committed with a great deal of force.
3 Better left in the active as the US is important.
4 Acceptable as it is or transformed.
  The couple was sent back to the States.
5 Both better transformed.
  Sunflowers *was painted by Van Gogh. It was bought for £24 million.* OR Sunflowers *was bought for £24 million. It was painted by Van Gogh.* (Even more likely would be: Sunflowers, *which was painted by Van Gogh, was bought for £24 million.*)
6 Better left in the active to show who did the action.
7 Better transformed to emphasise *cooperative.*
  The company was taken over by a cooperative formed by the staff.
8 Better left in the active.
9 Better transformed.
  It is thought that the serious crime rate is increasing.
10 Better left in the passive. (*Judge* is not important).
11 Better transformed to the active.
  My two cousins visited my new house last week.

12 Better left in the passive.
13 Better transformed to the active and changed slightly.
   I would have done it more quickly if you'd let me.
14 Better left in the passive.

9 This exercise practises the impersonal passive further. Read through the introduction with the students and make sure they realise that the two structures have exactly the same meaning and that the only difference is grammatical: the first uses the impersonal *it* as subject + a verb clause (see Unit 17 for more work on this) and the second has a personal subject + an infinitive. If necessary, refer students to the Grammar Reference section, and give them a few sentences to transform, for example:
People believe in John's innocence.
It is believed that John is innocent.
John is believed to be innocent.
Other sentences for practice:
People considered that it was the driver's fault.
It was considered that it was ... / The driver was considered to be /to have been at fault.
Everyone expects the Queen to attend the ceremony.
It is expected that the Queen will attend the ceremony. / The Queen is expected to attend the ceremony.
Everyone argued that the article was incorrect.
It was argued that the article was incorrect. / The article was argued to be / to have been incorrect.

* Ensure that the students are aware of the use of the perfect infinitive (*to have been*).
* Students make changes to the article.

Answers
1 It is alleged that he swindled ... / He is alleged to have swindled ...
2 It is said that he is a quiet man ... / He is said to be a quiet man ...
3 It was considered that he was an honest ... / He was considered to be an honest ...
4 It is thought that he may have taken the money ... / He is thought to have (possibly) taken the money ...
5 It is believed that his mother is in a home ... / His mother is believed to be in a home ...
6 It has been known for some time that Mr Gardner is in ... / Mr Gardner is known to have been in ...
7 It has been reported that Mr Gardner has been ... / Mr Gardner has been reported to have been ...
8 It is expected that the case will be heard ... / The case is expected to be heard ...

Further practice: Workbook Unit 6, Exercises 5 and 6.

Study skills

10 Semantic categorisation

The intention of this exercise is to help students to organise vocabulary in an effective way.

* Students complete the chart.

violent crime	non-violent crime	court/prison
stabbing	fraud	sentence
murder	burglary	capital punishment
rape	libel	appeal
mugging		imprisonment
assault		verdict
		judge
		convict

Notes: You might like to point out that *burglary* can be both non-violent and violent, though without any qualification it is usually understood as non-violent. Violent burglary is referred to as *aggravated* burglary. (*Burglary* is robbery from a house; *robbery* is from a person, bank, shop; *mugging* is assault on the street in order to steal money/a handbag etc.)

* Check the chart around the class.
* The second part of the exercise can be done for homework, with checking in class in the next lesson.

Listening skills

11 Note-taking

This is a useful skill for students to practise at this level, especially if they are likely to be studying or working in English at any point.

A
* Explain that students are going to hear something about a professional dilemma. Elicit examples of professional dilemmas. (Refer back to Exercise 2.)
* You can do this listening in one of two ways. If your students are likely to need a lot of help, play the tape once for them to listen only and think about the important facts given, discuss them, then play the tape again for students to take a few notes. If you want to emulate an authentic note-taking situation with more advanced students, play the tape only once, telling the students they have to note down the important facts while they are listening, then they can ask you a few questions to clarify if they wish.

Tapescript
BRIAN I work, or rather, used to work, for Bennett Electrics, as Technical Adviser. A few months ago, a new Personnel Manager, Marion Lynch, started working there. Although she hadn't got much experience, at first she was really good. She was clearly out to make a good impression, and she did. She was very friendly, always ready to put herself out for others, and always dealt with every problem quickly and efficiently. Then, a couple of months ago, she started getting sloppy, not putting through new pay rises on time, forgetting to renew car tax, that sort of thing. Last month a problem came up with my salary increase – it didn't happen when I was expecting it to and I got into debt with the bank. Anyway, to cut a long story short, I had a furious argument with Marion, who claimed that I was at fault and that I was just trying to give her a bad name, so I walked out. Fortunately, I've already found another job, but I really couldn't understand why the management allowed her to stay and get away with all the mistakes. She seemed to be getting on so well there, so I decided to try to find out what was going on. Anyway, I heard some gossip about her which explains all her actions, but it's very bad for the company. I really don't know whether I should tell someone at the company or not.

B
* Tell students to read through the summary and to complete as much of it as possible from their first listening. Make sure that they realise that they can write as many words as necessary in each gap.
* Students can check their answers in pairs if you wish.

C
* Play the tape again for students to listen and check their answers.

Answers
1 technical adviser   2 personnel manager   3 quickly and efficiently   4 sloppy/careless   5 forgetting to renew car tax /not putting new pay rises through on time
6 salary increase   7 got into debt with the bank
8 some information

Note: Allow students to phrase their answers differently, as long as they contain the correct information.

- Discuss the dilemma in the situation: Brian has found out some information which has a bearing on Marion Lynch's behaviour. If he tells the company, he could be harming Marion Lynch, but if he doesn't, the company could encounter more problems.

12 Multi-word verbs

- Focus students' attention on the verbs from the listening.
- Play the tape again so that students can listen to the verbs in context.
- Check the matching answers before students do the sentence completion.

Answers
Matching
be out to d   put oneself out g   deal with a
put through h   come up c   walk out e
get away with b   get on f

Sentence completion
1 getting on   2 puts himself out   3 walked out
4 came up   5 was out to   6 dealing with
7 get away with   8 put ... through

13 Listening to infer

- This exercise can be done in a number of ways. The simplest is the method suggested in the Students' Book. It can also be done as an integrated jigsaw activity by dividing the class into three and giving one group the reading to do (page 159) while the other two groups listen to the dialogue as suggested. They then all get together to discuss the dilemma.
- If you follow the method in the SB, make sure that the students are aware that they are only listening to one side of the conversation. You will find that they concentrate so much on their information that they cannot listen to the whole dialogue.
- After they have listened, get them to transfer information and to use the questions to work out what might have happened.

Answers
1 She asks if there is anything wrong with Marion.
2 Her work has been going downhill.
3 The company risks being sued.
4 That her mother died six months before she started at the company.
5 No.
6 It upset Marion a lot.
7 A couple of months before she started in the company.
8 She has had problems in finding somewhere to live.
9 Probably not.

- Students discuss the problem in pairs and decide what they think has really happened.
- Students read the report by the doctor to find out whether they were correct or not.
- Discuss what the doctor should do.

Tapescript
STEVE Jennifer, hi. You called me.
JENNIFER Yes, Steve. Have a seat. Don't worry, it's nothing serious. It's just, well, you're a friend of Marion's, aren't you?
STEVE Yes, we've known each other for years. We went to college together. Why, what's the problem?
JENNIFER Listen, I want you to know that this will be treated in the strictest confidence, but I've been worried about Marion, and I thought you might know if there's anything wrong.

STEVE Wrong. What do you mean? Do you think she's ill or something?
JENNIFER I don't know, Steve, but you must have noticed that things haven't been right lately. I mean, when she first started here, she was really good – very efficient, easy to get on with, a pleasure to have around, but over the last six weeks, well, things have gone really downhill.
STEVE Do you mean that business with Brian? That really upset her, you know. Perhaps she was in the wrong but he was hardly one of the easiest people to work with. When he got annoyed with someone he'd make their life hell, whoever it was.
JENNIFER Mmm. Well, it upset her too much, I think. Her swings of mood are really quite remarkable. Anyway, it's not just that; there are several other things that have caused problems recently, including one which could lead to us being sued. Look, Steve, if there's anything wrong, please tell me – I want to help, before it's too late.
STEVE Mmm. You know her mother died a couple of months before she started here ...
STEVE A couple of months! She told me that her mother had died about six months before she started here, she said that she'd been badly affected by that and that was why she'd been out of a job for so long.
STEVE Oh, yes, er, a couple of months, six months, I'm not really sure. But you're right, her mother's death did affect her badly, and she's had her problems since then, trying to find somewhere to live and other things.
JENNIFER Steve, I think there's something that you're not telling me. Now, if there are any problems I really should know, because things aren't looking very good for Marion, you know ...

Reading skills

14 Finding evidence to support/refute a statement

A
- Explain that the students will now read about a true dilemma of a completely different nature.
- Ask them to guess what the article might be about by looking at the photograph.
- Students skim the article quickly (allow only a short time) and answer the general questions.

Answers
1 Adoption is permanent; fostering is temporary.
2 They seem to be very nice, genuine people, concerned about their foster child.
3 Because the authorities felt he should grow up with a black family.

B
- Before the students read the article again, you may wish to preteach the following vocabulary: *counsel* (lawyer), *perverse* (going against what is accepted as normal or right), *judicial* (adjective from *judge*), *precedent* (a case which provides an example for the future).
- Students read more carefully to decide whether the statements are correct or not and to find evidence to support/refute them. This is a useful way of ensuring that the students read carefully.
- Check around the class.

Answers
1 CORRECT *showered with love and affection* (para. 3), *deep and binding love* (para. 4), *excellent care* (para. 5)
2 INCORRECT *had remortgaged their home* (para. 2)
3 CORRECT *their other adopted son* (para. 3)
4 INCORRECT *a rigid policy on placing children with families of the same cultural and ethnic background* (para. 4)

5 INCORRECT *one cannot but feel sympathy for them* (para. 5)
we have had lots of sympathy (para. 9)
6 INCORRECT *no court could come to that decision* (para. 8)

C ● Students complete the chart. (They will already be familiar
with some of the words from Exercise 10.)

the courts and the legal system	adopting children
Court of Appeal	foster parents
legal battle	adopt/adopted
counsel	long-term carers
judge	short-term carers
judicial review	1980 Child Care Act
case	

● Discuss the case with the students: do they feel that the
decision was correct?

Language awareness

15 This exercise looks at words which are near homonyms (i.e
they look and sound very similar). These are words which
English speakers often confuse. Unit 20 looks more closely at
homonyms, homographs and homophones.

● Students find the two similar words in paragraph 4, and try
to give their meanings.

Answers
counsel – lawyer (can also mean *advice*)
council – local governing body

● Divide the class into pairs and ask them to look at the pairs
of words together and decide what the differences are
between them. (They should not use a dictionary for this
exercise.)
● When they have discussed the ones they know, they can
turn to the pages in their books to find the other meanings.

Extension
● Students make sentences in their pairs to show the
difference between these words. You could give each pair
of students one pair of words only here to make the
exercise faster.

Language work

16 Connectives of contrast (1)

A   Identifying contrasts

● Students locate the idea in the text which is contrasted and
identify the connective in each case.

Answers
a *however*. It contrasts the Mellings' desire to make a
permanent home for David with the local authority's
decision.
b *but*. It contrasts the authority's policy with their lack of
attention to individual cases.
c *on the contrary*. It contrasts the suggestion that the Mellings
may not have given adequate care to David with the
reality.
d *instead of*. It contrasts the Mellings' needs with what they
are actually getting (sympathy).
e *while*. It contrasts the fact that the authority may agree with
the Mellings on an emotional level about their actions.

While introduces a clause. It might be worth pointing out
that *while* here is nothing to do with the *while* which links
simulataneous actions, often followed by the gerund.

Answers (to replacing exercise)
1 In the UK there are many children without parents.
However, it is difficult for childless couples to adopt. (*But*
is also possible here, combining the two sentences into
one.)
2 While everyone appreciates the reason for this decision,
few people agree with it.
3 We were unhappy about the changes but we didn't
complain. On the contrary, we decided to accept them
gracefully.
4 Instead of the settlement we wanted from the company, we
were offered something totally unacceptable.
5 The authority is well-meaning. However, it has disrupted a
young child's life. (Also possible with *but*.)

Note: Most of the connectives are possible if the sentences are
rephrased. The ones above are the most likely if the sentences
are not rephrased.

B ● The students now use the connectives to join sentences.
Allow any correct uses of connectives, as long as the
sentences have been reformulated correctly. Encourage the
students to use the connectives from 1–5 above as well as
those from the text. The most likely answers are given
below.

Answers
1 Many childless couples in the UK desperately want to adopt
a baby. However/Yet, inflexible adoption regulations ... /
Inflexible adoption regulations make adoption ...and
older. Nevertheless, many childless couples ...
2 The regulations are intended to ensure that children go to
good homes. On the contrary/However, they ensure ... /
Instead of this, they ensure ...
3 Couples often find it impossible to adopt in the UK. So,
instead of looking in the UK, they look abroad for their
families.
4 While this can be a solution for some, only the ... / This can
be a solution for some, but only the ...
5 Although/While adopting overseas has been an option for
sometime, the British Government ...

Further practice: Workbook Unit 6, Exercise 8.

Writing skills

17 Writing a summary (2)

The following tasks help students tackle summary skills in an
organised way.

● Go through the first part of the question with the students,
identifying the changes made in the model summary. They
should pick up the fact that the summary contains only the
chronological, salient facts in the first paragraph and a brief
description of the current position in the second paragraph.
Linkers they should identify: *some months later, where,
however, because, on the one hand, on the other hand*.
● Students look back at Unit 2 for the stages in writing a
summary and follow the steps to write a summary of the
text in Exercise 14.

Model summary
James and Lynne Melling have been fighting an expensive
legal battle to remain carers of their two-year-old foster child,
David, who has lived with them for most of his life. The local
authority has taken David from them to place him with a
family from the same cultural and ethnic background. While

the Mellings knew they were only short-term carers, they have become very fond of David and do not wish to lose him.

They requested an appeal against the decision of the local authority, during which the judge praised their care of the child, but decided that the local authority had acted correctly and that he could not allow the case to go any further. The Mellings were very upset after the hearing, especially as they had heard nothing of David since he had been taken away from them.

Further practice: Workbook Unit 6, Exercise 9.

Speaking skills

18 Expressing opinions formally

Some of the expressions given here are more formal than others. The more formal ones have an asterisk beside them in the answers.

- Get students to categorise the expressions and discuss which are more formal and which they might use all the time. They can add more to the list if they can think of any.

Answers
Giving an opinion
* In my opinion …
If you ask me …
I feel quite/very/rather strongly that …
Agreeing
* I'm totally in agreement with …
You're quite right. / X is quite right.
That's absolutely right.
Disagreeing
I'm afraid I can't go along with that.
I'm afraid I can't agree with …
* I think X is mistaken.

- Once you are sure the students are aware of the formality levels, get them to react to the statements about the article in their books, first in pairs, then in groups. Monitor for correct use/pronunciation of the phrases.

Final task

19 Debate

You can either do this exercise formally, as a debate, which gives students more opportunity to practise the language from Exercise 18, or you can do it informally if you wish.

- Make sure that all the students understand the motion and the procedure of the debate as described in their books.

A
- Divide the class into groups, either according to their initial feelings about the topic, or arbitrarily. Direct them to the help at the back of their books.

B
- Students discuss the questions and elect proposer/opposer and seconders. Make sure students are aware that the proposer/opposer and seconder should present different arguments.

C
- Make sure the students are clear how the debate is carried out, as described. The four speakers present their cases and then the debate opens to the class.

D
- The class votes to find out whether the motion is carried or not.

Extension
- The motion can be rephrased as a question for the students to answer in an essay for homework, e.g. *Do you agree that adoption of any available children should be open to all couples regardless of age, ethnic background, wealth or personality?*

Unit summary

Themes	School subjects; attitudes to education; different educational systems; schooldays
Structures	Verbs + infinitive or -*ing*; gerund/infinitive phrases
Vocabulary	Educational word groups
Pronunciation	British and American pronunciation
Skills	*Reading:* Understanding anaphoric reference
	Listening: Listening and transcoding to a chart
	Speaking: Checking and clarifying
	Writing: Recounting an event or experience

 ## Teaching notes

Introduction

1
- Read through the introduction and instructions with the class.
- When the students have completed the task ask them to report back to class, write the scores (column G) from each group on the board to find out the order of popularity of the subjects for the class as a whole.

2
- Students work in pairs to complete the matching task.

Answers
1 C (Adolf Hitler)   2 F (Sting)   3 B (Meryl Streep)
4 A (Queen Elizabeth)   5 E (François Mitterand)
6 D (Margaret Thatcher)

- Ask the students to name the people. Answers above in brackets.
- Briefly discuss whether they find the information surprising. Elicit the names of other famous people the class knows who may have had unusual educational backgrounds.

3 There is some challenging vocabulary in the newspaper article. This is dealt with in Exercise 5.

- Explain the reading task. Students should write down the three reasons in their own words.

Answers
(Four arguments are given for not going to university. Each student need only find three arguments, but elicit all four from the class as a whole.)
1 Many successful people believe they would have been less successful if they had gone to university.
2 Exotic experiences are more useful for a novelist than going to university.
3 People without degrees tend to be more original.
4 Being self-taught allows you to do things in your own way.

- Go through the follow-up questions with the whole class, eliciting suggestions and encouraging discussion.

Speaking skills

4 Checking and clarifying information

Although this is primarily a speaking skills exercise you should

point out to the class that it is also a test of their detailed comprehension of the newspaper article.

- Read out the dialogue yourself or ask two students to read it.
- Point out the key phrases used by the speakers:
  The author says ..., doesn't she?
  Not exactly, she actually says ...
- Divide the students into pairs and nominate Students A and B in each pair.
- Explain to the students that they will need to check the text very carefully to complete their mini-dialogues correctly, as all the prompt phrases are slightly incorrect.
- When they have finished, ask one or two pairs to read their dialogues to the class.

Vocabulary

5 Students should be able to work out the matching words and definitions by studying the words in context and by using a process of elimination.

Answers
1 i   2 f   3 b   4 g   5 h   6 c   7 e   8 j
9 a   10 d

Metaphors

- If students are unfamiliar with the term *metaphor*, you could write one or two well-known examples on the board:
  I'm dying for a drink. (I want a drink very much.)
  It's raining cats and dogs. (It's raining heavily.)
  This water's freezing. (This water is very cold.)
- Divide the students into pairs to complete the exercise.
- They should first study the phrases in context, then match each expression with a clue in order to work out its meaning. Finally they should write out the meaning of each expression in their own words.
- Pairs should compare answers in small groups.

Suggested answers
1 g treat a person as inferior
2 a Oxford or Cambridge University
3 a university
4 b very successful people
5 d measure precluding (not allowing) change or progress
6 c direct from working as a housewife
7 e unprejudiced/unbiased
8 f visited there

Language work

6 Verbs + *ing* or infinitive

There are a large number of verbs which are followed by EITHER the infinitive OR the -*ing* form. These can be found in grammar reference books and learnt by heart. This exercise concentrates on those verbs which can be followed by both forms, depending on meaning. Additional notes on these verbs can be found in the Grammar Reference section at the back of the Students' Book.

A
- Ask the students to read through the extracts and the sentences and underline the verbs and the forms which follow them.
- By studying the examples they have underlined they should

be able to work out the following rules:
When referring to an action/state that happened or began before the time of regretting, remembering etc. we use the -ing form.
I stopped worrying about it years ago.
When referring to an action/state that happens after the time of regretting, remembering etc. we use the infinitive.
I stopped to buy a newspaper on my way home from college.

- Ask the students to give you a few more examples of each type of meaning and put these on the board. If possible, the examples should refer to their own lives and experience.
  I remembered to bring a dictionary today.
  I remember going to the zoo when I was a child.

- Point out to the students that *go on and forget* follow the same rules and elicit one or two examples.
  I'm going on to study for a Master's after I've completed my first degree.
  Begin taking the malaria tablets one week before you leave and go on taking them for one month after you return.

B
- Follow the same procedure as above.
- The students should be able to work out the following rule:
  When there is no personal object we use the -ing form.
  When the verb has a personal object we use the infinitive.
  The college only allows smoking in the designated areas.
  The college only allows students to smoke in the designated areas.

- Elicit one or two more examples from the class. Point out that *forbid* and *permit* follow the same rules and elicit a few examples. Use these to check that students know how formal these two verbs are, and how strong *forbid* sounds, therefore, in statements like the one below.
  The school permits smoking in the coffee bar.
  I forbid you to use dictionaries in this test.

C   Answers
1 running   2 not studying   3 to use   4 teaching
5 practising   6 to take   7 to bring   8 going
9 to wear   10 to inform

Further practice: Workbook Unit 7, Exercise 5.

Reading skills

7   Understanding anaphoric reference

Note: There is further work on this subject, including cataphoric and exophoric reference, in Unit 20, Exercises 7 and 8.

- Read through the introduction and check that students understand the example.
- Ask students to complete the task. Point out that they will need to look back in the text to find out what these words refer to.

Answers
1 *them* universities
2 *they* people who have engineered their own education
3 *they* people who have engineered their own education
4 *it* going to university
5 *it* the mind
6 *them* the highlights

- Elicit from the class any other words which may be used to refer backwards and write these on the board. The most useful ones are listed below.
  he she him her this that these those the such

Listening skills

8   Listening and transcoding to a chart

Background information: The United Nations (UN) was set up after World War II (in 1945) with the aim of maintaining world peace and security and improving international cooperation on economic, social, cultural, and humanitarian issues. It now has about 160 members. The *Universal Declaration of Human Rights* is a document signed by all the member states indicating the minimum standards of human rights which they will enforce.

- Ask the class to tell you what they know about the United Nations and the *Universal Declaration of Human Rights*.
- Read through the introduction and the extract from the UN Declaration with the class and briefly discuss whether they agree with the principles expressed in the document.
- Ask the students to explain their understanding of free and equally accessible education. Elicit examples of countries where education does not fulfill these criteria.
- Refer students to the chart. They should study the 'Britain' column and then fill in the column for their country/countries.
- Play the interviews on tape. Students complete the columns for the United States and Japan.

Answers

The United States
4–5   pre-school
5–6   kindergarten
6–12   grade school (1st–6th grades)
12–14   junior high school (7th–8th grades)
14–18   high school
18–21   University (sometimes 5 years)

Japan
4–6   kindergarten
6–12   elementary school
12–15   junior high school
15–18   high school (optional)
18–22   University

Tapescript
Interview with Jamie Shambaugh
INTERVIEWER Jamie, can you tell me a little bit about your education?
JAMIE I began my education at the age of four, in America they have something that's called pre-school which lasts several hours a day and which your parents accompany you to for perhaps half the time..
INTERVIEWER Uh huh.
JAMIE And, basically that's just teaching you to be away from the home for you know a certain amount of time of the day, basically they don't really teach you much it's just sort of a social adjustment (um) which you have to make. Um, the age of five you enrol in kindergarten which is the lowest level of proper education and kindergarten is divided into afternoon and morning sessions and, um, you spend half the day. Um, I think basically that's mainly just to teach you being around other children and things.
INTERVIEWER So at what age does your actual formal education begin?
JAMIE Formal as in..?
INTERVIEWER Lessons, reading lessons, writing lessons.
JAMIE Oh, it begins actually the next year (uh hu) in first grade. You begin you know copying letters, you begin writing simple words
INTERVIEWER So that's at the age of six?

JAMIE   Probably, yeah (Yeah) and that's all printed writing (uh hu) and cursive comes the next year (yeah) cursive writing. Um, I think in the second grade you begin learning sciences as well, you have very simple science instruction in that same classroom, um, you're doing more reading then as well and you actually start doing history and you start picking up the more you know the various subjects which you'll be learning for the next ten years or so.

INTERVIEWER   Yeah.

JAMIE   That's when you begin – second grade. Then in third grade, fourth grade, fifth grade, sixth grade – those are all just advanced stages of the previous year, basically.

INTERVIEWER   Is there any name which is given to this group of years?

JAMIE   Grade school.

INTERVIEWER   Grade school.

JAMIE   Uh hu, yeah. Uh, in seventh grade and eighth grade is called junior high school. Basically these two years are more of a social transition, um, you have co-educational you know you know, gym classes (uh huh) and you have social functions such as dances and this type of thing and it's basically to sort of set the stage for high school (uh huh). You couldn't ...

INTERVIEWER   When do you make that transition to high school?

JAMIE   Uh, about twelve to thirteen. Okay? And then you went to high school usually at the age of fourteen. High school's fourteen to eighteen – it's four years.

INTERVIEWER   At what age do you leave school and start at college, normally?

JAMIE   Um, eighteen.

INTERVIEWER   And how long would you spend at university?

JAMIE   Um, oh the typical undergraduate degree lasts four years, um some people can do it in three, some people do it in five, um but generally four.

Interview with Ken Miki

INTERVIEWER   What sort of education did you have as a child, Ken?

KEN   Well, first of all I went to the kindergarten when I was four years old for two years. After that I went to the elementary school at the age of six for six years. After that I went to junior high school for three years.

INTERVIEWER   Right, so when did you leave junior high?

KEN   Um, when I was fifteen. After that I went to high school for another three years.

INTERVIEWER   Until you were eighteen?

KEN   Yes, and I went to a, university.

INTERVIEWER   Is that the uh, usual educational system for most people in Japan?

KEN   Yeah, I think so. I think I'm the typical case.

INTERVIEWER   What age can you leave school if you want to?

KEN   Theoretically at the age of fifteen, after finishing junior high school we can leave, but I think most people go to high school.

- Divide the class into small groups to compare their charts and discuss the follow-up questions. When they have finished, elicit feedback from all groups.

Pronunciation

9 British and American English

Note: You should reassure students that there are only a few differences between American and British English pronunciation (fewer than between Castilian Spanish and South American Spanish or between Portuguese and Brazilian Portuguese, for example). This exercise aims to familiarise students with those differences that do exist.

A • Read through the instructions and play the extracts on tape. The students should notice that the underlined words are pronounced differently by American and British speakers. The pronunciations are as follows:

proper: American /prɒpɜ:r/   British /prɒpə/
afternoon: American /æftɜːnuːn/   British /ɑːftənuːn/
half: American /hæf/   British /hɑːf/

- The students should be able to work out the two most important differences:
1 pronunciation of /r/.
2 pronunuciation of letter *a*.

B • Explain the task. Students will hear first the British and then the American pronunciation of five groups of words. The words in each groups follow a pronunciation rule which the students must work out. Students can begin by underlining the individual sound in each word which is pronounced differently.

- Play the tape. Elicit the answers and put them on the board.

Answers

A	British /ɑː/ American /æ/	(letter *a*)
B	British /ə/ American /ɜːr/	(ending -*er*)
C	British /t/ American /d/	(letter *t*)
D	British /aɪl/ American /əl/	(ending -*ile*)
E	British /juː/ American /uː/	(letters *u, ue* and *ew*)

- If you want your students to learn to produce the American pronunciations, you can play this section of the tape again, using the pause button to allow the students to listen and repeat.

C • Students listen to the tape and decide whether they are hearing the British or American pronunciation.

Answers

1 *half* British	9 *better* British
2 *after* British	10 *missile* American
3 *bath* American	11 *fragile* British
4 *proper* American	12 *agile* American
5 *mother* British	13 *due* British
6 *lover* American	14 *tune* American
7 *water* American	15 *new* American
8 *winter* American	

Vocabulary

10 Educational word groups

- If students are unfamiliar with this type of exercise, explain item 1 as an example: *edifice* is the odd word out, because all the other words are names of educational institutions, whereas *edifice* means a *large building or construction*.
- Allow students to use dictionaries.

Answers

1 edifice (educational institutions)
2 co-educational (things you do at school)
3 cursive (types of studying)
4 compulsory (types of school)
5 academic (types of educational institution)
6 course (types of qualification)
7 pre-school (stages of childhood)
8 professor (types of student)

11 • Read through the brief introduction and divide the class into two groups, A and B. Each group should read their own passage only and answer the five comprehension questions (the questions are the same for both groups, but the answers will be different) checking their answers with other members of their own group.

- Go around the groups quietly, checking that they have the right answers. They are unlikely to have any difficulties.

Answers
Jilly Cooper
1 Boarding school.
2 Upper or middle class.
3 Not very strict.
4 She was naughty, spoilt and outrageous.
5 It has made her outrageous.
Derek Jameson
1 A public elementary school.
2 Working class.
3 Very strict.
4 He was weak, always bullied.
5 He laughs a lot now to take away the pain of his childhood.

- Now ask students to form pairs so that each student has a partner from the other group. They should use their answers to tell their new partners about the passage they have read.
- Read out the three statements to the class and ask students to discuss the statements in their pairs, using evidence from the articles they have read to back up their opinions.
- Elicit feedback and, if the subject interests the students, open it up to a general discussion on discipline, classroom atmosphere and/or private education.

Language work

12 Gerund or infinitive phrases

- Read through the introduction and elicit the answer.

Answer
The form usually only used in formal written English is the infinitive phrase.
To complain to your parents was impossible in those days.

- Ask students to explain when each form is used and elicit the following rules, writing the examples on the board.
An infinitive or gerund phrase can be used as the subject of a sentence. Gerund phrases are usually used for general actions while infinitive phrases usually refer to a specific event/situation.
Complaining to your parents was impossible in those days.
To complain to my parents was impossible when I was a child.
Infinitive phrases are usually only used in formal writing. In conversational English it is more usual to use an introductory *it* construction.
It was impossible to complain to my parents when I was a child.

- Now ask students to complete the re-writing tasks.

Suggested answers
Language teaching policy
People say learning a foreign language is easy when one is young. Acquiring a language is something we all do in our infancy without even thinking about it. Thus we believe that studying a foreign language in kindergarden is a vital first step to eventual mastery. Starting at the age of five or six is ideal.

Mertonleigh school
To study at Mertonleigh is to experience a unique and stimulating environment. To learn in our quiet and contemplative surroundings is to take part in a centuries-old scholarly tradition.

Further practice: Workbook Unit 7, Exercise 6.

Writing skills

13 Recounting an event or experience

Note: This exercise follows from the work on past tenses and linkers in Unit 2. This skill is developed further in Unit 12.

- Ask the students to complete the sequencing task.

Answers
1 an introductory link between the past and present
2 an explanation of the background
3 a description of the characters involved
4 a narrative account of the event
5 an explanation of how she feels about it now

- Read through the instructions with the class. Explain that they must use the headings to plan their account (using notes) before they begin writing.
- Students can base the account on a true personal experience, they can invent a story or they can use the picture for inspiration.
- Go around and check their plans. The account can be written up for homework.

Further practice: Workbook Unit 7, Exercise 7.

Final task

14 Decision making

This is a challenging decision-making and information-gap exercise. You should allow at least 30 minutes for the exercise. You may find it helpful to study the students' information on pages 164 and 172 of the Students' Book before beginning part B of the exercise.

- Divide the class into groups of three or four and read through the introduction.

A
- Explain the task. Each group must decide how many hours to devote to each school subject out of a total of 24 possible hours. Once they have agreed on this, they must make a list of the subjects and the number of hours they wish to devote to each, checking that the total comes to 24. Check that the groups are making reasonable decisions and balancing the subjects fairly.
- If groups are unable to decide, you can suggest the following solution.

Art 2 lessons	History 3 lessons
Biology 1 lesson	Literature 3 lessons
Chemistry 1 lesson	Music 1 lesson
Computer studies 3 lessons	Physics 2 lessons
Economics 3 lessons	Sports 3 lessons
Geography 2 lessons	

Total 24 lessons

B
- Now nominate Students A, B and C in each group. Try to give role C to students with good organisational and communication skills. Groups with 4 students will have two Student Cs.
- Explain that each group is now going to plan the school timetable to fit in the subjects/hours they have decided on.
- Students should turn to their information and study it carefully before they begin exchanging information (orally) in order to plan the timetable.
- Monitor the groups and give assistance as necessary.
- Some groups may find it impossible to work out a timetable for their chosen subjects. If so, they should be prepared to amend their earlier decisions about the number of hours to devote to each subject.

● Groups which followed the suggested list of subjects above
  should be able to work out the following timetable.

WINTERBROOK HIGH SCHOOL: FOURTH YEAR TIMETABLE						
LESSONS	9 – 10	10 – 11	11 – 12	1 – 2	2 – 3	3 – 4
Monday	English Ms Gray	Chemistry Ms Bingham	Economics Ms Terry	Economics Ms Terry	Economics Ms Terry	Maths Mr Karl
Tuesday	Literature Mr Carlton	Literature Mr Carlton	Literature Mr Carlton	Geography Mr Denton	Maths Mr Karl	Biology Mr Sutton
Wednesday	Geography Mr Denton	English Ms Gray	Music Mr Carlton	Sport Ms Smith	Sport Ms Smith	Sport Ms Smith
Thursday	Computer studies Ms Lean	Computer studies Ms Lean	Computer studies Ms Lean	English Ms Gray	Physics Mr Sutton	Physics Mr Sutton
Friday	History Ms Bingham	History Ms Bingham	History Ms Bingham	Art Mr Denton	Art Mr Denton	Maths Mr Karl

Unit 8 Round the World

 ## Unit Summary

Themes	Round-world trips; Jules Verne; international travel
Structures	Groups of nouns; inversion after negative adverbials
Vocabulary	Travel and transport; idioms (in Workbook)
Skills	*Reading:* Recognising tone and purpose
	Listening: Listening to form judgements
	Speaking: Paraphrasing
	Writing: Physical description
Pronunciation	Stress patterns in compound words

Note: Dice are required for the final activity in this unit.

 ## Teaching notes

Introduction

1
- Read through the introduction with the class. Ask the students if any of them have been on similar trips and elicit one or two of their experiences.
- Divide the students into small groups to discuss the three questions.
- Elicit answers and put them on the board. Students/groups should give reasons for their choices. Let the students discuss/decide which are the three most and least favoured destinations for the class as a whole.

2
- Divide the class into pairs and nominate Students A and B in each pair. Explain the situation: Student A is a travel agent, Student B is considering a round world trip. Read through the Student B information with the class and ask Student As to turn to page 164/5 of the Students' Book to find their itineraries/prices.
- Check that the students understand the rules: the trip must begin and end in London, and travel must be in one direction only. Stopovers can only be made at those cities marked on the map.
- Allow 10 to 15 minutes for the students to complete the task and then ask pairs to report back to the class.
- Students should work out which is the most popular itinerary and discuss the reasons for this.

3 **Background information:** *Around the World in Eighty Days* was published in 1873. Jules Verne was a French writer who is regarded as the father of science fiction, a reputation based on his earlier novels *Voyage to the Centre of the Earth* and *Twenty Thousand Leagues Under the Sea.* His work has always been very popular and many films have been made of his stories. (There is more information about Jules Verne in the Workbook Unit 15, Exercise 1.)

- Elicit from the class anything they know about *Around the World in Eighty Days* and Phileas Fogg. If any of them has read the book or seen the film, they should tell the class what they remember.

A
- Explain to the class that a flyleaf is the inside flap of the paper cover of a hardback novel, usually giving a description of the novel and a brief synopsis of the story.
- Ask the class to read the flyleaf of Jules Verne's book only (NOT Michael Palin's book) and answer the three pre questions.

Answers
The three main characters are Phileas Fogg, his manservant Passepartout, and the detective, Fix.
Phileas Fogg tries to go around the world in 80 days to win a bet he has made at the Reform Club.
Some of the problems which occur on the journey are: a detour to save an Indian widow from *suttee* (ritual death on the death of her husband), saving Passepartout from Red Indians, and storms.

B
- Divide the class into pairs to discuss the differences and complete the chart with their ideas. There are no right or wrong answers to this and you should encourage students to come up with their own ideas.
- Ask one or two pairs to feedback their ideas to the class.

C
- Ask students if they have heard of Michael Palin and elicit anything they know about him.

Background information: Michael Palin is a British writer, actor and comedian. He first became famous for his role in the BBC comedy series *Monty Python's Flying Circus* in the 1970s. He has written and starred in several TV series and films, including *The Life of Brian* and *A Fish Called Wanda.* In 1988 Palin re-created Phileas Fogg's journey around the world for a TV series and wrote a bestselling book about the experience.

- Now ask the students to read Palin's flyleaf and compare the flyleaf description of his journey with their ideas (from their charts) by listing any similarities and differences.
- Ask the pairs to explain why Palin's journey was different (to elicit the point that Palin was deliberately trying to re-create a 19th-century journey, not a 20th-century one).

Vocabulary

4 Travel and Transport

A
- With a weak class you might prefer students to complete this exercise in pairs or small groups.

Answers
Jules Verne
1 nostalgia   2 manservant   3 zest   4 quarry
5 detain   6 suttee
Michael Palin
7 state cabins   8 deck   9 sacks   10 barge
11 cockatoo   12 liqueur

B • You can make this exercise more interesting for the students by making it a competition, the winner being the student who finds the most words.

means of transport	adjectives	nouns connected with travel
ocean liner dhow steamer train aircraft ferries freighter container ship	breath-taking brilliant marvellous delicious regulated exciting feverish engaging French resourceful loyal assiduous guilty incredible quixotic simple golden regular crowded open creaking signed blind bizarre dirty unparalleled difficult full frank no-holds-barred great	detour route encirclement journey boarding (also a verb) schedule sea travel timetables bunks passports visas customs forms carnets frontier

Further practice: Workbook Unit 8, Exercise 2.

Study skills

5 Adjective collocation

• Read through the explanation with the class. They should have no difficulty understanding the concepts.

Answers

The implied noun, which *exciting* and *breathtaking* describe, is *journey*.
Phrases which are not possible in English: *a loyal journey*
a loyal nostalgia
Suggested rule: The adjective *loyal* collocates with nouns which describe people.

• Point out to the students that the adjective *loyal* can also be used to describe domestic pets.
• Explain the collocation chart to the students. The exercise should be done in two stages. Firstly students should complete the chart with examples from the flyleaves. Then they should compare their ideas with a partner and together think of other words with which the listed adjectives can collocate, writing an example sentence for each.

Answers

Note that these answers only include the collocations from the flyleaves.

ADJECTIVE/NOUN COLLOCATION (TYPE OF NOUN DESCRIBED)			
person	event	written account	means of transport
engaging (manservant)	breath-taking (journey)	frank (account)	crowded (ferries)
resourceful (manservant)	marvellous (journey)	full (account)	crowded (Red-Sea ferries)
loyal (manservant)	exciting (journey)	no-holds-barred (account)	creaking (container ships)
assiduous (detective)	incredible (adventures)		open (dhow)
guilty (party)	feverish (boardings)		
blind (barber)	quixotic (detours)		
	bizarre (ritual)		

Language work

6 Groups of nouns

Compound nouns often present difficulties for students because dictionaries often disagree on whether some are written as one word or as two words with (or without) a hyphen. The best advice is to use a reliable monolingual dictionary and follow its conventions consistently. Because the creation of compound nouns is one of the main ways in which English vocabulary develops, it is inevitable that there will be differences of opinion.

A • Ask students to divide the examples into three types and then match each of the types with the definitions which follow.

Answers
a bank robbery, manservant
b Verne's story, Fogg's schedule
c the adventure of the eighty days, a warrant of arrest

B • Explain the task and read through the example with the class. If students are still having difficulties they can refer to the information in the Grammar Reference section at the back of the Students' Book.

Answers
1 Jules Verne's reputation is based on the fact that he virtually invented the type of book known as science fiction.
2 Fix's suspicion is that Fogg is a bank robber.
3 Circumnavigation is much easier nowadays because of jet aircraft.
4 Palin's journey is made more difficult by the number of customs forms he has to fill in.
5 Timetables seem to be much less reliable now than they were in Jules Verne's time.
6 Palin's task was to use only those forms of transport which had been available in the nineteenth century.
7 The purpose of the journey undertaken by Fogg was to win a bet with his fellow club members.
8 Palin's diary records many of the dangers of sea travel including engine failure and storms.

Further practice: Workbook Unit 8, Exercises 6 and 7.

Pronunciation

7 Stress in compound words

A • Students should predict the stress pattern in the words.
• Play part A on the tape for students to check their answers.

Answers

manservant housewife bank robbery film crew
jet engine blackbird grandmother pair work

B • Play part B on the tape and ask students to answer the questions.

Answers

Sentence **a** contains a compound word (English teacher).
In sentence **a** the word *English* is stressed, in sentence **b** the word *teacher* is stressed.
The general rule is that the main stress is usually on the first word or part of the compound.

C • Read out sentences 1a and 1b as a model for the class. Stress the underlined part as below:
  a I saw a blackbird in the garden.
  b I saw a blackbird in the garden.
• Ask the students to repeat the sentences, checking that they are able to distinguish the stress patterns.
• Divide the students into pairs to practise reading the sentences. Monitor and check that they are using correct stress patterns for the compound words.

Reading skills

8 Recognising tone and purpose

At this level students should be developing a feel for the style of texts and an ability to judge their purpose. The flyleaf of a novel is the part of a book a reader will look at when browsing in a bookshop. Its purpose therefore, is to inform the reader about the content of the book and to persuade him or her to buy it. This style of text is a form of publicity and students should recognise the enthusiastic and exaggerated tone of the language used.

Extension

• Ask the students to look at other texts in *Distinction* Students' Book and comment on their tone and purpose. Suitable examples are:
1 Text extracts from *The Book of Heroic Failures*, Unit 1, page 9. (Humorous non-fiction anecdotes, to amuse readers.)
2 *Punishment takes many forms*, Unit 2, page 20. (Magazine article, serious but non-academic tone, to inform readers and provoke discussion.)
3 Personal letter, Unit 9, page 74. (Personal letter to a friend, informal and friendly tone, to act as a means of social communication between friends.)
4 Text extracts from linguistics book, Unit 10, pages 76–7. (A text book, formal and academic tone, to educate and present research results.)

9 • Divide the students into pairs and explain the task. Read through the list of items and check understanding.

Note: *Stockings* nowadays usually refers to a tight-fitting silk, nylon or wool garment which covers the foot and leg, worn by women. In the nineteenth century, *stockings* were thick long socks worn by men. A *macintosh* is a waterproof coat.

• When pairs have made their lists, they should compare these with Michael Palin's list on page 159 of the Students' Book.

• Form the students into small groups to discuss the similarities and differences between the three lists, and to try to explain them.
• This exercise can lead into a more general discussion of the differences between travel in the nineteenth century and the present day.

Listening skills

10 Listening to form judgements

A • Read through the introduction and explain the numbering task.
• Play the tape. (N. B. On the tape Terri's story precedes Simon's.)

Answers

Tijuana [6] New Haven [4] London [3]
Singapore [X] Moscow [2] New York [X]
Hong Kong [1] California [5]

B • Play the tape again for students to complete the gap-filling task.

Answers

Simon obtained a special visa which allowed him to 1 *work in the States for a limited period*. Unfortunately he didn't know that this visa 2 *is only valid* for three months. As a result he got into a lot of trouble at the 3 *immigration office on the Mexican border* in Tijuana. Now he thinks it's very foolish to travel without 4 *checking all your documents in advance*.
Terri bought her ticket to Hong Kong after she saw an advertisement in 5 *a magazine*. The flight was delayed and arrived 6 *late* in Moscow. She couldn't get on the next flight because her ticket was only valid for 7 *the twice-a-week flight*. Terri had to spend three days in the hotel. She couldn't go out because she didn't 8 *have a Russian visa*.

C • Divide the students into pairs.
• Explain that students must now use the information they have heard to form their own judgements about the situation described.
• Once they have made their decisions they should compare these with other pairs'.

Suggested answers

a You should be very careful about buying cheap tickets. Check that they are valid for all flights and check the arrangements for alternative flights if you are delayed, try to avoid stopovers if you can. Check that in-flight service (meals etc.) is included.
b Check that you have visas for all the countries you are passing through, in case you get delayed. You should find out how long the visas last and how they can be renewed, some cannot be renewed. Once you are in a foreign country do not leave it until you have all the documents you need or you might not be allowed back in. You should be very careful about working (or telling the immigration officer you plan to work).

Tapescript

TERRI Did you see that television series with Michael Palin?
SIMON The one where he went around the world in eighty days?
TERRI Yeah.
SIMON Yeah, it was really good. You know, that's something I've always wanted to do.
TERRI Me too. Mind you, you have to put up with a lot of hassles. I mean, I went to Hong Kong last year and it was one long disaster!

SIMON   Really?

TERRI   Yeah, I was stuck in Moscow for three days!

SIMON   How on earth did that happen?

TERRI   Well, it was like one of those bucket shop tickets, you know, from the back of a magazine. I went down to this little place in central London, in Soho and paid cash.

SIMON   But they're usually OK aren't they?

TERRI   That's what I thought at the time. Now I know better! I mean the plane was delayed two hours leaving Heathrow and we were doing a stopover at Moscow. It was Aeroflot, like mega-crummy, no drinks, terrible service... so we arrived late at Moscow, in the middle of the night, and we all went into the transit lounge and after about two hours this official came in and told us we'd missed the connection to Hong Kong, we'd have to stay the night in the airport hotel ...

SIMON   But why?

TERRI   The late departure from Heathrow apparently.

SIMON   So, what was the hotel like?

TERRI   Grim... more like a prison really. Anyway, the next morning I went down to reception and asked what was happening. Disaster! They'd checked my ticket or something and decided it wasn't a proper Aeroflot one, only valid for the twice-a-week flight, not the daily flight. So I had to sit there and watch all the other passengers go off to catch the next plane to Hong Kong while I was stuck in this terrible hotel.

SIMON   Well, a good chance to explore Moscow.

TERRI   No way! I didn't have a Russian visa, of course, so they wouldn't let me out. I had to stay there for three days. The pits! No TV, no newspapers, no phone lines and the food was gross. All because I had this cheapo ticket.

SIMON   I guess you won't be buying cheap tickets again.

TERRI   You're not wrong!

SIMON   You know I had a similar sort of experience in the States.

TERRI   Uh huh?

SIMON   Yeah, when I was an exchange student. See, I had this special visa, a J1 Visa, in my passport, which entitles British students to work in the States for a limited period – it's a kind of reciprocal thing with the UK.

TERRI   Mm, I think I heard about that before.

SIMON   Yeah, I was in New Haven ...

TERRI   At Yale?

SIMON   Yeah, well, after the semester I went over to California to work, you know, get some money together to do some travelling. I did that for about six weeks and set off for Mexico. A real experience I can tell you! It was much more expensive than I'd expected and I got some sort of stomach bug, so I had to head back to the US.

TERRI   Problems at the border?

SIMON   Exactly! Well, I was a bit scruffy, my clothes hadn't been washed for ages and, of course, I'd been ill. So anyway, I got the bus back to the border at Tijuana and showed my passport to the immigration guy. Well, he saw the visa and he was like, you know, really suspicious. So I told him I wanted to go back to see a doctor and then to try and earn some money. Well, that was obviously the wrong thing to say! Suddenly all these other officers turned up and I was bundled into this back room and searched, I mean completely strip-searched, for drugs I suppose.

TERRI   Jeez!

SIMON   Yeah, it was pretty scary! I kept saying 'I'm British! I'm British!' but I think they just thought I was an illegal Mexican immigrant trying to get into the country. I was sure I was going to be locked up or, well, who knows? But then the first guy came back and he'd been checking my passport on the computer or something and, of course, he found out it was genuine. The trouble was, the J1 visa's only valid for three

months, and it's not renewable, and I'd already been in the States for over six months!

TERRI   So how did you get out of it?

SIMON   Mm, luckily I had my return ticket to London, so I showed that to them and they let me go through ... after giving me a lecture about not working in the States before I left. Quite a relief, but it does show you how risky it is to leave the country without checking all your documents, specially if you plan to work.

TERRI   That's true. There's lots of places where you can't get visas except in advance. I guess you should have read the small print on the visa.

SIMON   Mm, easy to say with hindsight!

TERRI   Well, looks like we both learnt the hard way!

Speaking skills

11 Paraphrasing

Paraphrasing is an important skill for students. In everyday English it is impractical to report what we hear, read and see exactly. We have to summarise and put things into our own words. Paraphrasing thus involves recognising and reporting the key points. This also allows us to add our own interpretation and opinion to what we are reporting.

● Read through the instructions carefully with the class.
● Divide students into A/B pairs to complete the task.
● Elicit the answers and ask the students to explain the clues.

Answers

Verne	Palin	Situation
B	F	Bombay
D	C	trains in America
E	A	crossing the Atlantic

Clues
Verne's extracts are written in the third person, Palin's are written in the first person (like a diary).
Extracts A, B and F mention location in the text.
Extracts D and E contain out-of-date vocabulary (*dressing-rooms, hoisting sail*), so are probably by Verne.
Extract C mentions aircraft, so must be by Palin, as aircraft didn't exist in the nineteenth century.

Language work

12 Inversion after negative adverbials

● Read through the examples and elicit answers to the questions.

Answers
The subject/verb order has been reversed.
The writer has used this construction to add emphasis – a stronger feeling of negativity.

● Elicit or explain the grammar rule: the subject and auxiliary verb are inverted. If there is no auxiliary verb *do/does* or *did* are used.
  I rarely go to parties. → *'Rarely do I go to parties.*
● Point out to the students that this construction is used in formal written English. It is not usually used in spoken English.
● Read through the list of negative adverbials. If you have a strong class you can elicit further examples of negative adverbials and put these on the board:
  not (+ object)   *seldom   nobody   hardly   scarcely*
  No sooner ... than   Not only ... but also   Only after
  Only in   Only since   At no time
  Under no circumstances   In no way   On no account
● Introduce the sentence transformation exercise and go

through the example to check understanding before students complete the sentences.
Students may wish to refer to the Grammar Reference section at the back of the Students' Book.

Answers
1 Rarely had Palin been so tired.
2 Never before had Passepartout had such an adventure.
3 Not since the invention of the jet engine has such a journey been possible.
4 Nowhere can you escape timetables and schedules.
5 Not until airfares become much cheaper will world travel be possible for everyone.
6 I have rarely read such an exciting adventure story.
7 You would not find such colourful ceremonies anywhere.
8 Palin had never had such a difficult challenge.

Further practice: Workbook Unit 8, Exercise 7.

Writing skills

13 Physical description

A   • Read through the descriptions and check understanding of vocabulary.

Note: *Bogies* are four-wheeled undercarriages fitted at either end of train carriages to enable them to turn corners.

   • Ask students to look at the chart and check that they understand the categories and examples.
   • Students should add further examples from the extracts to the chart.

Answers

Descriptive feature	Examples
comparing similar objects	a sort of long omnibus owes much to aircraft design like the bullet train unlike the trains in China
showing the position and relationship between objects	rows of seats open coach formation two-tiered between them was an aisle linked together by gangways convoy
describing colour, material, shape or construction	moulded seats a lightweight shell silver, red and blue livery neatly-designed
describing the function of objects	fold-down tables dining-cars sleeping cabins dressing-rooms saloon-cars observation-cars refreshment-cars

B   Students should refer to the photograph of a jumbo jet interior on page 65 of the Students' Book to complete this exercise.

   • Divide students into pairs to complete the notes.
   • Explain that the task is to write notes describing all the items they can see in the photograph and their own experience and imagination, using the examples in the chart as models.
   • Encourage students to use dictionaries for the exercise. If students are unfamiliar with the vocabulary used in describing the parts of a cabin interior, you may wish to put these words on the board:
   overhead locker   safety belt   reclining seat   cloth padded   headset   armrest   footrest   folding table overhead lamp   plastic   vinyl   carpet   emergency exit   gallery   video   screen   headphones (socket) legroom   aisle   window

   • Pairs should compare notes and add new words/notes to their lists.

C   • Read through the introduction and the advertisement with the class. The writing task can be given as homework.

Further practice: Workbook Unit 8, Exercise 9.

Final task

14 The Round the World Game

Note: A pair of dice are required for each group. Each student will also need a token. If necessary, these can be made from small pieces of coloured paper or card, or from small items such as rings, earrings, coins etc.

   • Ask students to turn to page 156 of the Students' Book.
   • Read through the instructions with the class, including the example questions on page 160 of the Students' Book. Explain to the class that if they disagree about a particular question they should ask you to come over and adjudicate.
   • Divide the class into groups of 3 or 4 to play the game, re-arranging tables etc. as necessary.
   • 20 – 30 minutes should be adequate to complete the game.

Unit summary

Themes	Fast food; famous dishes; diet and health; restaurants and recipes
Structures	Emphatic devices; *actually* and *really*
Vocabulary	Food and drink; multi-word verbs with particle *off* (in WB)
Skills	*Reading:* Re-ordering jumbled paragraphs *Listening:* Listening and comparing *Speaking:* Expressing opinions *Writing:* Writing a personal letter
Pronunciation	Emphatic stress

Teaching notes

Introduction

1
- Elicit anything the students know about the reputation of British food. Explain that many British dishes have unusual names. Students are going to work out the names and ingredients of the five dishes in the picture.
- Read through the instructions with the class.
- Divide the students into groups of five and nominate Students A – F. If you have an odd number, students can double up roles.

Answers
Toad in the hole sausages in batter, Picture C.
Bangers and mash sausages and mashed potato, Picture A.
Cornish pasty meat and potato in a pastry shell, Picture D.
Spotted dick sponge pudding with currants, Picture B.
Welsh rarebit cheese and tomato on toast, Picture E.

- Ask students if they have tried (or would like to try!) any of the dishes.

2
- As a warm-up, ask the class to identify and discuss the eating places in the photographs.

Background information:
Photo A: Pizzaland is a chain of inexpensive pizza houses, also serving other simple dishes such as garlic bread or spaghetti, and wine, beer, juice or coffee. The restaurants are modern in decor. A take-away service is also available.
Photo B: Fish and chip shops traditionally sell their food, wrapped in newspaper or brown paper, to customers over the counter, but it is possible to eat at simple tables in some places. They serve chips and either peas or baked beans with everything: fish in batter, sausages, burgers and pies. They often sell tea, coffee or soft drinks but no alcohol.
Photo C: Chinese restaurants can be found all over Britain, ranging from the very expensive to the cheap and cheerful. They serve rather westernised dishes from China and other countries in the Far East.
Photo D: Burger bars like this one can be found in city/town centres, railway stations etc. all over Britain. They sell burgers in baps (bread rolls) with sauces and pickles, hot dogs and hot or cold drinks. The food is for instant consumption, but facilities for this are rarely provided.

Photo E: Indian restaurants are very popular. As Chinese restaurants, they range from the expensive to the cheap and cheerful, offering Tandoori (spiced, baked meat) dishes, curries and rice dishes. Most offer restaurant or take-away service.
Photo F: French restaurants, or bistros, are to be found in many town and city centres. Informal in atmosphere, the food is often quite expensive but good, as is the wine. Bistros are popular with working people at luchtime and with trendy couples, families and young people in the evening and at weekends.

- Introduce the questionnaire. Students complete individually.
- Students work in small groups (3 – 5 students) to compare their questionnaires and work out the preferences of the group as a whole.
- Groups report back to class in order to work out the preferences of the class as a whole.

3 In this and later exercises, students will hear about different types of restaurant in Britain. If they are not familiar with these, it will help if you explain the background.

Background information: American-style hamburger and pizza restaurants are popular in Britain (these are often multi-national chains and students may be familiar with these from their own countries). There are also many so-called *ethnic* restaurants, most commonly Chinese, Indian, Greek and Turkish. On the tape students will hear about *kebabs* – a Turkish dish comprising lamb in slices or chunks either on a skewer or inside pitta bread with salad. Most of these restaurants offer facilities for customers to eat the food on the premises or to take it home – this is known as *take-away* (*take-out* or food *to go* in American English). Some restaurants also deliver take-away food to the customers' own homes.

- Read through the instructions with the class. Ask students, in pairs, to write down their definition of fast food with one or two examples. Do not give any help at this stage.
- Explain the listening task then play the tape.

Answers
Five characteristics
1 You don't really sit down to eat.
2 You can be served quickly.
3 You don't have to wait.
4 Food comes quickly.
5 It's pre-prepared.
Examples
McDonald's and Burger King; little kebab take-aways and Greek places.

Tapescript
TONY Um, I'm going to ask a few questions about fast food and your eating habits. But first, em, what do we understand about *fast food*. If someone asks you if you like it, what kind of things are you thinking of?
DIANE I'd first think of um, places like McDonald's and Burger King [Uh huh] burger places, erm, basically where you don't really sit down to eat, erm ...
[MARK Well I suppose fast food ...]
LOUISE Where you can be served quickly ...
MARK Yeah, you don't have to wait [That's right] – it sort of comes quickly, it's pre-prepared or ...
JANET Yeah, so even like the little kebab take-aways and things and the Greek places – I suppose you'd think of under

fast food as well ...
DIANE   Mm, mm.
TONY   But if, if the food is cooked more on the premises by the person who runs the restaurant, but is then served quickly, is it still fast food?
JANET   I would think of it as fast food, I think, yes, yes ...
[MARK   Yes, I think so.]
TONY   Okay.

- Students should compare the characteristics described on the tape with the definitions they wrote earlier.
- Ask students whether they agree with the ideas on the tape. Elicit a definition of fast food from the group which everyone can agree on and write this on the board.

Reading skills

4   Re-ordering jumbled paragraphs

- Read through the introduction with the class and elicit any opinions and/or experiences which students have had.
- Students individually read the text extracts and complete the numbering task.
- Students compare their answers and discuss the clues with a partner.

Answer
C A F E D B
Clues: Dates in the text; the introduction and conclusion are obvious because of the mention and position of the book's title.

5
- Explain the task. Students should complete the chart in note form rather than complete sentences.

Answers
1955 – McDonald brothers sell first burgers at California drive-in movies.
        – Ray Kroc buys their names and recipes and opens first restaurant in Des Plaines, Illinois.
1967 – Opening of first restaurant outside USA.
1972 – Sales exceed $1 billion.
1974 – First McDonald's opens in Britain.
1984 – Over 200 McDonald's in Britain
        – McDonald's serving 18 million customers a day
        – Ray Kroc dies
1990 – McDonald's opens its largest restaurant, in Moscow
Now – World's largest restaurant chain. Over 11,500 restaurants in 52 countries.

- Discuss the text with the class. What do they think is the reviewer's opinion of the book. What do they think is the reviewer's opinion of McDonald's?

Vocabulary

6   Food and drink

A
- Explain the task and divide the students into pairs. The exercise can be more fun if you introduce a competitive element by telling students that the aim is to be the pair with the most words on their lists.
- Ensure that students write their lists on a piece of paper.

Suggested answers
(The lists in the charts at the top of the next column contain only those words introduced in the previous exercises. Some items can be put under more than one heading.)

hot dishes	snacks	ingredients
fried chicken	sandwiches	shellfish
bangers and mash	cornish pasty	pasta
spotted Dick		
toad in the hole		
Welsh rarebit		
Cornish pasty		
pizza		
hamburgers		
fish and chips		

hot drinks	non-alcoholic drinks	alcoholic drinks
tea	Pepsi	wine
coffee	fruit juice	beer
	mineral water	

B
- Students exchange their lists and re-categorise the words from the lists they have been given under the new headings, adding their own words.
- After a few minutes ask one or two pairs to read out their lists. In a multilingual class you may get some interesting or unusual items. If so, write these on the board and ask the pair to explain them to the class.

Further practice: Workbook Unit 9, Exercise 5.

7
- For the first part of the exercise, it may help students to explain the differences between the items if you put the following questions on the board.
  Cooked or not?   Use oil or fat?   Use oven or grill?
  Hot or cold?   Is it cut up? How?
- Students can work in pairs or small groups.

Answers
fried   cooked in boiling fat or oil
grilled   cooked directly under or over great heat
roast(ed)   (usually used for meat) cooked in a hot oven or over/in front of a hot fire, with the food being basted periodically with the fat and juices that come out
stir-fried   lightly fried in a small amount of fat/oil while being frequently stirred
steamed   cooked in hot steam rising from boiling water
sautéed   cut into thin slices and quickly fried
shredded   cut into long thin pieces
sliced   cut into even lengths
chopped   cut up into very small pieces
charbroiled   grilled over a charcoal fire
baked   cooked by dry heat in an oven
chilled   cooled down to a temperature slightly above freezing
poached   gently cooked in boiling or hot liquid (e.g. water or wine)
boiled   cooked in boiling water

- For the second part of the exercise students may wish to use examples from their own national cuisines. The suggested answers below relate to well-known British or international dishes.

Suggested answers

sautéed potato	stir-fried vegetables
chilled soup	chopped onions
chopped parsley	fried chicken
roast beef	sliced carrots
charbroiled hamburgers	grilled fish
shredded cabbage	

Listening skills

8   Comparing

A   **Note:** This is an intensive listening exercise which is best done in a language laboratory. If you do not have access to one, you should be prepared to play the tape several times in order for students to answer successfully.

● Pre-teach these names of British restaurant chains.
Burger King   Wimpy   Perfect Pizza
● Explain the task and ask the students to read through the statements. Check understanding of *cholesterol* (pronounced /   /), a substance which, if present at high levels in the blood (as a result of eating a lot of meat, saturated fats, cheese, cream etc.) can affect blood pressure and trigger heart disease.

● Play the tape.

Answers
Ticked statements: 1, 2, 5, 7, 8

B   Students may need to listen several times to find the answers.

Answers

1a FALSE	1b TRUE	1c TRUE
2a TRUE	2b TRUE	2c FALSE
3a FALSE	3b TRUE	3c TRUE

Tapescript
See page 181 at the back of the Students' Book.

C   ● Explain the task and ask students to write down the statements individually.
● Now divide the class into small groups to discuss their opinions and to draw up a short list.
● Groups report back to the class.

Language work

9   Emphatic devices

This exercise presents emphatic devices for recognition and production by students. The device of fronting, which is common in very informal conversational English, is not dealt with here. At this level students are unlikely to be able to use it appropriately. However, you may wish to present the following examples for recognition only.
She may be patient, but she isn't sympathetic ➤ *Patient she may be, but sympathetic she isn't.*
I don't like his attitude. ➤ *His attitude I don't like.*
They sell nice things here. ➤ *Nice things they sell here.*

A   ● Read through the examples and explain the matching and underlining task.

Answers

a   repetition of intensifiers
You are in the centre of town waiting to see a film which starts in half-an-hour. Suddenly you feel <u>very, very</u> hungry.
b   emphatic reflexive pronoun
Phenomenal growth and success – a large part of which seems to be due to the rigorous standards imposed by Ray Kroc <u>himself</u>.

c   emphatic use of *so*
... when I eat the food I think, oh, this is <u>so</u> disgusting I don't know why I came ...
d   exclamations
... after I've had it I think <u>oh God!</u> It was horrible, ...
e   emphatic use of auxiliary verb
... I think people <u>do</u> probably think it's, it's even less healthy than it is, ...
f   emphatic use of question tags
... it's all cholesterol and fat, <u>isn't it?</u>

● Elicit why and when the different forms are used. Put the answers on the board.

Answers
To emphasise a particular person or thing: reflexive pronoun.
To emphasise an adjective: repetition of intensifiers and use of *so*.
To emphasise an action or state: auxiliary verbs and question tags.
To emphasise surprise or emotion: exclamations.

● Ask students to think of further examples of auxiliary verbs and intensifiers, exclamations and reflexive pronouns. Elicit and write these on the board.
auxiliaries: *will/shall   have*
intensifiers: *far   much   really*
exclamations: *Oh Lord!   Oh no!*
reflexive pronouns: *herself   themselves   ourselves   yourself*

● Point out we can use *such* rather than *so* to emphasise a noun or adjective and noun combination.
It was so disgusting. / It was such a disgusting meal.

B   **Answer**
JIM   I *do* believe that was the worst meal I've ever eaten.
ANN   That steak was *so* overcooked, *wasn't it?*
JIM   And the vegetables were *really, really* soggy.
ANN   And the bill was *far, far* too expensive. Didn't you say Monica recommended it *herself?*
JIM   Yes, she said she eats here *herself* every day.
ANN   *Oh God!* She must be mad!

C   ● Elicit the answers.

Answers
A and C are emphatic sentences.
(Type A is used if you want to emphasise the verb.)

● Write the basic constructions on the board.
What + verb clause + *is/was* + noun
It is/was + noun + *that/who* + verb clause
● Ask the students questions and ask them to respond using the emphatic constructions.
Maria, was it President Bush who was assassinated in Dallas?
(No, it was President Kennedy who was assassinated in Dallas.)
José, what annoys you? Is it quiet students?
(No, I don't mind quiet students. What annoys me is talkative students.)
Noriko, you love Beethoven, don't you?
(No, what I love is Mozart/it's Mozart that I love.)
● Students can practise making mini-dialogues like this in pairs.

D   ● Students should write the answers individually to check they can manipulate the constructions.

Answers
1   What infuriates me is bad manners.
2   It's Italian cuisine that my boyfriend loves.
3   What I hate is overcooked vegetables.
4   What they despise is people who won't try new recipes.

5 It was during the summer holiday that I tried lots of new restaurants.
6 It's salad that she always prepares for lunch.
7 It's my parents who are going to try out that new pizzeria next week.
8 What gets on his nerves is people who don't leave a tip.

Further practice: Workbook Unit 9, Exercise 7.

Pronunciation

10 Emphatic stress

A
● Point out that, in speech, stress is much more important in conveying emphasis than is the construction one chooses. You can demonstrate this by reading out the three sentences from Exercise 9 above and varying the stressed word.
What makes me feel <u>ill</u> is fish and chips.
What makes <u>me</u> feel ill is fish and chips.
What makes me feel ill is <u>fish</u> and chips.
The listening and matching task will check whether students are sensitive to this feature.
● Students should read the five questions carefully.
● Play the tape and check answers.

Answers
a 5 b 3 c 1 d 2 e 4

Tapescript (also in the Students' Book)
1 My partner opened a vegetarian restaurant <u>yesterday</u>.
2 <u>My partner</u> opened a vegetarian restaurant yesterday.
3 My partner opened a <u>vegetarian</u> restaurant yesterday.
4 My partner <u>opened</u> a vegetarian restaurant yesterday.
5 <u>My</u> partner opened a vegetarian restaurant yesterday.

B
● Each student should write out the five questions in a different order.
● Divide students into A/B pairs.
● Student A reads out the answer *My partner opened a vegetarian restaurant yesterday* five times, using different sentence stress each time to suit questions a–e, but in random order. Student B then says what the order of the questions was. Students then reverse roles and continue practising.

C
● Explain to the students that they are now going to combine the use of emphatic stress with the emphatic constructions studied in Exercise 9.
● Students should look at questions a – e in section A while they listen to the tape.

Answers
1 b 2 e 3 c 4 d

Tapescript (also in the Students' Book)
1 It was a vegetarian restaurant that my partner opened.
2 It was my partner who opened a vegetarian restaurant.
3 It was yesterday that my partner opened a vegetarian restaurant.
4 What my partner did was open a vegetarian restaurant.

D
● Explain that the four statements are just prompts, they are not emphatic. Students, working in pairs, should make them emphatic and then write suitable questions for them.
● If some students are unsure of the task, put the Pizza Hut sequence (from the answers below) on the board as an example.
● When students have made their questions and answers they should change partners. Each student should read the answer only to his/her new partner. The partner should be able to work out the question being answered.

Suggested questions/statements and responses
What restaurant did your best friend go to last night?
– It was Pizza Hut that my best friend went to.
Your best friend went to Pizza Express, didn't she?
– No, it was Pizza Hut that my best friend went to.
What can't your teacher stand?/Is there any food your teacher really dislikes?
What my teacher can't stand/really dislikes is Chinese food.
When do you love eating Italian food?/You love eating Italian food midweek, don't you?
– It's at the weekend that I love eating Italian food.
I think Burger King makes the best hamburgers. / Who makes the best hamburgers?
– It's McDonald's who make the best hamburgers.

Language work

11 *Actually* and *really*

A
● Students read the extracts while they listen to them on tape.
● Students discuss and attempt to answer the questions. With a weak class this will be more successful if done in small groups.

Answers
Which word makes a verb stronger? *really* (C)
Which words introduce something unexpected and reinforce opinion? *actually* (B and F)
Which word makes a whole sentence less emphatic? *really* (D)
Which word makes a verb less emphatic? *actually* (A and E)

● Elicit the answer to the final question and put the answer on the board.

Answer
When *really* comes after a verb, it makes it less emphatic (e.g. A and E).
When *really* comes before a verb, it makes it more emphatic (e.g. C).
When *really* comes at the end of a sentence, it makes the whole sentence less emphatic (e.g. D).

● If the class is not clear about this put the following example sentences on the board.

Less emphatic
sentence: They weren't interested in my photographs really.
verb: They weren't really interested in my photographs.
More emphatic
verb: They really weren't interested in my photographs.

Tapescript
See Students' Book, page 73.

B
● Students should complete the task individually and then compare their answers in pairs.

Answers
1 a I don't *really* think much of her cooking.
  b He doesn't *really* feel very well.
  c That fried chicken wasn't *really* very good.
2 a I don't *actually* agree with that.
  b Well, I *actually* think pizzas are very unhealthy.
  c You'll *actually* find that some fruit is very fattening.
3 a I *really* think fish and chips aren't healthy.
  b Sometimes I *really* feel like a huge juicy burger.
  c They *really* are overweight.
4 a It's not much of a restaurant *really*.
  b I don't fancy a heavy meal *really*.
  c I think that shellfish is rather overpriced *really*.

Further practice: Workbook Unit 9, Exercises 8 a and b.

Speaking skills

12 Expressing opinions

A • Use the questions to generate a brief class discussion on fast food and health.

B • Students read the tapescript on page 181 of the Students' Book and make a note of the phrases used by the participants to introduce their opinions. Tell them they should be able to find at least five phrases.

Answers
I think ...   I don't think ...   I feel that ...   I can't say I ...
I suppose ...   I must say ...

 • Now elicit any further phrases students may know and write these on the board.
   In my opinion ...   I believe ...   If you ask me ...
   I guess ...   I'd say ...

C • Read through the instructions and explain the task. Point out that the aim of the exercise is to exchange opinions and to persuade each other so that a joint decision can be reached.
 • Students work in groups of four or five to complete the task. The exercise is more effective if you impose a time limit of no more than ten minutes.

D • Groups compare their charts and work out which dish got the most stars for the class as a whole.

Writing skills

13 Writing a personal letter

Note: You may like to contrast this letter with the formal letter in Unit 3 (page 26). At this level students should be familiar with the conventions of informal letters (layout, salutations etc.). If necessary, quickly revise this by asking the class to analyse Jane's letter. They should note the position of the sender's address and the omission of the addressee's address and surname.

 • Read through the introduction.

 • Ask students to read the letter and underline any features which they consider informal. Elicit these and write them on the board.
   Dear .... (use of first name rather than surname)
   Love, Jane (use of *Love* rather than *Yours sincerely* and omission of surname)
   use of contractions
   use of exclamations
   use of direct questions
   use of informal vocabulary: *kids   your place*
   use of idiomatic expressions: *We're on quite a tight budget   I'm not exactly the world's greatest cook!*
   I'd love to ...   ... that would be great

 • Remind students to use these features in their replies.
 • Elicit the class's opinion on what should be contained in the reply and note the following points on the board.
   Thank her for her letter.
   Say how pleased you are that they are coming.
   Give news about how you/your family are.
   Give information about babysitters.
   Give information on places to eat (lunchtime and evenings): names, how to get there, opening times, approximate cost, type of food etc.
   Give best wishes to Jane and family.
 • The letter can be written as homework.

Further practice: Workbook Unit 9, Exercises 9 and 10.

Final task

14 The Restaurant Game

This game takes about twenty minutes with an average class.

 • Read through the introduction with the class.
 • Divide the class into two halves: customers and restaurant owners. The two groups should move to opposite sides of the classroom. Sub-divide the restaurant owners into more or less equal numbers of As, Bs, Cs and Ds.
 • Ask the customers to look at the task sheet on the relevant page of the Students' Book. Each customer should work individually. They should read the information and work out the questions they need to ask the restaurant owners. Insist on them writing out these questions before allowing them to begin the game.
 • Ask the restaurant owners to turn to the relevant pages of the Students' Book and study their information sheets. Each student should work individually. Each restaurant owner should take a piece of paper, write the name of his/her restaurant on it, and display it on their desk.
 • Once these preparatory stages are completed, the customers should stand up and go over to the restaurant owners' desks, asking their questions of A, B, C and D in turn.
 • The winner is the first student to successfully complete their task sheet by finding the most suitable restaurant for each of the six situations.

Correct answers (for Customers' tasks)
1 L'Escargot
2 New York New York
3 Pizzeria Italia
4 Grandma's Kitchen
5 Grandma's Kitchen
6 New York New York

Unit 10 Talk to the Animals

 Unit summary

Theme	Language awareness unit covering types of language and communication
Structures	Defining and non-defining relative clauses
Vocabulary	Vocabulary connected with animals; categorising; animal idioms (in WB)
Skills	*Reading*: skimming and scanning
	Listening: finding words and phrases
	Speaking: expanding and exemplifying
	Writing: sentence and paragraph construction
Pronunciation	rhythm in relative clauses
Language awareness/Study skills	Writing a definition of language

 Teaching notes

Introduction

1 The still from a TV advert on the first page of this unit presents the topic of whether animals can talk or not. It comes from a series of advertisements for a brand of tea, each of which focusses on the chimpanzees behaving like humans.

● Discuss the first questions in open class and establish whether the students think that animals can 'talk'. They will probably want to differentiate between 'talk' and 'communicate' at this point.

● Students discuss the speech bubbles in pairs or small groups and decide if they agree with them or not.

● Play the short section on tape by Mike Down, which addresses the issue of whether animals can communicate. Ask students to summarise his opinion and say whether they agree with it or not.

Tapescript

MIKE DOWN   Well, it's not a question of feeling. I mean, animals do communicate, all animals communicate, even the simplest animals, even something like an amoeba, a tiny one-celled animal that you can only just see if you've got very good eyes; even these animals communicate. There ... the only question is how complicated the communication is. Simple animals communicate just a few bits of very simple information, whereas very advanced animals, like ourselves, communicate vast amounts of extremely complex information. But all animals communicate, without exception. Even plants communicate, although at a very, very different level.

Answer

He believes that all animals, however simple, communicate.

Language awareness

2 Defining language

This exercise gets students thinking about what exactly language is.

● In pairs, students write a definition of language. As well as the prompts given in the exercise you may want to ask them to think about speech, words and sentences, body language and meaning.

● Discuss the definitions and write some of the best ones on the board.

3 Students match the animals with their names.

Answers

A grasshopper   B sheep   C nightingale   D bee
E parrot   F Alsatian dog   G Siamese cat   H dolphin

● Play the sounds on tape. Students match with the animals.

Answers

1 Siamese cat   2 sheep   3 nightingale   4 bee
5 Alsatian dog   6 parrot   7 dolphin   8 grasshoppers

● Students discuss whether or not they think the sounds represent some kind of communication, and if so, what. They then decide whether the animals in question are using language, according to their definitions in Exercise 2.

Reading skills

4 Skimming and scanning

This exercise provides practice in reading and understanding the gist and detail of texts without understanding every word. Encourage students to do A and B without using a dictionary.

A This part of the exercise asks students to skim the texts quickly to match paragraphs with headings.

● Give a time limit of about two minutes for students to look through the texts very quickly. They should only be looking for the basic subject of each text to match it with the headings.

Answers

1 g   2 e   3 a   4 c   5 f

(Students should be able to discount the distractors both from the content of the paragraphs and because their tone/register is wrong.)

B The students now read the texts again, quite quickly, but this time scanning for specific information. They do not need to understand every word to do the task.

● Students complete the chart.

Answers

animal	communication	what the system lacks
bee	dancing	flexibility
wolf	facial expressions, movements of tails and growls	creativity
monkeys and apes	sounds and gestures	expressing abstract concepts
parrots and mynah birds	imitating words	meaning or understanding
European robin	song	flexibility/variation of meaning
spider	gestures	creativity

- If the students need to ask about or look up any vocabulary, they can do so at this point.
- Students compare these systems to their definitions of language from Exercise 2.

5 This exercise summarises the information about language in a passage by Descartes. The language of this passage is quite difficult and the students may need some help.

- Students write a short summary of the differences as explained in the extract.

Model summary

Every human being can express abstract thoughts and emotions, while no animal can.

- Students discuss the idea expressed here.

Language work

6 Defining relative clauses

Both types of relative clause are dealt with in this unit: defining relatives here and non-defining in Exercise 11. Some aspects of the use of relative clauses have not been dealt with within the unit, for example, the use of prepositions with relative clauses, but these are addressed in the Grammar Reference section at the back of the Students' Book.

A ● Students look back at the texts and complete the examples of relative clauses.

Answers

1 There is no other animal ... which can do the same.
2 ... forming of them a statement by which they make known their thoughts.
3 They have no way of expressing the anger they felt yesterday.

● Students match the clauses with the statements about them.

Answers

a 1   b 2   c 3

● Explain if necessary:
In number 1, the pronoun (*which*) refers to *animal*, which is the subject of the relative clause.
In number 2, the pronoun (*which*) refers to *statement*, which is the object of the relative clause (*they* is the subject).
In number 3, the pronoun is not necessary (though *which* and *that* are both possible), as it would refer to the object of the relative clause.

● Students now look back through the texts to find examples of each type of clause discussed: where the pronoun refers to the subject, where it refers to the object and where it is not necessary.

Answers

a The pronoun refers to the subject of the clause.
A study of higher animals also reveals no 'language' systems that are creative in the same way ... (Text 1)
A bird that has learnt to say ... (Text 3)
The song studied was that which signalled ... (Text 4)
... natural movements which betray passions ... (Text 6)
b The pronoun refers to the object of the clause.
... their signals are highly stereotyped and limited in terms of the messages which they convey. (Text 1. The pronoun could be omitted here.)
c The pronoun is not necessary (and not used).
But that's all (that) *they can do.* (Text 1)

● Students find the relative starting with what and decide what the pronoun refers to.

Answer

The birds imitate what they have heard.
What refers to 'everything which'. (*What* can only be used in this way to refer to an abstract object.)

Extension

- If you wish to look at the use of prepositions with relative clauses here, you can start with example 1 ... *by which they make known their thoughts*. In formal speech/writing the preposition precedes the pronoun and introduces the clauses, but in informal speech/writing, the preposition is put at the end of the clause: *...which they make known their thoughts by.* (The latter word order would sound odd here because of the formality of the language.)
- You may wish to use these example sentences for further transformation practice.
This is the desk at which I sit (which I sit at).
She's the girl with whom I went to Paris (who(m) I went to Paris with).
There was an old lady on the train, for whom I gave up my seat (who(m) I gave my seat up for).
That's the hole through which you post the receipts (which you post the receipts through).

B Students make relative clauses joining the sentences. They will have to make quite a few changes to the sentences given to link them as relatives, so the first three relate very closely to the texts in order to help students become confident with these transformations.

Answers

1 A study of higher animals reveals no language systems that are creative in the way human language is. / A study of higher animals reveals language systems, none of which is creative in the way human language is.
2 The song was studied which signalled the robin's possession of a certain territory. / The song which signalled the robin's possession of a certain territory was studied.
3 The birds imitate what they have heard.
4 The animals which the scientists studied did not have real communication systems.
5 Humans communicate in a manner which is highly creative and flexible.
6 The people around the man did not understand what he tried to say.

C Students complete the text with pronouns where necessary.

Answers

1 which/that   2 which   3 who/that
4 who/which/that/–   5 who/that/which
6 who/that/which   7 that/who/–

Note: It is possible to use either *who* or *which* for animals. *That* can be used for people, animals and objects. Where it is possible to omit the pronoun (when it refers to the object of the relative clause), it usually sounds more natural to do so.

Further practice: Workbook Unit 10, Exercises 5 and 6.

Listening skills

7 Finding words and phrases

A This exercise requires students to listen for specific words as they are listening. The listening is quite difficult as the speaker is very familiar with his subject and uses a lot of vocabulary that will be unfamiliar to students. (He does, however, expand and paraphrase quite a lot.) This first task aims, therefore, to familiarise students with the listening in a fairly simple way, before they start listening for the more difficult content.

● Read through the introduction with the students and check that they are familiar with the names of animals and their pronunciation. (More difficult ones: orang utan /ɒræŋuːtæn/, piranha /pərɑːnə/.)
● Play the tape once. Students do the exercise.

Answers

1 ant   2 bee   3 lion   4 cheetah   5 zebra
6 orang utan   7 gorilla   8 chimpanzee

Tapescript

(The asterisks show the best places to rewind during the next exercise.)

INTERVIEWER Right. You're talking about social groupings here, could you tell us something about the ways animals form into groups?

MIKE DOWN Yes, er many, many animals are very solitary animals; the only times they get together is when they mate, or when they're bringing up their young. The majority of animals are solitary, but a very significant group of mammals and insects, like ants and termites, bees and wasps, are very social and they group together because in a group it's much safer: you can defend yourself more easily if you're in a group, you can find mates more easily if you're in a group, and you can change the world around you by working with the others if you live in a group. Solitary animals have a much more difficult time in many ways.

INTERVIEWER You mentioned lions and other carnivora earlier on. Do they group very much?

MIKE DOWN Yes. Most cats in fact don't group. Er, lions and, to a lesser extent, cheetahs are the only cats that group together – a group of lions is called a pride – and you might get anything up to fifteen or twenty lions in a pride. A pride of lions would have perhaps two or three males, perhaps a dozen females, and then the cubs. But the real lion group consists of females with their cubs. The males tend to stay for a few years and then they get kicked out by a group of younger males that comes in and take over. *

INTERVIEWER Right. What about other animals such as the … you've got here zebras, for example, and the apes as well, do they …

MIKE DOWN Yes. Well, zebras form temporary groups. Most of the year they're basically on their own, although you will get groups of mothers looking after their foals, but at one time a year, when the females are ready to mate, then the males move in, and the males fight one another very vigorously: they will try and bite each other, they will try and neck-butt each other and the biggest, strongest males see off the others, and they're the ones that collect a little group of females around them and mate with those females. But once mating is finished, and the babies are beginning to develop inside the mothers' bodies, then off the males go and live solitary lives again for the rest of the year. *

INTERVIEWER And how about the apes?

MIKE DOWN Ah, well, now you're talking about the group of animals that we belong to, and apes – some apes – live in very, very big and complicated social groups. Not all – orangutans, for example, big apes that live in Indonesia and Malaysia – they're very solitary and one adult may meet another adult only once every two or three years, when a male and a female mate, and then, the only relationship then will be between a mother and her baby. The baby will stay with the mother for two or three years, four years, five years even, learning from the mother, learning what sorts of foods to eat, what the signs of danger are, and then when the baby grows up, off it'll go, and live its own, solitary life. The reason why orangutans are solitary is because there's not very much food in a forest and if there was a big group of orangutans all the food would just run out. * But, leaving Asia and going to

Africa, then you find very social apes. Now, gorillas, for example, gorillas live in unimale groups.

They used to be called harems but the technical term is unimale because there's one male within the group; one male, and then around him will be anything up to six, seven, eight, nine females, plus all the babies. And that one male in the group is the silverback gorilla, and he's much bigger and stronger than the others. He's got silvery fur on his back and the others won't challenge him and he'll lead the group slowly through the forest, settling down every night and moving on the next day, finding food. So that's a unimale group, but if you move a little bit further west, into West Africa, you'll start to come across chimpanzees. * Now they're a bit smaller than gorillas; they spend a lot of time in the trees, whereas gorillas are down on the ground, and chimpanzees are much more closely related to us than they are to gorillas. They're our closest living relatives. Now chimps live in multimale groups; in other words you'll get, oh, anything up to six, seven, eight males, then you'll get two or three times that number of females, a dozen, two dozen females, plus all the youngsters, so we're talking about groups that can be as big as forty or fifty or even sixty. Now, a chimpanzee group – multimale group – is a very flexible type of group: it constantly splits into smaller groups, off they go for a few days, back they come, reform, break up again and within that group the males tend to hang around the outside, protecting the group, fighting off rival males that might want to come in and mate with the females, but they tend to come and go to some extent. The on-going core of the chimpanzee group consists of females with their young, and sometimes sisters will actually work together to bring up their young collectively. Yes, so apes are very, very social animals indeed.

B ● The students will now have to listen more intensively to hear and note down the types of groups formed. With a weaker group you may wish to stop the tape and replay sections frequently. The asterisks in the tapescript above show the best places to stop and rewind.
● Pre-teach the following if necessary:
mate (produce young), *carnivores* (meat-eating animals), *solitary* (on one's own), *harem* (group of females living/mating with one male only), *youngster* (young child/animal)

Answers

animal	type of group	description
lion	multimale/pride	two or three males, a dozen females and cubs. Real group = females and cubs.
zebra	temporary	mother and baby only
orangutan	– (they're solitary)	
gorilla	unimale/harem	one male (silverback), 6–9 females, babies
chimpanzee	multimale	6–8 males, 1–2 dozen females, youngsters many males, often splitting into smaller groups and then reforming

● Discuss with students why they think animals form different types of groups, and which types they imagine would be more successful.

C The next extract is for much less detailed listening.

- Divide the class into pairs. Students discuss their ideas of why animals form social groups.
- Discuss as a class and write the suggestions on the board.
- Play the next extract. Students listen for gist and to find out if their suggestions were right.

Answers
safety, protection, hunting, division of labour (some animals are on the lookout while others rest), hygiene, building up social relationships and a social hierarchy

Tapescript
INTERVIEWER Interesting, yes. You mentioned earlier the main reasons for groupings are safety, erm, protection, erm, hunting presumably. Are there any other reasons that animals group together?

MIKE DOWN Yes, well, you mentioned hunting – of course, hunting in a group is much easier than hunting on your own, especially if you're a small animal. Er, dogs, for example, hunting dogs in Africa, wolves in north America and Northern Europe. They're quite small animals but they can bring down very big animals and the only reason they do this, why they do this, is because they hunt as a team, as a pack. Now, when it comes to defence, the boot is on the other foot. Er, it's also helpful if you live in a group because if you live in a group, some members of the group can go to sleep, some members of the group can feed their babies, some members of the group can lower their heads and graze away on the grass without worrying too much, while other members of the group are on the lookout.

INTERVIEWER I think you mentioned earlier, or in your notes, something about hygiene being an example as well?

MIKE DOWN Yes, well, social animals also clean each other, er, this ... in birds it's called preening and in rodents and carnivores and primates it's called grooming. It means that an animal can clean other members of the group and that other members of the group clean it. But it's much more than just hygiene: it's also building up relationships, building up friendships, lessening tensions, er, within the group. Most animals have a personal space around themselves that they don't like other animals to get, to get in. Human beings are the same: we don't like people putting their faces too close to ours – when they do it's usually a sign of threat, it's a sign that they are trying to frighten us when they put their faces very close to us. But when animals groom each other, when they stroke each other, when they tickle each other, when they pick each other's fur, erm, they're lessening those aggressions and they're trying to build up friendships and that's very, very important in social animals – it's important in all animals as all animals have to mate – but social animals get close to each other not just when they mate but when they're protecting each other, when they're helping one another, in different ways. So, what grooming does is build up these friendships, and then, having built up the friendships it helps to establish, to set up a pecking order, what we call a hierarchy, within the group because the dominant members of the group tend to get groomed whereas the lower-ranking members of the group tend to do the grooming. So everybody knows his or her place within the group by this grooming going on.

Extension
- If you want students to listen a bit more intensively to this passage, ask them to find the words for the following:
  a team of dogs/wolves (*pack*)
  to eat grass, used for horses, zebras etc (*graze*)
  cleaning (*preening* of birds, *grooming* of rodents, carnivores and primates)
  actions which promote closeness/cleaning (*stroking, tickling, picking*)

- Discuss as a class how closely you think the reasons for social grouping resemble the reasons for humans forming social groups.

8 Vocabulary extension

A • Students complete the sentences.

Answers
A group of lions is called a *pride*. A baby lion is called a *cub*. A group of wolves is called a *pack*. A baby zebra is called a *foal*.

- Play the tape again only if necessary. Students can use a dictionary to complete this.

B • Students use the list of words to make a chart of the nine animals, names of their groups and their young.

Answers

animal	group	young
lion	pride	cub
zebra	herd	foal
cow	herd	calf
dog	pack	puppy
goat	herd	kid
goose	flock	gosling
sheep	flock	lamb
whale	school	pup
wolf	pack	cub

Further practice: Workbook Unit 10, Exercise 3.

Speaking skills

9 Expanding and exemplifying

A • Students read through the items and try to remember how Mike Down explained them.
- Play the edited tape for students to listen if necessary.

Tapescript
(The first four items come from Exercise 7A/B, the last two from Exercise 7C.)

1 The majority of animals are solitary, but a very significant group of mammals and insects, like ants and termites, bees and wasps, are very social and they group together because in a group it's much safer ...

2 Ah, well, now you're talking about the group of animals that we belong to, and apes – some apes – live in very, very big and complicated social groups. Not all – orang-utans, for example, big apes that live in Indonesia and Malaysia – they're very solitary ...

3 Now gorillas, for example, gorillas live in unimale groups. They used to be called harems but the technical term is unimale because there's one male within the group; one male, and then around him will be anything up to six, seven, eight, nine females, plus all the babies.

4 Now chimps live in multimale groups; in other words you'll get, oh, anything up to six, seven, eight males, then you'll get two or three times that number of females, a dozen, two dozen females, plus all the youngsters, so we're talking about groups that can be as big as forty or fifty or even sixty.

5   Yes, well, you mentioned hunting – of course, hunting in a group is much easier than hunting on your own, especially if you're a small animal. Er, dogs, for example, hunting dogs in Africa, wolves in North America and northern Europe. They're quite small animals but they can bring down very big animals and the only reason they do this, why they do this, is because they hunt as a team, as a pack.

6   So, what grooming does is build up these friendships, and then, having built up the friendships it helps to establish, to set up a pecking order, what we call a hierarchy, within the group because the dominant members of the group tend to get groomed whereas the lower-ranking members of the group tend to do the grooming.

Answers

1   ... like ants and termites, bees and wasps ...
2   ... big apes that live in Indonesia and Malaysia.
3   ... unimale, because there's one male within the group.
4   ... in other words, you'll get anything up to six, seven, eight males ...
5   ... hunting dogs in Africa, wolves in North America and northern Europe.
6   ... what we call a hierarchy.

● Ensure that students can see how these *expanding* devices are used and ask if they can think of any others, such as *What I mean is..., as in ..., that is/that means i.e. ....*

B   This task gives controlled practice in the use of expanding and exemplifying, by providing students with terms that their partners won't know.

● Discuss the attitude to pets in the students' country/countries.
 Which animals are the most common pets?
 Do they live inside or outside?
 Are they expected to do any 'work' for their keep, (such as guarding the family or catching mice)?
 How do they think their attitude compares to the British attitude to pets?
● Divide the class into pairs. Students turn to the relevant pages.
● Students read their texts and the definitions with them.
● In pairs, the students read each other their texts, explaining where necessary.

Extension

● To practise this skill further, get students to make notes individually about something they are very interested in. (The notes could be done at home.) They should also note down some terms that are likely to be unfamiliar in English to the other students. They then give short 'speeches', either to the class or in groups, about their topic, making sure they explain where necessary. Students listening should note down any new words and their meanings – their comprehension of new words will show the speaker how clearly he/she has explained the new vocabulary.

Vocabulary

10 Categorisation

The purpose of this activity is to get students thinking about categories, and about how they can be organising vocabulary.

● Students work individually to divide the animals into categories. Check as they are doing this. The most logical categories are: insects, mammals, birds; those with fins, wings, legs; pets, farm animals, wild animals; those which live in water, on land, in the air.

● Students compare their categories in pairs, justifying their reasons for particular categories and choosing the 'best' one. They then work in groups of four and do the same.
● They brainstorm more animals in their groups and add them to their categories.
● You could ask them to do this on pieces of paper, then to swap them around the class so that other students can see the organisation and pick up names of other animals.

Language work

11 Non-defining relative clauses

This exercise looks at the second (and less common) type of relative clause.

A   ● Students look at the two sentences and answer the questions about them.

Answers
Sentence 1 specifies a particular song. Sentence 2 gives extra information.

● Tell students that the pronouns used with non-defining relative clauses are the same as those with defining relatives, except for *that*, which cannot be used in non-defining clauses. (The commas are dealt with in Part B of the exercise.)
● Students do the combining exercise.

Answers
1   Cruft's dog show, which is held in spring (every year), is the highlight of the dog breeder's year.
2   Some people, who have lived with their pets for a long time, think they can understand their pets' facial expressions.
3   Humans have devised a lot of complicated communication systems, all of which involve symbols of some kind.
4   Some apes, who have been trained from birth, have mastered certain simple ways of communicating with humans.
5   Some higher level mammals, who live in groups, are very social.
6   Some animals, (who are) usually living in a human environment, come to rely on the company of humans rather than their own kind.

Note: Students have to decide in each case which information is the 'extra' information (usually the less central/important item). Encourage students to embed the relative (put in the middle of the sentence) wherever possible, especially in the longer sentences. It would be natural in sentence 6 to omit the pronoun and verb. See Unit 3 (substitution and ellipsis) and Unit 15 (participle clauses) for more examples of this.

B   This exercise helps to show students the difference between the two types of relative.

● Students read the sentences and work out the difference between them.

Answers
1   In the first only some animals were moved into different cages; in the second all the animals were moved.
2   In the first we were looking specifically for a cat which was black and white with green eyes, and we bought the first one which fitted the description; in the second we bought the first cat we saw. (It was incidental that it was black and white with green eyes.)

● Focus attention on the commas: they are only used in non-defining relatives.

Note: This exercise may cause difficulty for students whose language does not make the distinction or uses commas in exactly the opposite way. It is best not to labour the point in these cases, as they will hardly ever have to differentiate. Be sure, however, to emphasise the difference between providing defining information and incidental information.

Further practice: Workbook Unit 10, Exercises 5 and 6.

Pronunciation

12 Rhythm in relative clauses

● Play the tape. Students listen and mark the stress and pauses on the sentences in Exercise 11B.

Answers
1   The 'animals who were moved into different 'cages became much 'healthier.
    The 'animals, (*pause*) who were moved into different 'cages, (*pause*) became much 'healthier.
2   We bought the 'first cat we saw which was 'black and 'white with 'green 'eyes.
    We bought the first cat we 'saw, (*pause*) which was 'black and 'white with 'green 'eyes.

● Discuss the differences. In non-defining relatives: the rhythm is interrupted; we pause before the relative clause, and after if appropriate; there is a stress on the word preceding the relative clause.
● Play the four sentences. Students insert commas if necessary.

Answers
1   We stopped at the first hotel which had a bathroom. (defining)
2   I gave a tip to the waiter who had served our table. (defining)
3   I bought the cheapest computer which had a colour monitor. (defining)
4   He decided that the black suit, which didn't have a waistcoat, was the most suitable. (non-defining)

● Ask students to say the first three as if they had non-defining relative clauses in them, and to say 4 as if it had a defining relative clause in it.
● Students work in pairs to read out some of the sentences in this and the previous exercise, 11B. They should vary their pronunciation to give both defining and non-defining sentences.
● Students write their sentences into relative clauses. Check that they are doing it correctly.

Answers
Student A
1   My dog, who/which waits at the door with my slippers when I come home, is both very clever and very useful.
2   My pedigree cat who/which has got a blind eye won first prize in a cat show recently.
Student B
1   I bought the horse which was trained to jump.
2   My aunt owns a really pretty parrot, which can say 'Pretty Polly' and 'Goodbye'.

● Students dictate their sentences to each other, then check that they are correct.

Writing

13 Sentence and paragraph construction

This exercise gives further practice in relative clauses and also in linking sentences to form a paragraph. The students can choose the way they link the sentences quite freely.

● Students rewrite the sentences in order to make relative clauses. You may wish to do this orally.
● Students then form the sentences into a paragraph.

Model answer
Have you ever seen a person who looks like their animal? It is said that people who live closely with their animals start to look like them. For example, I have an elderly neighbour who owns a little pekinese dog, which she takes everywhere with her. Now, the pekinese, which has a very squashed face, is a particularly ugly kind of dog, and, unfortunately, the old lady's face, which always used to seem quite attractive to me, now seems very wrinkled and squashed. This may be pure coincidence; I certainly hope so as I have a bulldog, which is an extremely ugly animal!

Final task

14 Words and meanings

This exercise looks at ways of interpreting meaning from an invented language.

● Start by focussing attention on the still from *Watership Down* (by Richard Adams, 1972). Do the students know the film/book? If so, discuss the storyline; if not, tell the students that it is about a group of rabbits who leave their warren (refer students to Exercise 9B for a definition) when they sense great danger, and the story is about their search for a new home. The extracts come from the early part of the book, when one rabbit is describing what actually happened to the warren once most of them had left.

A   This first part of the exercise involves guessing meaning from the context.

● Students read the extract from the book and use the clues in the context to work out the meaning of the words in italics.

Answers
the Threarah   the elder of the warren (indicated by his age)
silflay   eating above ground (the verb *feed* gives a clue)
ni-Frith   noon (most of the morning is the clue)
hrududu   car, lorry (men were getting out, it was standing)

● Get the students to think about the three 'things' the narrator describes. Read through the questions with the students to help them here.

Answers
big, long, heavy
long, thin, bending
The rabbit couldn't see or think, so the air must have been contaminated.
Metal cylinders, hosepipes, poisonous gas. The men are gassing the rabbits in their warrens.

Extension
● If your students enjoy this kind of exercise, give the following 'rabbit words' and definitions for the students to work out.
    1   *tharn*: the rabbits experience *tharn* when they look into the lights of a *hrududu*. (the trance rabbits experience with fear)

2 *elil:* the rabbits also experience *tharn* when they meet *elil*, such as foxes or some big birds. (enemies)

3 *Frith:* the *hrududu* have lights as bright as *Frith; ni-Frith* is the middle of the day. (the sun)

4 *iron road:* a certain kind of *hrududu* travels on an *iron road.* (railway)

5 *owl time:* when *Frith* is no longer in the sky (night)

6 *to stop running:* what a rabbit does when injured very badly and unable to recover. (to die)

B This task gets students to think about the concepts behind words.

- Divide the class into groups of three or four.
- Students look at the first part of the task and try to imagine what the compound nouns refer to.

Suggested answers
sight improvers *glasses, contact lenses*
a clothes smoother *an iron*
fire water *whisky, brandy* etc.
valuable paper *money*
a sleep interrupter *an alarm clock*
wailing wood *a violin, a guitar* (any wooden musical instrument)

- In the same groups students now think of compound nouns to describe the objects given. This could be done as a team competition, with a time limit of about ten minutes. The groups then hand you their expressions and you read them out, with the class voting for the best one for each concept.
- The groups think of phrases for two other items. They then give their phrases and the other groups try to guess what they refer to. This could also be done competitively, with points given both for writing concise phrases and for guessing correctly.

 Unit summary

Themes	The history of the cinema; films
Structures	Reported speech and reporting verbs
Vocabulary	Film genre, film history and film production; reporting verbs; film idioms (in WB)
Skills	*Reading:* scanning, skimming and ordering; analysing text
	Listening: identifying attitude, speaker and function
	Speaking: comparing a spoken and written film review
	Writing: writing a film review
	Pronunciation: attitudinal intonation
Language awareness/Study skills	Suffixes; word formation

 Teaching notes

Introduction

1
- Discuss the introductory questions with the students. Keep the discussion quite general here as the students will get a chance to talk about their favourite films in Exercise 13.
- If you wish, you could introduce the topics here of types of film (i.e. genres) and movements in film (i.e. Hollywood mainstream compared to New Wave, Avant Garde, etc.). How much you discuss here depends on your students' interest in the topic.
- Explain the phrase *film buff* (someone who is interested in and knowledgeable about the film world) and introduce the quiz.
- Divide the class into groups of four. If the number of students does not divide into groups of four, have some groups of three with one student (A, B or C) reading the questions on page 81 as well as looking at the back. Explain the procedure: Student D reads out the questions. The groups try to answer the questions, using the prompts at the back only if necessary.
- Allow ten to fifteen minutes for the quiz. **Do not give the students the answers when they have finished**, as finding the answers provides the motivation for reading the text in Exercise 2.

Reading skills

2 Skimming and scanning

A This text is long and full of information which will be used through the unit. The exercises have therefore been developed to lead students through it in a systematic way.

- Tell students to skim through the text quickly, purely to check their answers from the quiz. Tell them not to look up any vocabulary during reading and give them a time limit of about eight minutes to find all the answers to the quiz.
- Students compare their answers in pairs when they have finished.

Answers
1 Thomas Edison
2 one or two minutes

3 British
4 type
5 John Wayne
6 Ronald Reagan
7 Oscar
8 *Citizen Kane*
9 Alfred Hitchcock
10 Italy
11 *Throne of Blood*
12 Bombay, India
13 *Who framed Roger Rabbit?*
14 Sony

B This exercise requires the students to read the text again a little more carefully to give headings to the paragraphs.

- Tell students to read the text again and decide on the best heading for each paragraph.

Answers
para 1   D The Development of Early Cinema
para 2   F The Hollywood Studio System
para 3   C The Film Star
para 4   J Film Directors
para 5   A Cinema from Other Countries
para 6   I New Developments in Film
para 7   H The Future of the Cinema

C This final section requires the students to read the text much more carefully to get an idea of the chronology suggested.

- This would be the appropriate time to answer any questions regarding vocabulary from the text. Items most likely to be unfamiliar, and to be needed in the understanding of the passage are: *ingeniousness* (cleverness), *era* (age, period), *founder* (someone who starts something), *set* (the scenery and props of a film), *vie* (compete), *accolade* (award, praise), *herald* (announce, come before).
- Students re-read the text in order to put the events in chronological order.

Answers
f 1   a 2   d 3   c 4   e 5   b 6

Vocabulary

3 Finding categories

A
- Refer back to Unit 10, Exercise 10 for notes on categorising vocabulary.
- Students scan the text for words related to the cinema and categorise them. They can choose a number of different categories. If you wish to guide the students, suggest the following: genres, film history, film technology, film production, stars, studios, cinema, film criticism, directors, films, movements in film.

Note: If you're short of time, leave out the categories which refer to names, i.e. studios, stars, directors and films.

Suggested answers
genres   *gangster, horror, melodrama, musical, thriller, film noir, cartoon*
film history   *kinetoscope, sound movie, Hollywood, studio system*
film technology   *frames, project, (low-key) lighting, camera angles, special effects, animation*

film production *production companies, stars, studios, sets, directors, producers*
stars *Charlie Chaplin, Rita Hayworth, Humphrey Bogart, Marilyn Monroe, John Wayne, Ronald Reagan*
studios *United Artists, Warner Brothers, Universal, Columbia, (Disney)*
cinema *box office (takings), B-movie*
film criticism *Oscar, critics*
directors *Orson Welles, Alfred Hitchcock, Ingmar Bergman, Akira Kurosawa, Pedro Almodovar*
films *Citizen Kane, Psycho, Frenzy, Throne of Blood, Ran, Star Wars, Who framed Roger Rabbit?*
movements *German Expressionism, French New Wave, Italian Neo-realism*

- If your class is interested in film, you may like to get them to add more words to some of the categories above, especially that of genre, as they will need the names of more genres for part B of this exercise.

B
- Focus attention on the ten film titles. Check that students recognise each of them. In a monolingual class, you can discuss them as a whole class; in a multilingual class, divide the class into nationality groups for them to discuss the films.
- Students decide which genre each film belongs to.
- Check with the class and then ask students to add another example to each genre.

Answers
1 *The Sound of Music* musical
2 *Dracula* horror
3 *The Silence of the Lambs* thriller (horror)
4 *Scarface* gangster
5 *Snow White and the Seven Dwarfs* cartoon
6 *Alien* science fiction
7 *Love Story* romance
8 *Ghostbusters* comedy
9 *Raiders of the Lost Ark* adventure
10 *Gone with the Wind* historical (melodrama)

Further practice: Workbook Unit 11, Exercise 3.

Study skills

4 Word formation and suffixes

A This exercise helps students to see the relationships between nouns, verbs and adjectives.

- Tell students to fill in the chart. They can check back in the text to find some words. (Not all the words are in the text.)
- Put the grid on the board and students call out/come up and write in the answers.

noun	verb	adjective
achievement	achieve	
commercialism (commercial also possible = advert)	commercialise	commercial
development	develop	developed/ing
entertainment	entertain	entertaining
ingenuity		ingenious
innovation	innovate	innovative
popularity	popularise	popular
production	produce	productive
technology		technical/technological

B This section extracts common suffixes from the chart and analyses their use.
- Students copy and complete the chart with words from the text.

-ity	-ism	-ment	-ology	-ion
reality	racism	movement	technology	animation
popularity	expressionism	development	sociology	impression
possibility	Realism		psychology	innovation
				production
				competition
				Depression
				interpretation
				tradition
				sophistication

- Students match the suffixes with the explanations.
Answers
1 *-ity*   3 *-ism*   5 *-ology*
2 *-ment*   4 *-ion*

Note: Ensure that students are aware that the suffixes may involve spelling changes in the root.

- Students add more nouns to the lists.

C Students complete the words with suffixes.
Answers
1 psychology   3 arrangement   5 rarity
2 optimism   4 abolition

Extension
- In groups, students can choose other words with the suffixes and write sentences to describe them, which can then be given to other groups to solve.

Further practice: Workbook Unit 11, Exercise 5.

Listening skills

5 Listening to identify attitude

A
- Tell students that they are going to listen to a review of *The Silence of the Lambs*. Find out if they know the film and, if so, what they can tell you about it.
- Students read the questions about attitude.
- Play the review once only for students to think about the attitudes. (This is how they would be listening to a review on the radio.)

Answers
The reviewer's attitude towards:
a very positive (*slick, tense thriller; refreshing, if you see only one film this year make sure it's this one*)
b also positive (*expert direction*)
c also positive (*outstanding performances*)
d negative (*could have been gory, violence, shock tactics*)

- Discuss the point about Hollywood treatment of horror films (all violence and shock). If students have seen this film, ask if they agree with the review.
- Play the review again for students to list the words/phrases which helped them. (See **Answers** above.)

Tapescript

See pages 181 – 2 of the Students' Book.

B Listening for gist

This helps to prepare students for writing a review in Exercise 6.

- Play the review again for the students to listen for the topics. (Combine this with the second listening in A if you wish.)

Answers
1 an introduction to the film
2 the plot
3 details of the two main actors
4 the feminist aspects of the film
5 the reviewer's recommendation

Writing skills

6 Writing a film review

This whole exercise leads students towards writing a film review by getting them to analyse and compare the language used in the spoken review they have just heard and the written review they need to complete in 6A.

A This is a gapped text which focusses students' attention on the structure of a written review.

- Students read through the text and complete it with words from the review they have listened to.

Answers
1 murderer/killer
2 psychoanalyst/psychologist
3 childhood
4 gruesome/gory
5 direction
6 imagination
7 performances
8 feminist
9 determination
10 psychological

B • Discuss the questions generally with the students. They should be able to answer them from their own knowledge of English.

Answers
Differences: contractions, colloquial language, less complex grammatical constructions in spoken language.
Written language is more formal.
We are more likely to use latinate vocabulary and more formal register in written language.
We use more complex grammatical constructions in written language, e.g. embedded and subordinate clauses.

- Divide the class into pairs. They each look at the relevant text and complete the chart.

Answers

aspect of language	spoken	written
the order in which information is presented	background to film, plot, actors, feminist angle, recommendation	plot, background, actors, feminist angle, recommendation
length of sentence	fairly short, with some subordination, but not much	some very long sentences, e.g. those starting *Lecter, an eminent ...* (line 4) and *Viewers whose ...* (line 28)

formal/informal language	informal, e.g. addressing audience as *you*, contractions, referring to personal opinion	formal, e.g. no contractions (see grammatical constructions)
vocabulary	some colloquialisms, e.g. *smash, obviously* (to state a point), multi-word verbs	all neutral or formal, many latinate adjectives e.g. *impeccable, mundane, implicit*
grammatical constructions	impersonal *it* constructions, e.g. *It's interesting that ..., It's refreshing ...,* imperatives, e.g. *make sure ...,* conditionals, e.g. *If you see only one film this year ...*	use of adverbs, e.g. *interestingly* and *surprisingly,* passives, lots of participle clauses, e.g. *Starling, played to perfection by ...,* relatives, e.g. *... during which she is persuaded*

- Tell students that the order of presentation of the information is probably more normal in the spoken review, but it is possible to change the order in written reviews, as the reader can always refer back to the plot etc.

C • Students now focus on the written review. They can read it again to answer the questions. (You may find that most of these questions have already been answered.)

Answers
a lines 28-32
b lines 12-14
c lines 14-21
d lines 1-11
e lines 22-27
tenses: present simple (often passive) and continuous
adjectives and adverbs: used a lot
subordination: used a lot

D • Students now listen to the review of another film with a view to writing a review of the film. If you prefer, omit this section and ask students to write a review of a film they know well/have recently seen.
- Students listen to answer the questions. They compare answers with their partner.

Answers
plot: See tapescript below.
genre: romantic comedy
director: Peter Weir, who has had successes with *Picnic at Hanging Rock* and *Witness*
actors: Gerard Depardieu, draws on his unconventional background, compassionate and good performance as a composer; Andie McDowell, good performance as a horticulturalist
opinion: witty, amusing, well worth seeing

Tapescript
REVIEWER Now, our second film this afternoon is a totally different kettle of fish. *Green Card* is a romantic comedy directed by Peter Weir. Weir has had great successes in the past with *Picnic at Hanging Rock* and *Witness*, and *Green Card* is likely to carry on the tradition.

The two lead roles in the film are taken by an unlikely pair: Gerard Depardieu as a penniless composer in New York looking for a way to extend his visa, and Andie McDowell as a horticulturalist looking for the apartment of her dreams, and certainly not looking for Depardieu! She finds her dream apartment, but it has only one hitch – the owner will let it only to a married couple. Enter a mutual friend who sees a

way of solving both problems at once by setting up a
marriage of convenience. Depardieu and McDowell take an
instant dislike to each other, get married and immediately
part, hoping never to see each other again, but when the
Immigration Department starts investigating the validity of
their marriage, that all has to change ...

The plot is fairly predictable; you can imagine the farcical
situations that arise from the couple's forced cohabitation,
and the final outcome is also fairly predictable, but the clear
mismatch of the two lead characters and a witty script make
for a gentle and amusing comedy.

The two main performances are very good, with Depardieu
drawing on his own unconventional background to play the
talented slob with a lot of compassion. The film also looks
somewhat critically at both the American Immigration
Department and at New York's intellectual society. It's
certainly a film well worth seeing if you find yourself with a
spare evening.

Well, that's all for this week. Next week I'll be back with
news of ...

● Students discuss in pairs what would go into a written
  review and in what order.
● Students write the review.

Model answer
Green Card is a romantic comedy starring Gerard Depardieu
and Andie McDowell and directed by Peter Weir, already
noted for his direction of *Picnic at Hanging Rock* and
Witness.

Set in New York, the plot is a rather unlikely tale of a
marriage of convenience between a penniless French
composer, Gerard Depardieu, wishing to extend his
American visa, and a young horticulturist, Andie McDowell,
who has found her dream apartment, but it can only be let to
a married couple.

After the wedding the couple part, hoping never to see
each other again, as they have taken an instant dislike to each
other, but they are soon forced back together in order to
prove the validity of the marriage to the American
Immigration Department. The comedy in the film, ranging
from the gently comic to farce, centres on this forced
cohabitation and its predictable outcome.

This seemingly trite plot is secondary, however, to the witty
script and excellent performances by the leading actors.
Depardieu, charismatic as ever, seems to draw on his own
unconventional background to bring great comparison to his
character, a talented slob. Andie McDowell is equally
convincing as the liberated, intelligent horticulturist and it is
the combination of these two performances that makes the
film amusing and entertaining.

This is not just a film about personal relationships, however.
The situation that the main characters find themselves in is a
vehicle for critical consideration of the American Immigration
Service, while the characters themselves provide an ironic
insight into New York intellectual society.

Green Card, therefore, gives the viewer an entertaining
insight into American life. While not being one of the major
releases of the year, it is a film well worth seeing for its witty
script and the very talented performances by the actors in the
leading roles.

Further practice: Workbook Unit 11, Exercise 10.

Reading skills

7   Reading for detail

This reading passage is the vehicle for presentation of the
language work on reported speech.

● Discuss the questions about Jodie Foster with the students.
  Remind them that she was the main protagonist in *The
  Silence of the Lambs.*
● Students read the text to check whether their answers were
  correct.
● Students answer the true/false questions.

Answers
1   TRUE.
2   TRUE.
3   FALSE. She feels that she can't work if she is given too much
     respect.
4   FALSE. They have explored the darker side of life.
5   FALSE. She thought it wasn't a part that would win her
     another Oscar.
6   FALSE. Her role is that of a hero.
7   FALSE. It gained a nomination.
8   TRUE.

Language work

8   Reported speech

A   Students find the equivalent sentences in the interview.

Answers
1   ... she said that it wasn't a part that she thought would win
     her another Oscar, but that when she'd read the script a
     couple of years before she'd felt compelled to do it.
2   'I decided early on that I wasn't going to make any dumb
     comedies, so my films didn't do that well ...'

● Students look at the sentences and underline the changes
  in tenses, pronouns and time adverbials. Discuss them with
  the class.

Answers
1   Tenses shift one tense further into the past. (backshift)
2   Pronouns change to refer to the person speaking. (E.g. here
     I becomes *she.*)
3   Time adverbials can no longer have a reference to the time
     of speaking. (E.g. here *a couple of years ago* becomes *a
     couple of years before.*)

● Make sure students feel happy about the changes (referring
  them to the Grammar Reference section if necessary), and
  then explain the exercise. Student B has a text in reported
  speech, which he/she must rewrite in direct speech.
  Student A has the same text in direct speech, which he/she
  must rewrite in reported speech. Do not let the students
  know at this stage that the texts are the same.
● Students rewrite their texts. They can do this in groups:
  divide the class into two groups, A and B, which can then
  split into smaller groups.
● When they have finished, each A joins a B to compare
  texts. Each should have written a very similar text to the
  one their partner has been working with.

B   This section looks at the times when the tenses do not shift back.

● Discuss whether there were any points in the texts where
  they might not have changed the tense. Refer them to the
  explanations.

Note: *was going to* does not change in reported speech, as
had been going to suggests that the action did not happen for

some reason.

- Students rewrite the sentences in reported speech.

Answers

1 They said they had seen quite a lot of films when they were/had been living in the city.
2 He said he likes/liked spending the whole weekend in front of the TV, watching videos.
3 She said she hadn't accepted the part in his new film because it was/had been an extremely harrowing role and she had felt unable to take it on.
4 They said when they had arrived in Hollywood it was already the film capital of the world. (*had been* is unlikely here; *had become* would be possible)
5 She said she always went to see his films because she thinks/thought he is/was an extremely good actor.

Further practice: Workbook, Unit 11, Exercises 7 and 8.

Listening skills

9 Identifying speakers

A You may find that your students know very few of the films in the top twenty. Don't worry if this is the case: the point of this top twenty is to lead into the students making one for themselves in the final task.

- Discuss the top twenty. Make sure that the students are aware of the pronunciation of the films on the list.
- Play the conversation on tape. Students tick the films they hear.

Answers

Citizen Kane (1), *The Godfather* (5), *L'Atalante* (7), *Raging Bull* (8), *Psycho* (14)

- Ask students to discuss the opinions of the people on tape regarding the top twenty. (Don't play the tape again yet.)

Answers

It's really a top twenty for film buffs. Perhaps there should be one based on cinema attendance.

- Discuss whether students agree with those opinions.

Tapescript

DIANE What do you think of the top one, the first film according to this, ... the top film according to the critics is *Citizen Kane*.
TONY Well, I think that's always the top film according to just about everybody, isn't it?
DIANE Do you think so? Would you say that? What do you think of it?
TONY Um, I'm not sure if I've seen it, actually [Well, yes], but, I mean, it's ...
JANET It's one of those films you always think you have seen, and you're never sure ...
DIANE You've seen it!
JANET Have I seen it?
DIANE We went to see it in Germany together.
JANET Ah, well, there you are, you see. I have seen it. I've obviously forgotten already.
MARK I think it's the sort of film that people involved in the film business like, [Yes] because it's got so many ... it started so many things; it was the first film to do so many things, but for ordinary members of the public [Yes] that doesn't really matter, you know, I mean, they're more interested in what's entertaining ...
TONY Well, I think when it first came out, when it came out, it wasn't very popular, in fact, was it? [No, you're right.] It wasn't a box office hit [Mm] at all. But probably a lot of these weren't box office hits. [That's true, yeah. That's right.] And

the films which have been seen by most people are probably not in the top twenty. [Mm, yeah.]
LOUISE Yeah, 'cos that's what I thought when I looked through it. I thought, 'My goodness ...'
DIANE Well, I think there are one or two in this [Where is *Jaws*?] that are considered entertainment films. What about *The Godfather* and *Raging Bull* [Yes, OK] I would've thought they're considered entertainment films.
LOUISE I'm, I'm very surprised *Raging Bull* is in there.
DIANE Why? Didn't you like it?
LOUISE I did like it, but [I don't think it would have been a ...] I don't think it would be [a popular film] there if you asked people in the street what were their top twenty films. I don't think they'd include *Raging Bull*.
DIANE But then, if you asked people in the street, half these films wouldn't be included because people ... unless they're, they're interested in film per se, they're not going to know a lot of these films that are very old. They're not going to know films that are not their own language like, um, *L'Atalante*.
TONY But wouldn't it be more sensible to have a top twenty based on the attendance in cinemas [Yes] of people who've seen these films?
LOUISE I think that would be my criticism of this ...
DIANE ... but surely the whole idea of something like this is basically for people who are interested. It's saying, you know, these are the films that you should have seen, [Yes] which I think is quite OK.
LOUISE Yes, I think that's true, it would be useful as a ...
JANET That's maybe true if you're ...
LOUISE ... a hit list.
JANET That's right, but some of these films on here are ... for example, *Psycho*, which I think had a, ... an immense effect on people at the time; I'm not so sure if young people nowadays would be quite so impressed by it, because, with the recent special effects in the cinema and things, maybe *Psycho* seems a little bit tame. I don't know.
LOUISE Oh, I don't think *Psycho* could ever seem tame. [I don't know, no.]
JANET I don't know, [I disagree] I think in, ... with some of the things that they're producing now, I think for some people it could seem a little bit tame.
DIANE It depends on what ... what you understand by tame, and what you understand by violence as well, because some of these films that are out these days – I don't know many of the blood and guts films these days – but the thought of just watching people exploding ... it's nothing, whereas in *Psycho* it's all in the imagination. Even the shower scene in *Psycho* is very much in the imagination; you never see the knife touch her skin, her body. You never see it – it's all a series of juxtaposed images, and that's what's so good about it. You can't take away from Hitchcock the fact that he's one of the greatest directors that's ever lived.
JANET No. I certainly wouldn't want to take that away from him, but I certainly know now that if it came onto television I wouldn't watch it, not because, not because I've seen it so many times, but just because I know about it, it's so famous. I ... I just, I wouldn't have the inclination to watch it any more. I don't think ...
LOUISE Gosh, I'm completely the opposite. I wouldn't watch it but I wouldn't watch it because I find it so disturbing. [Mm]
MARK Oh, I would. I'd tell anyone to watch it actually, because it's so full of ...
LOUISE It's a brilliant film ...
MARK ... it's just psychological terror.
LOUISE No, I would tell everyone, too, yeah, I think everyone should watch it, but it's like, um, the sort of ...(*fade*)

B This section of the exercise looks at identifying speakers. The students can use the information given to help them identify the speakers.

- Play the tape again for students to answer the questions; you may need to play it twice so that students can get used to the voices, or stop it regularly.

Answers
1 TRUE.
2 TRUE.
3 FALSE. It is Diane who says this.
4 FALSE. It is Tony who says this.
5 TRUE.
6 TRUE.
7 FALSE. It is Mark who says this; Janet is not impressed by *Psycho*.

10 Identifying function

This exercise takes certain extracts from the film and matches them to their functions in speech. This introduces some of the reporting verbs needed for Exercise 12.

- Students listen to the statements from the conversation and match them to their functions.

Answers

agreeing 3   recommending 7
asking 1   reminding 2
asserting 6   suggesting 4
explaining 5

Tapescript
1 What do you think of the top one?
2 You've seen it ... we went to see it in Germany together.
3 That's true, yeah. That's right.
4 But surely the whole idea of something like this is basically for people who are interested.
5 ... in *Psycho*, it's all in the imagination. Even the shower scene in *Psycho* is very much in the imagination.
6 You can't take away from Hitchcock the fact that he's one of the greatest directors that's ever lived.
7 I'd tell anyone to watch it actually.

- Play the extracts again. Students answer the questions.

Answers
1 That Hitchcock is one of the greatest directors.
2 That the horror in *Psycho* is all in the imagination.
3 For anyone to watch *Psycho*.
4 That she had seen *Citizen Kane* (in Germany).

Pronunciation

11 Attitudinal intonation

This exercise aims to help students perceive and produce certain attitudes in intonation.

A
- Tell students that they are going to listen to some more extracts and responses. They should concentrate on the responses, which are very short.
- Play the extracts. Discuss the questions in the class.

Answers
1 emphatic agreement, reassures the speaker
2 weak agreement, helps the conversation along
3 agreement, simple 'listener tactic'
4 conceding a point, no real feeling
5 strong agreement, taking the floor
6 firm agreement
7 disagreement, but not offending the speaker
8 disagreement, conceding a point, allowing another opinion

Tapescript
1 I think it's the sort of film that people involved in the film business like ...
   Yes.
2 It wasn't popular in fact, was it?
   No, you're right.
3 It wasn't a box office hit at all ...
   Mm.
4 What about *The Godfather* and *Raging Bull*?
   Yes, OK.
5 But wouldn't it be more sensible to to have a top twenty based on the attendance in cinemas ...
   Yes.
6 It's saying, you know, these are the films you should have seen.
   Yes.
7 I don't think *Psycho* could ever seem tame ...
   No, I disagree.
8 ... I wouldn't watch it because I find it so disturbing.
   Mm.

B
- Explain that students rate the strength of feeling in the responses (according to the intonation) on a scale of 1–10, with 10 being the strongest.
- Play the extracts again for students to rate the feeling. They can compare what they have done in pairs.

Answers
(These are approximate and answers anywhere near these numbers are acceptable.) See chart below.
- Ask students if they notice any patterns. They should notice that the greater variations in pitch express stronger feeling.

word/phrase	strong feeling 10 ---- 9 ---- 8 ---- 7 ---- 6 --- 5 ---- 4 ---- 3 ---- 2 ---- 1 ---- 0 weak feeling
1	8
2	4
3	3
4	6
5	9
6	7
7	7
8	2

C This section practises intonation of *Mmm*. This enables students to concentrate on the intonation and not worry about words.

- Explain the listening to the students and play the tape as many times as they wish to hear it.

Answers

strongest 4 and 6,   weakest 1

- Students write five invitations for this evening. They should all start in the same way, such as *Would you like to ...?* or *Shall we ... tonight?*
- Divide the class into pairs and explain the exercise: A reads his/her invitations to B, who responds only with *Mmm*, but making his/her enthusiasm clear by the intonation. A decides which invitation(s) B is most interested in, and checks with B. They then swap roles.
- Monitor and encourage exaggerated intonation.

Language work

12 Reporting verbs

A
- Read through the introductory notes and explain to the students that it is often more natural to use the range of functional reporting verbs given than to use *say, tell* etc. when reporting speech.
- Students do the initial transformation. Check that they have understood.

Answers

She suggested that the whole idea of something like that was for the people who were interested ...
She explained that in *Psycho* it was/is all in the imagination.

- Students report the statements from Exercise 10. These are the ones they heard on the tape.

Answers

1 She asked what he thought of the top one.
2 She reminded her that she had seen it, that they had gone to see it in Germany.
3 He agreed that a lot of them hadn't been box office hits.
4 She asserted that you/one couldn't take away from Hitchcock the fact that he was one of the greatest directors that had ever lived.
5 He'd recommend anyone to watch it.

B
- Students practise reporting with different verbs by reporting a dialogue on tape. If you want to speed this up, divide the class into A and B, and get the groups to transform alternate sentences.

Tapescript

DIRECTOR Right, everyone. We're all here and we're ready to roll. Into positions for the scene in the restaurant and ... hang on, where's Dennis? Sam, could you go and check the dressing room, please. Oh, here he is. Late again, Dennis. You're always late these days.
DENNIS I'm sorry. Let me explain. I had to take my daughter to school and I got stuck in the traffic coming back.
DIRECTOR That's just not good enough, Dennis. I'll have to think about replacing you if this continues.
DENNIS Oh come on, be reasonable. It hasn't happened that much, only about three times.
DIRECTOR Yes, you're right, but it's three times when the cameras have been set up and we've all been here and we haven't been able to start. It's beginning to cost both time and money.
DENNIS I know. I am aware of that. I appreciate your problem.

DIRECTOR Seriously, Dennis, if you want to stay in this game you ought to consider getting a childminder or something.
DENNIS You're right. I'll think about it, and I will try to get here in time in future.
DIRECTOR OK. Right everyone, into position, and don't forget to keep out of the way of Camera 3 for this scene ...

Model answer

The director asked Sam to look for Dennis. When Dennis arrived the director complained that he was always late. Dennis apologised and explained that he had had to take his daughter to school and had got stuck in the traffic coming back.

The director complained that it wasn't good enough and he warned Dennis that he would have to think about replacing him if that behaviour continued. Dennis denied that it had happened very much, only three times, and the director agreed but explained that it had been three times when the cameras had been set up, everyone had been there and they hadn't been able to start. He added that it was beginning to cost both time and money.

Dennis accepted that there was a problem and the director advised him to consider getting a childminder. Dennis agreed and said he would think about it. He promised to try to get there in time in future. The director then continued with the filming and reminded everyone to keep out of the way of Camera 3 for that scene.

C
- Students complete the chart with the verbs they have been using.

Answers

Verb + infinitive	Verb + -ing	Verb + object infinitive	Verb + *that*
refuse agree promise	suggest recommend advise deny apologise (for)	ask remind advise	suggest remind agree assert recommend explain complain warn

- Remind students of the chart in their books.

Final task

13 A top ten films list

A
- Remind students of the top twenty in Exercise 9. Ask individual students to note down their favourite three or four films.

B
- In groups they compile a top ten.

C
- Follow the instructions in the Students' Book to create a class top ten.

Extension
- Students choose a film from the top ten and write a review of it.

Unit summary

Theme	Famous fakes and frauds
Structures	Modal verbs of probability and certainty; modal perfects
Vocabulary	Words with negative connotation; idioms of reality and illusion; technology (in Workbook); multi-word verbs with particle *through* (in Workbook)
Skills	*Reading:* Identifying degrees of probability and certainty
	Listening: Checking and clarifying information
	Speaking: Persuading and convincing
	Writing: Narrative accounts
Pronunciation	Assimilation

 ## Teaching notes

Introduction

1
- Divide the students into pairs to discuss the pictures and decide which are real and which are fakes.
- Pairs compare their answers with other pairs, trying to agree on their decisions.
- When students have made up their minds they can turn to page 160 of the Students' Book to find out about the pictures.
- Elicit reactions to the pictures and the information. Were the students surprised? Expand into a brief discussion of what is meant by a fake and elicit further examples from the class.
- Elicit the following and write on the board:
  fake document/object/work of art which seems genuine but is not
  forgery the act of copying a document/signature/bank note etc. with criminal intent; a copy which is designed to deceive
  forger person who commits forgery
  fraud criminal deception; person who pretends to be something/someone they're not
  hoax less serious trick played on one or more people, for a relatively harmless e.g. humorous motive, not usually for personal gain

2
- Discuss the introductory question with the class, eliciting any knowledge they have.

Background information: Evolution is a theory, accepted by many (but not all) scientists, which explains how life evolved or developed from the earliest organisms to modern humans. It was developed by the English naturalist, Charles Darwin (1809 – 1882), in the book *On the Origin of Species by means of Natural Selection*, published in 1859. According to this theory, modern man is descended from the apes. Since 1859, scientists have been searching for the remains of early humans, seeking to prove and explain this process.

- Read through the introduction and questions with the class.
- Pre-teach:
  humanoid human-like
  anthropoid ape-like
  fossil skeleton or imprint of an ancient plant or animal preserved and found in rock
  paleontology the study of fossils and their implications
  skull bones of the head
- Students read both documents and answer the questions

Note: The students will have a chance to discuss their reactions to the documents and theories in Exercise 4B, following a closer examination of the texts. Do not pre-empt this by allowing them to discuss their opinions at this stage.

Answers
1 He claims that the remains combine a humanoid skull with an ape-like jawbone, the teeth being worn down in a way only possible with human jaw movement, thus proving a half-way stage between man and the apes.
2 Sir Piers argues that the skull and jawbone may not be connected, or the teeth may be the result of natural deformation, or it may be a fake.

Study skills

3   Analysing and gap-filling

This exercise takes students through one of the step-by-step elimination techniques used to complete vocabulary gap-filling exercises (based on parts of speech rather than meaning). If the class is proficient in this area you may wish to go straight to section C.

A   Answers
establishment noun   *geology* noun
prestigious adjective   *fossil* noun   *predicted* verb
eminent adjective   *evolution* noun
frenzied adjective   *descendent* noun
anthropoid adjective   *descent* noun
interpretation noun   *ancestry* noun
proof noun   *enthusiasm* noun   *cloud* verb
evidence noun   *amassed* verb   *coincidence* noun
sensationalist adjective

B   Answers
1 adjective   2 noun   3 noun   4 noun
5 adjective   6 noun   7 adjective   8 noun
9 verb   10 noun   11 noun   12 noun

C   Answers
1 eminent   2 evolution   3 fossil   4 evolution
5 anthropoid   6 descent   7 prestigious
8 judgement   9 amassed   10 evidence
11 interpretation   12.coincidence

Reading skills

4   Identifying degrees of certainty/probability

A
- Read through the introduction and explain the task. Check understanding of the four categories: impossible, possible, probable and certain. Point out the importance of the phrase *according to the relevant text* – students should not consider their own interpretation at this stage.
- Go through the example, asking the students to find and underline the relevant sentence in the text (it is the last sentence of first paragraph), and explaining how the verb form *could provide* indicates that the writer thinks this is

possible rather than probable or certain.
* Students follow the same procedure for the other statements. Check they write down the verb phrase and degree of probability for each statement as this will be needed in Exercise 5.
* Students should compare their answers with a partner.

Answers

1 POSSIBLE. Verb form: *could provide*
2 IMPOSSIBLE. Verb form: *could not be...*
3 CERTAIN. Verb form: *must prove...*
4 CERTAIN. Verb form: *must be...*
5 PROBABLE. Verb form: *should revolutionise...*
6 CERTAIN. Verb form: *would...*
7 IMPOSSIBLE. Verb form: *cannot be made...*
8 POSSIBLE. Verb form: *could be...*
9 POSSIBLE. Verb form: *might be...*
10 POSSIBLE. Verb form: *might not be...*
11 POSSIBLE. Verb form: *may be...*
12 CERTAIN. Verb form: *will serve...*

B
* Students should spend a few minutes discussing the four questions and then report back to class. There are no fixed answers.
* Use the report back stage to initiate a brief discussion of their ideas and then ask the students to turn to page 161 of the Students' Book to find out the full story.

Language work

5 Modal verbs of probability/certainty

A
* Students should copy the chart onto paper and complete the columns with the verb forms they have noted in the previous exercise.

Answers

Impossible	Possible	Probable	Certain
could not be	could	should	must
cannot be	might		will
	might not		
	may		

* Elicit answers to the questions and write these on the board.

Answers

The negative of *must* in this context is *can't* or *couldn't*, not *mustn't*.
The negative of *could* in this context is *might not*, not *couldn't*.
Rank order: *May* is slighty more positive than might or could, although there is little real difference. *Might* is arguably the least positive.

B
* Elicit anything the students know about Vincent Van Gogh.

Background information: Vincent Van Gogh (1853 – 1890) was a Dutch post-impressionist painter and a friend of Gauguin. His talent was unrecognised during his lifetime and he spent many years in mental asylums, eventually committing suicide. His most famous paintings are *Sunflowers*, *The Yellow Chair* and *A Cornfield with Cypresses*. Although he never sold any paintings and died penniless, his works are now amongst the world's most popular and valuable pictures.

* Explain the task. Pre-teach:
self-portrait picture/photo of oneself painted/taken by oneself

provenance (proof of) the history of an object, in particular who has owned it from the time of its creation to the present day.
* Students complete the re-writing exercise and then compare their answers.

Answers

SELF-PORTRAITS MAY NOT/MIGHT NOT BE BY HAND OF VAN GOGH
...three self-portraits up to now accepted as being painted by Vincent Van Gogh may/might/could be fakes.
'Three of them cannot/could not be guaranted as genuine.'
There are rumours that the pictures may/might/could be withdrawn from public display.
Any picture which is not traceable to one of these sources must be considered dubious.
...the majority of art historians should/would support his view that the brushstrokes are haphazard.
...the self-portrait in London's Courtauld Gallery must be genuine.

Further practice: Workbook Unit 12, Exercise 7.

Speaking

6 Persuading and convincing

For the purpose of this exercise it is better not to give the students any further information about the pictures. At the end of the exercise, to satisfy their curiosity, you can give them the information printed below.

A
* Ask the students to describe the painting and guess its artist. They may recognise the style of Jan Vermeer (1632 – 75), a Dutch artist famous for his depictions of domestic interiors in 17th-century Holland.
* Read through the dialogue with the class and elicit answers to the questions.

Answers

(Open question. Don't tell the class whether the picture is genuine or not at this stage.)
A is trying to convince B that the painting is a fake. B is trying to put counter-arguments.
Some of the devices they use are:
phrases to elicit agreement.
Don't you think ...?
Don't you agree ...?
question tags to elicit agreement.
They're ..., aren't they?

B
* Divide the class into pairs and nominate A and B in each pair.
* Read through the instructions with the students and check they understand their roles.
* Monitor the pair work, checking that the students are using the persuading/convincing devices outlined above.
* When the pairs have finished ask them to report back with their decisions. Did they decide the pictures were fakes or not?
* Now tell them the following:
Picture A is a fake Vermeer, painted by one of the world's greatest forgers, Henricus Van Meegeren, in about 1936.
Picture B is, as far as we know, genuine.
Picture C is an Italian fake dating from the 18th century. The head is facing the wrong way and comes from another statue.

Listening skills

7   Checking and clarifying information

Note: This is a particularly demanding intensive listening exercise which is most effectively done in a language laboratory. If you do not have access to one, be prepared to play the tape several times for students to complete the tasks.

A   Elicit anything the students know about Adolf Hitler and the famous diaries fraud without going into too much detail.

Background information: Adolf Hitler (1889 – 1945) was an Austrian who founded the German Nazi party and was a dictator in Germany during the Second World War (1939 – 45). He committed suicide in an underground bunker in Berlin in 1945 as the Russian army entered the city. He wrote Mein Kampf (My Struggle) in 1923 and many people believe he kept a secret diary during the war. Because there are many unanswered questions about his life, the discovery of such a diary would be a significant historical event and of great financial value.

* Read through the introduction and ask the students to read the summary, checking understanding.
* Pre-teach:
  memorabilia relics/objects (usually of little financial value) connected with an event or experience in the past
  syndication rights the formal, legal right to reproduce and use a copyright work (book, printed document, TV or radio programme, film) already produced by someone else/another company for an agreed payment to them

B   * Explain the checking/correcting task and play the tape.
* With a strong class, do not check their answers at this stage, but move straight on to section C.
* With a weak class you may prefer to check that they have found all the mistakes and then play the tape again for them to make corrections. The thirteen mistakes are underlined below.

Answers
THE STORY OF THE HITLER DIARIES
1945 Adolf Hitler sends a plane containing a mysterious locked trunk to Berlin. It was shot down somewhere. Heidemann visits Fritz Stiefel, a collector of Nazi memorabilia, and sees a Hitler diary.
1980 Heidemann sets out for West Germany to search for the site of something and eventually discovers a number of crashed planes in a village.
1981 (January) Heidemann 'discovers' Kujau and hears his story about his fictional father.
1981 (January) Heidemann starts 17 regular visits to Kujau, swapping suitcases for each instalment of the diaries. Some experts in the United States and Sweden confirm the handwriting as being unquestionably that of Adolf Hitler.
1983 (April) World-renowned forger Hugh Trevor-Roper confirms the authority of the diaries.
1983 (April) Stern has collected the full set of diaries and begins some sort of negotiations for the German syndication rights with the world's leading publishing companies.
1983 Forensic test results are published, exposing the diaries as clever and brilliant fakes. Kujau and Heidemann on trial somewhere are sentenced to over fourteen years for fraud.

C   * Explain the additional information task and play the tape.
* Students should double-check their summaries with a partner or in small groups.

Model summary
THE STORY OF THE HITLER DIARIES
1945 Adolf Hitler sends a plane containing a mysterious locked trunk from the bunker in Berlin to a safe haven in Salzburg; it was shot down in the middle of a remote forest in East Germany.
1979 Heidemann visits Fritz Stiefel, a collector of Nazi memorabilia, and sees a Hitler diary.
1980 (November) Heidemann sets out for East Germany to search for the site of the crash and eventually discovers a number of graves in the village of Boernersdorf.
1981 (January) Heidemann 'discovers' Kujau and hears his story about his fictional brother.
1981 (January) Heidemann starts 27 regular visits to Kujau, swapping suitcases full of cash for each instalment of the diaries.
1982 Handwriting experts in the United States and Switzerland confirm the handwriting as being unquestionably that of Adolf Hitler.
1983 (April) World-renowned Hitler scholar Hugh Trevor-Roper confirms the authenticity of the diaries.
1983 (April) Stern has collected the full set of diaries and begins secret negotiations for the international syndication rights with the world's leading publishing companies.
1983 (May) Forensic test results are published, exposing the diaries as amateurish and blatant fakes.
1985 (July) Kujau and Heidemann on trial in Hamburg are sentenced to over four years for fraud.

Tapescript
See page 182–183 of the Students' Book.

Vocabulary

8   Words with negative connotations

Note: The first part of this exercise can be made more challenging by asking the students to find more words by listening to the tape again, rather than allowing them to read the tapescript.

* Read through the introduction. If students are not familiar with the concept of negative connotation write the following chart on the board:

POSITIVE	NEUTRAL	NEGATIVE
inexpensive	cheap	worthless
slim	thin	skinny
scrupulous	careful	pedantic

Students should be able to see how words can have a similar meaning but carry different connotations. Elicit a few more examples from the class.
* Students add words from the radio programme to the lists.

Answers

features of modern international publishing	features of the fraud	the forged diaries	Gerd Heidemann	Conrad Kujau
credulity	deception	worthless	ambitious	small-time
greed	intrigue	ineptly forged	unscrupulous	petty
	farce	amateurish	gullibility	notorious
		blatant		

- Students now look at the second chart and put words from the lists into the correct columns. Encourage them to use their own knowledge or dictionaries to complete it.

Answers

noun	adjective	adverb
deception	deceptive	deceptively
notoriety	notorious	notoriously
greed	greedy	greedily
amateur	amateurish	amateurishly
blatancy	blatant	blatantly
gullibility	gullible	gullibly
farce	farcical	farcically
ineptitude	inept	ineptly
unscrupulousness	unscrupulous	unscrupulously

Pronunciation

9 Assimilation

Note: This exercise only covers word-boundary assimilation of final /t/ before the sounds /k/ and /p/, and final /d/ before the sounds /b/, /k/ and /g/ in connected speech. The aim is to act as an introduction and to make students aware of this feature of spoken English.

Extension

- If you wish to cover the feature in more detail you may find the following chart useful:

  /t/ before /b/ changes to /p/   e.g. that bag /θæp bæg/
  /t/ before /j/ changes to /ʃ/   e.g. can't you? /kɑːntʃuː/
  /d/ before /j/ changes to /dʒ/   e.g. would you? /wʊdʒu:/
  /d/ before /m/ changes to /b/   e.g. good morning /gʊb mɔːnɪŋ/
  /n/ before /m/ changes to /m/   e.g. thin man /θɪm mæn/

A
- Read the introduction and play the extracts on tape.
- The students should be able to hear that the underlined final /t/ in the words has disappeared and become assimilated with the first sound of the following word.
- Elicit the answers.

Answers
a The final /t/ changes to /p/.   b The final /t/ changes to /k/.
c The final /t/ changes to /k/.

- If the students have difficulty hearing the assimilation, put the following on the board and read the items aloud.

  that /θæt/   *that plane* / θæp pleɪn/

B
- Write the following definition on the board.
  Assimilation the replacement of one sound by another that is similar to adjacent sounds.
- Some students may feel that assimilation is somehow wrong or lazy. Point out that it is a common feature of rapid spoken English; it is NOT due to laziness or sloppy speech.
- Explain the task and play the tape, several times if necessary.

Answers
1 I believe he's on that plane.
2 We had to work under extremely strict conditions.
3 He's rather a fat person.
4 I prefer very hot curries.
5 Only five pounds! That was a good buy.
6 She's got a bad cold.

7 Jim's the head gardener.
8 That was a very sad ballad.
9 What a beautiful old carpet.
10 There's a famous Vermeer in the Red Gallery.

- Students listen and repeat. Check that they make the assimilations correctly.

C
- Let students discuss the questions in pairs or small groups. Play the tape again if they need to check their ideas.

Answers
When /t/ is followed by /p/ or /k/ it changes to that sound. When /d/ is followed by /b/ or /g/ it changes to that sound. The combination of sounds is different in items 6 and 9: /d/ is followed by /k/ and it doesn't change to /k/, it changes to /g/.

Writing skills

10 Narrative accounts

A
- Discuss the questions with the class.

Answers
In exercise 7A the events are listed in chronological order whereas in the radio review the speaker gives the beginning and end of the story first, and then fills in the events of the story in a series of *flashbacks*. Another difference is that the events in the summary are written in the present tenses whereas they are described in the past tenses in the radio review.
The advantages of chronological order are that it reflects the way time passes in real life and is therefore easy to understand.

- Elicit and discuss the answers.

Answers
a The past tenses are usually used (past simple/continuous/perfect) to tell a story, although in some narratives, such as anecdotes or jokes, the present tenses are used to create a feeling of immediacy, spontaneity and excitement. It is also usual to use the present tenses when we are describing the plot of a book or film, and often, but not always, when we are summarising a narrative.
b Linking words are used to show the various relationships between events: This can be a relationship of time sequence, cause and effect, conditionality and so on.
c Time references allow us to place narrative events in historical perspective and in sequential relationship to each other.

B
- Explain the task. Students can use the corrected summary of the story in Exercise 7 as a skeleton from which to build their narrative. They should use past tenses.
- Students can work individually or in groups, using one of the methods for group writing outlined in the introduction.
- As this is a fairly controlled narrative, it can be corrected by the students themselves. They should exchange their accounts and, working in pairs, check each other's work.

Model answer
The story of the Hitler diaries fraud began in 1945 when Adolf Hitler sent a mysterious trunk of personal documents on a plane to Salzburg. The plane crashed in a remote forest near the village of Boernersdorf.
   Twenty-five years later Gerd Heidemann, a journalist on Stern magazine, met Fritz Steifel and saw a 'Hitler diary' in his collection of Nazi memorabilia. Stiefel told Heidemann that he had bought the diary from an antique dealer in Stuttgart named Konrad Kujau. Heidemann visited Kujau and heard his story about his brother, a general in the East German

army, who had obtained the diaries from peasants who had rescued them from the burning wreckage of a plane which had crashed outside their village in 1945. Heidemann visited East Germany and found several graves near the village of Boernersdorf. This convinced him that Kujau must be telling the truth, so he decided to buy the diaries from Kujau on behalf of his employers, the German magazine *Stern*.

Because it was illegal to export Nazi documents from East Germany, Kujau was able to convince Heidemann that everything would have to be done in secret, with payments in cash and no receipts. Starting in January 1981, Heidemann made 27 visits to Kujau, swapping suitcases full of cash for each instalment of the diaries. By April 1983 he had collected the full set and had paid Kujau over four million dollars. *Stern* began secret negotiations with leading international publishing companies and asked several Hitler experts to check the diaries. They were all convinced that they were genuine, and several newspapers began publishing extracts from the diaries, which were also sent for forensic tests at the Bundesarchiv. It was when these results came out, in May 1983, that the truth emerged. According to the forensic scientists the diaries were undoubtedly fakes. Kujau and Heidemann were arrested and found guilty of fraud in 1985, receiving sentences of four years.

Further practice: Workbook Unit 12, Exercises 9, 10 and 11.

Language work

11 Modal perfects

A • Students study the extracts and answer the questions.

Answers
(Both phrases are examples of modal perfect forms.)
1   *Must have been trying* is the modal perfect progressive form (modal verb + *have been* + present participle).
    May have been is the modal perfect simple form (modal verb + have + past participle).
2   *Must have been* is used to make a deduction about the past of which you are certain.
    May have is used to make a deduction about the past which is probable but not certain.

• Ask students to complete the matching task.

Answers
1   *must have*   2   *can't have*   3   *might have*
4   *may have*

• Write this chart on the board and elicit the modal perfect forms from the class.

MODAL PERFECTS
CERTAINTY	must have		
PROBABILITY	would have		
POSSIBILITY	may have	might have	could have
IMPOSSIBILITY	can't have	couldn't have	

B • Students look at the photograph and discuss the questions in pairs, using modal verb forms.

Suggested answers
It must have been taken at the beginning of the twentieth century/It may have been taken in the nineteenth century.
It might have been taken by one of the girl's friends or relatives.
The creatures could/might be fairies.
The creatures might be playing with the girl.
It can't be genuine.

• Ask pairs to report back to class.

C • Students complete the task individually.

Answers
1   can't have existed   2   must have been lying   3   can't have been playing/can't have played   4   must have faked
5   may/might/could have combined   6   may/might/could have made   7   may/might/could have painted   8   must have been

Further practice: Workbook Unit 12, Exercise 7.

Vocabulary

12 Idioms of reality and illusion

• Elicit the meaning of the sentence from the students.

Answer
The sentence means that the management of *Stern* were not suspicious, although they should have been.

• Point out that *smell a rat* is an idiom which means *suspect that something is wrong*.
• Students complete the matching exercise, checking their matches with a partner.

Answers
a 7   b 10   c 11   d 3   e 4   f 9   g 8   h 1
i 12   j 2   k 6   l 5

• Students use idioms from the list to make sentences about the situations.

Suggested answers
The fact that Kujau knew about the plane crash was a red herring / The plane crash was an open secret.
Stern counted their chickens before they were hatched.
Kujau took Heidemann for a ride / Kujau pulled the wool over Heidemann's eyes.

Extension
• Ask students if they know of any recent scandals or crime stories which have been in the news. Elicit two or three and write them on the board. As a brief game, ask students in small groups to make as many sentences as they can about the events, using idioms from the list. The group which makes the most correct sentences within a set time wins.

Final task

13 The Strange Case of the Mulahabad Diamonds Fraud

Note: This is the second Sherlock Holmes reading jigsaw in *Distinction*. The first, *The Murder of Michael Roe*, is in Unit 2, Exercise 13, page 22 of the Students' Book. See the teaching notes on page 21 for background information on Sherlock Holmes and a step-by-step guide to organising the activity. This is more challenging and will take at least 25 minutes with an average class.

Solution
The man who died in Sir Hugh Drummond's house was Corporal Tom Cabmoll, an old soldier of the Norfolk regiment (the tatoo of HONOUR OR DEATH on his arm is the regimental motto). In India in 1860 Cabmoll had stolen ten diamonds from a Hindu temple in Mulahabad. Soon after the crime, the diamonds were discovered in his bed and the officer commanding his unit, Colonel Tosh, sentenced him to 25 years in Calcutta Military Prison.

While Cabmoll was awaiting trial, Colonel Tosh substituted fake diamonds for the real ones. The change was discovered when the diamonds were returned to the temple, but the military police assumed it was Cabmoll who had switched the stones before his arrest and given them to an accomplice.

Over the next 25 years, Colonel Tosh sold a few diamonds every time he was in London, and bought a house in an expensive area. Meanwhile Cabmoll was in prison. He knew someone was selling the stones because, every time some appeared on the market, the military police interviewed him.

Colonel Tosh retired to London. Cabmoll was released from prison and came to London to find his diamonds. By checking the dates on which they had been sold against the times when Colonel Tosh was in London he must have worked out that it was Tosh who had switched the stones.

Colonel Tosh clearly expected Cabmoll to come for the diamonds, so he kept the remaining ones hidden in a wooden box in his bedroom. Inside the box he kept one or more poisonous snakes, which he fed every day with live mice, and he slept with a revolver under his pillow.

When Cabmoll burgled Colonel Tosh's house in search of the diamonds, the colonel was in hospital and his son, who knew nothing about the diamonds, was in bed asleep. Cabmoll knocked him out and thoroughly searched the house, eventually finding the box in the bedroom. He put his hand into the box and was bitten by the snake.

Having served in India, Cabmoll knew that the only remedy for such a snake bite was to immediately amputate the limb into which the poison had been injected. So he ran to the next-door house, which happened to belong to Sir Hugh Drummond, seized the axe and cut off his hand. He was too late and died a few minutes later.

Unit summary

Themes	Unusual weather conditions; environmental issues
Structures	Ways of predicting; revision of conditionals; mixed conditionals
Vocabulary	Environment, climate and geography; multi-word verbs with particle *down*; positive and negative bias; weather idioms (in WB)
Skills	*Reading*: predicting; interpreting attitude; following cause and effect links *Listening*: understanding cause and effect links; listening for detail *Speaking*: speculating *Writing*: hypothesising; expressing cause and effect
Pronunciation	Sentence stress

 Teaching notes

Introduction

1   This unit deals with weather issues and the environment. The introductory exercises are a way of getting students to focus on the topic.

- Ask students to look at the title and the photos and to predict what the unit will be about. Ask if students understand the pun in the title (*whether/weather or not*).
- Discuss the instructions with students and whether they experienced any strange weather conditions in the period mentioned. Do not go into details as this is dealt with in Exercise 2.
- Students read the eight headlines. If necessary, draw to their attention the clues in the headlines as to the places, such as: 1 *Home Counties* refers to the area around London; 3 the type of tourist trade threatened is clear because of the use of *mild*; 4 the country referred to must be very large if it can contain a lake bigger than Britain, etc.
- Students match the headlines and places.

Answers
1 a   2 d   3 b   4 f   5 c   6 g   7 h   8 e

Note: There may be problems with numbers 5 and 6. Make sure students are aware that this is purely a 'fun' exercise and it does not matter if they get some wrong.

- Students can check their answers and read more about the weather conditions on page 161. This can be done in pairs/groups. One students turns to the back and the others ask questions about the weather conditions, e.g. *Where was the inland sea? How big did it become?* The student looking at the back either answers from the information or says *I don't know.*

2 ● Focus attention on the photographs of weather conditions. Discuss what each one shows.

Answers
top left: hurricane/storm   top right: tidal wave
bottom left: forest fire   bottom right: avalanche

- Run through the names of certain types of weather conditions for the students. This will be useful for the unit. Useful vocabulary is:
  storm, hurricane very severe storm
  typhoon small, violent tropical storm
  flood when a large amount of water covers land that is normally dry
  tidal wave exceptionally large incoming wave, often very destructive, also known as *tsunami*
  drought lack of water
  gale strong wind, not necessarily associated with a storm
- Students work in small groups to discuss the questions. Open this up to a brief class discussion before going on.

Reading skills

3   Predicting and interpreting attitude

A   **Background information:** This newspaper article concerns the October 1987 storm in the southern part of the UK. This was a very sudden storm of huge force (often referred to as a hurricane) which raged for several hours one night in October and caused irreparable damage. Vast areas of land were ruined, especially in terms of trees – large numbers of very old, irreplaceable trees were destroyed – and a lot of damage was done to property. Fortunately, very few people died as it took place during the night and had died down significantly by the morning.

- Go through the prediction questions one by one with the students, discussing (but not checking) answers as you go along.
- Students read the whole text and check their answers.

Answers
1   Advertisements somehow connected with global warming.
2   Because they were inaccurate and sensational.
3   (1) The government (it's sensational); (2) the government; (3) scientists; (4) an advertising agency.
4   That environmental problems were the cause of the 1987 storm.

B ● Before students read the text carefully, you may wish to go through some of the more difficult vocabulary and any concepts that demand knowledge of Britain.
  global warming the gradual increase of the Earth's temperature due to the greenhouse effect
  greenhouse effect the effect caused by certain gases which build up in the atmosphere and trap the heat and rays of the sun, acting like a greenhouse
  undermine weaken someone's position
  watchdogs literally dogs who guard a building, often used of agencies who keep controls on certain industries, e.g. advertising
  the Meteorological Office the authority responsible for weather forecasting
  greenhouse gases gases which contribute to the greenhouse effect
  energy conservation saving energy, e.g. using less electricity, using cars less
  overstate exaggerate
  flimsy not very strong
  copywriters people who compose the wording of adverts/publicity materials

- Students read the text. Once they are aware of the meanings of the environmental concepts, they should not have any problems.

Answers
1 FALSE. *Scientists said the campaign, ... amounted to unscientific scare tactics* (paragraph 2); whole of paragraph 4; whole of paragraph 5.
2 TRUE. *... the campaign, which links the greenhouse effect to extreme weather conditions ...* (paragraph 2); slogan in paragraph 3.
3 FALSE. *'We would regard them* [the storms] *as natural events and there is no evidence whatsoever to say that they aren't.'* (paragraph 5); *'There is no way you could say that a particular storm was caused by the greenhouse effect'* (paragraph 7); *the claims were based on 'flimsy' evidence* (paragraph 8).
4 FALSE. *... he was disappointed that advertisements with a positive message ... had overstated the case* (paragraph 7).
5 TRUE. *Chris Denny, the account manager, said scientists did not know what changes in climate to expect. 'Inevitably advertising picks on dramatic images ...'* (paragraph 8).

C ● Discuss the questions with the students. They should give an impression-based answer first, then look through the article to find evidence of his attitude.

Answer
We can infer this from certain words and phrases he uses, such as *sensational, scare tactics, 'flimsy' evidence*.

Note: Do not go into a lot of detail here as the next exercise looks at the specific vocabulary used to show bias.

Vocabulary

4 Positive and negative bias

In articles such as the one the students have just read, the bias of the writer is put across more by the words chosen than by what he actually says. This exercise looks at some of the words with a view to examining bias.

A ● Students write three headings in their books: *campaign, adverts* and *photos*. They then write down under each heading the words and phrases which describe it. Tell them that they will be looking mainly for adjectives.

Answers
the campaign
unscientific
scare tactics
flimsy evidence

adverts
inaccurate
sensational
misleading
positive message
overstated the case

photos
vivid
memorable
dramatic

● Students match words from their lists to the definitions.

Answers
1 *misleading*
2 *overstated the case*
3 *inaccurate*
4 *unscientific*
5 *scare tactics*
6 *memorable*

B ● Discuss the questions with the students.

Answers
positive: *positive message, vivid, memorable, dramatic*
negative: *all the others*
The balance is much more towards the negative, which gives us the idea that the writer's attitude is rather negative.

● Point out that the words which are positive mostly describe the photos and their impact, not the campaign itself.

Extension
Note: Students will do more work on negative bias in Unit 19, Exercise 6.

● If you wish to do some more work here on negative bias, you can give students the following pairs of words, and ask them to explain which one of the pair is the more negative, and why, using a dictionary if necessary.
propaganda – advertising
helpful – obsequious
widespread – ubiquitous
gushing – emotional
childlike – childish
affected – sophisticated
thrifty – mean
ingenuous – gullible

Language work

5 Predicting the future

This exercise looks at different ways of making predictions.

A ● Students complete the sentences from the text.

Answers
1 Any rise in temperatures could make the weather calmer.
2 If left unchecked, global warming is likely to change existing weather patterns.
3 The second advertisement warns that greenhouse gases would throw the world's climate out of balance.

● Go through the general questions with the students.

Answers
Could is used most in the text.
This is probably to express that the predictions are not at all certain; it is also used when a writer wants to be tentative.
Would is used to express quite a strong possibility. It is probably used here as a 'contracted conditional', meaning that greenhouse gases would throw the world's climate out of balance if we continued using them. It is a veiled threat to the reader.

Note: Conditionals are dealt with in detail later in this unit.

B ● Ask students to list other ways of predicting the future. They should be able to list all the following:
will (probably, certainly, definitely, etc.)
may/might/could (to show different degrees of doubt)
is likely /unlikely to
is possible/probable that ...
I expect/doubt that ...
● Divide the class into small groups. This can be done by making sure there are four groups (or eight in a large class) and that each one chooses one of the topics. (Make sure that each topic is covered.) Three groups will have serious topics, and one will have the light-hearted, final topic. They then discuss the topics, using a variety of predicting phrases.
● Open the discussion to the class. Each group presents its ideas and the class discusses them.

Listening skills

6   Understanding cause and effect

Cause and effect is one of the more difficult logical linking sequences in English, and there is therefore a lot of emphasis on it in this unit, starting passively with this listening exercise.

A   • Focus students' attention on the pictures and make sure they know the names of the geographical features depicted (A = archipelago, B = ice cap, C = dairy farmland).
   • Discuss with students what they might hear on the tape about these subjects.
   • Play the dialogue once for students to check their ideas.

Answers
ice caps: likely to melt
archipelagos (Maldives here): likely to be submerged
farmland (in southern England here): likely to be turned into crop (arable) not dairy farmland

Tapescript
INTERVIEWER Anne, thank you for joining me in the studio this afternoon. Today's phone-in, as you know, has concentrated on the government's advertisements about global warming. In response to the adverts, a spokesman from your office stated that there was no real link between the recent storms and global warming. Is that right?
ANNE LAWSON I believe he said that there was no evidence to suppose that they weren't natural events. I personally think that it is too early to start linking one-off storms, hurricanes and droughts with the greenhouse effect, but that does not mean to say that we should be taking its possible consequences lightly.
INTERVIEWER So you think that there are likely to be noticeable changes in the weather because of the greenhouse effect and global warming?
ANNE LAWSON Yes, almost certainly so. All the predictions so far are really based on informed speculation. As the article stated, we predict that there will be a rise of 1°C in Britain's temperatures by the year 2025, which could result in weaker storms and calmer weather ...
INTERVIEWER And if your predictions are conservative ...
ANNE LAWSON If, and it's a big if, they are conservative, then there'll certainly be more developments. There is, of course, evidence that the ice caps are melting, and there are some forecasts that estimate a rise in sea level of between 24 and 38 centimetres by the year 2030.
INTERVIEWER Which would have certain effects ...
ANNE LAWSON Naturally. It's conceivable that some low-lying geographical areas could be submerged. Take, for example, the Maldive Islands in the Indian Ocean. This is an archipelago of 1190 islands, the highest point of which is only three metres above sea level. Should there be a considerable rise in sea level, many of these islands would be in grave danger. It goes without saying, of course, that areas currently susceptible to flooding are likely to be the first to suffer in the event of a rise in sea level – Bangladesh, for example, is extremely vulnerable – intense storms and high winds bring serious flooding almost every year. Do you remember the tidal wave in the Ganges Delta in 1988 which destroyed or damaged the homes of about 25 million people? Unfortunately, a vicious circle comes into operation here. People whose land has been destroyed by flooding often move inland, forests are cleared for agricultural purposes and the resulting deforestation is thought to contribute to global warming as more carbon dioxide is allowed to escape into the atmosphere.
INTERVIEWER What about the changing climate generally, perhaps closer to home?

ANNE LAWSON Well, it will take a lot to make significant changes in the worldwide climate, but if the Arctic ice cap were to melt completely by 2090 – a scenario thought feasible by some – the entire weather pattern of the northern hemisphere would change, with the equatorial climate moving north to cover the north of South America and the West Indies, with the grasslands moving north to cover the whole of North Africa and the Arabian Gulf, and with the desert belt moving into Europe – covering Spain, the South of France, Italy, Greece and Turkey.
INTERVIEWER And what effect would this have on Britain?
ANNE LAWSON Britain might well start to enjoy a Mediterranean climate, with winter temperatures of about six or seven degrees Centigrade, and a summer average as high as 25°C, with temperatures regularly going above 35°C.
INTERVIEWER I imagine the population would welcome that possibility with open arms!
ANNE LAWSON Maybe, but I doubt that the farmers would! It would mean a complete change in the produce that could be farmed, with the south being able to produce a few hardy crops only, such as maize, and the tradition of dairy farming would have to move to the north of the country and to Scotland. In addition, we would have to contend with an increase in the numbers and types of insects, pests and diseases ... (*fade*)

B   • Explain that students have to complete the chart with the effects or causes of some of the things mentioned on the tape.
   • Play the dialogue again; students complete the chart.

Answers

cause	possible effect
1 increase in greenhouse gases →	change in weather patterns
2 rise in temperature →	calmer weather
3 ice caps melt →	rise in sea level
4 rise in sea level →	[1] flooding of vulnerable areas [2] submerge low-lying geographical areas
5 ice caps melt completely by 2090 →	total shift in weather patterns in the Northern hemisphere
6 change in climate in Britain or change in climate of Northern hemisphere →	change in type of farming or change in climate in Britain

C   • Focus students' attention on the second chart.
   • Play the dialogue again if necessary.
   • Students look back at the text to add more words to the chart.

Answers

environment	weather	geographical features
global warming	storm	ice caps
greenhouse effect	hurricane	archipelago
deforestation	drought	island
environmental pollution (text)	flood	delta
greenhouse gases (text)	high winds	grasslands
	tidal wave	desert
	lightning (text)	
	thunder (text)	

- If students do not yet know all the words in the chart they can do the pairwork exercise. If they are familiar with them all by now there is no need to do the exercise.

Further practice: Workbook Unit 13, Exercises 3 and 4.

Speaking skills

7 Speculating

A - Ask students if they can remember what language was used in the dialogue to speculate, and which phrases from Exercise 5 they heard. If possible, do this without playing the tape again.

Answers
All of the following were used: *likely to, will, could, there'll certainly be, it's conceivable that, would, might well, I doubt if …*

- Students look at some of the phrases which have been extracted and decide which are more or less possible.

Answers
more probable: 1, 3, 4, 5
less probable: 2

B - Divide the class into groups and explain the two parts of the exercise. Allow about ten minutes for the groups to speculate. Monitor to check that there is a variety of prediction being used.
- Discuss the predictions as a class.

Vocabulary

8 Multi-word verbs

- Focus attention on the verb *cutting down* in the extract. Students supply the meaning of the particle (*collapse/destruction*), using their chart if necessary. (They had this meaning of the particle *down* in Workbook Unit 6, Exercise 7.)
- Students complete the sentences. They should make a note of any particles which they think mean something different.

Answers
1 pouring (here the particle has the literal meaning of *down*)
2 pulled
3 burnt
4 brought
5 puts
6 broken

7 closed
8 wind (here the verb means *relax*)
The verbs in sentences 2, 3, 4, 5, 6 and 7 all have the meaning of *collapse/destruction* (sometimes metaphorical).

- Students enter any new meanings/examples in their charts.

Reading skills

9 Following cause and effect links

A This is the second exercise on cause and effect. It asks the students to recognise cause and effect in text and to create links if they can.

- Students read through the quotes quickly and try to group them together. This may vary from individual to individual: there are no correct answers, as long as students can justify their groups, e.g. 6, 8 and 10 all concern the Arctic ice cap; 2, 5, 6, 9 and 11 all concern changes in the weather patterns.
- Check that students do not have too many problems with the vocabulary in these extracts.

B - Students read through the quotes again and complete the chart. Ensure that they realise they can write more than one effect if necessary.

Answers

cause	effect
global warming	hotter and drier summers, melting of Arctic ice cap
emission of greenhouse gases	rise in sea level, disappearance of many Arctic species
melting of ice caps	change in weather pattern of the Northern hemisphere, disappearance of ice around the North Pole within a century
rise in sea level	islands in grave danger
climate change in Britain	change in agriculture possible in the country, appearance of insects such as the mosquito

- Divide the class into groups to discuss the causes and effects. They should write a few first conditional sentences, for example:
If the ice caps melt, there will be a rise in sea level/the ice around the North Pole may melt completely.
- Students discuss any links that can see from the right to the left columns, and make sentences, e.g. if there is a change in weather pattern in the Northern hemisphere, there will be a climate change in Britain.

Language work

10 Revision of conditionals

Note: We have assumed that students will be quite familiar with the basic conditional forms, therefore these exercises concentrate on presenting mixed conditionals.

A - Students find and write down examples of the conditionals.

Answers
FIRST CONDITIONAL: quote 1 *… if the emission of greenhouse gases continues at the present rate, the increase in temperature will be enough …*; quote 4 *If drastic measures*

are not taken ..., it is likely that ... (here the phrase *it is likely that ...* fulfils the function of a future form)
SECOND CONDITIONAL: quote 6 *if the Arctic ice cap were to melt..., the entire weather pattern of the Northern hemisphere would change*; quote 7 *If much of Britain were to experience ..., there would be ...*
THIRD CONDITIONAL: quote 5 *... the total would undoubtedly have been heavier if the the gale had happened during the daytime.*
CONDITIONAL USING A MODAL IN THE MAIN CLAUSE: quote 2 *If the loss of even the scant annual rainfall of Cape Verde were to become ... could save a way of life.*
CONDITIONAL WITH INVERSION INSTEAD OF THE *IF*-CLAUSE: quote 3 *Should there be a considerable rise in sea level, many of these islands would be in grave danger.*

* Revise quickly the grammatical structures of the three main conditionals. Refer students to the Grammar Reference section at the back of the Students' Book if necessary. Point out the use of the comma when the *if*-clause comes first.

B ● Students complete the sentences as they wish, using the correct conditionals. Accept any accurate, sensible answers.

Suggested answers
1 ... the world's rivers and seas will become even more polluted. (First)
2 ... would have been killed/injured. (Third)
3 ... we would be able to take all our rubbish there. (Second)
4 ... the sun's rays were not so harmful. (Second)
5 ... the world's fish supply will eventually run out. (First)
6 ... I wouldn't have believed it. (Third)

11 Mixed conditionals

A This exercise presents some of the more common types of mixed conditionals, i.e. conditionals which take different combinations of tenses from the three main ones. It is worth bearing in mind that many of these are not true mixed conditionals, but have a change of tense in the main clause to suggest degree of tentativeness/certainty. The Grammar Reference section outlines the main mixed conditional types.

* Ask students what they think mixed conditionals may be.
* Read the introduction, which explains mixed conditionals, with them.
* Ask students to supply the tenses and conditional parts in the example. (*if*-clause: past perfect; third conditional; main clause: *would* + infinitive; second conditional)
* Explain that this is possibly the most common type of mixed conditional, and that it expresses a past cause with a present effect. Another common example is: *If he hadn't robbed the bank, he wouldn't be in prison now.* Contrast this with: *If he hadn't robbed the bank, he wouldn't have been sent to prison.*
* Students read back through the quotes to complete the chart.

Note: The students are likely to find the discussion part of this exercise very difficult; make sure they understand that it is an awareness-raising exercise and that they will not be expected to produce more than the two or three most common mixed conditionals.

Answers

	if-clause: verb	main clause: verb
e.g.	Past perfect (3rd conditional): 'had not discovered'	would (2nd conditional): 'would not be able'

8	present simple (first conditional): 'assumes'	could + perfect infinitive (third conditional): 'could have melted'
9	present perfect (first conditional): 'has been'	would + infinitive (second conditional): 'would expect'
10	past simple (second conditional): 'were to be'	would + perfect infinitive (third conditional): 'would have disappeared'
11	present simple (first conditional): 'increase'	could + infinitive (second conditional): 'could establish'

* Students study the chart and try to work out why the conditionals have been mixed, and how uncertainty is shown.

Answers
8 The *if*-clause takes a present hypothesis but with a result projected by a certain time (i.e. use of the future perfect).
9 The *if*-clause takes a hypothetical cause that includes both present and past (present perfect) and expresses uncertainty about the hypothesis by using the second conditional form in the main clause, i.e. expressing improbability.
10 The *if*-clause suggests improbability of the hypothesis (*were to be*), the main clause projects a result by a certain time (see quote 8).
11 The *if*-clause is a straight first conditional hypothesis, the verb in the main clause (*could*, second conditional) expresses the writer's uncertainty about the result of the hypothesis.

B Students apply their charts to some 'rules'.

* Students read through the true/false 'rules'. Make sure they understand what to do and that they should be looking at all the quotes, not only 8–11.
* They look back at their charts to work out whether, according to the examples they have been examining, the rules are correct.

Answers
1 TRUE. (See quotes 2, 8, 11.)
2 FALSE. (It is actually possible, but very rare, as in *If we could have spent more time with him, he might have settled in better.* It is more common in American English.)
3 TRUE. (See quote 3; also possible in the first conditional, as in *Should he arrive on time for once, we'll get the early train.* In the third conditional the verb is simply inverted: *Had they not put the car in the garage for an inspection, they could have been killed.* Inversion is quite formal.)
4 TRUE. (See quote 8.)
5 FALSE.

12 Further practice of conditionals

A This is an analysis exercise to help students recognise the differences between certain types of conditional.

* Divide the class into groups or pairs. Students discuss the pairs of sentences together.

Answers
1 In a, it is possible that he will arrive on time; in b it is improbable. (In b we accept either that he has a reputation for being late, or that circumstances are likely to prevent his arriving on time.)
2 Sentence a refers to the present (I don't have enough money); sentence b refers to the past (I didn't have enough money).
3 Sentence a focusses on the present result of a past action;

sentence b focusses on the past result. (In a we know the person is still living in the city; in b the main clause could be referring to a time in the past.)

4 Sentence a refers to a present sentiment (I like her) and a past result of that sentiment; sentence b refers to a past sentiment (I liked her) which may no longer be true.

5 In a it is still possible that the city may become the crime capital of the world (the main clause is a future perfect construction), because of the present tense in the *if*-clause; in b the increase has stopped, so the result of the *if*-clause is no longer possible – it is purely hypothetical.

● If the students have had any difficulty with these items, refer them to the Grammar Reference section.

B ● Make sure students realise that items 3 and 4 should contain mixed conditionals. With reference to item 3, tell them that the death penalty was abolished in the UK in 1965.
● Students complete the sentences in their pairs/groups.

Answers

1 People would be much happier if they didn't worry about money.

2 If the steam train hadn't been invented, there wouldn't have been an industrial revolution.

3 If the death penalty hadn't been abolished in the United Kingdom in 1965, it would/might be a safer place today.

4 If consumers continue to demand good quality wooden furniture, the rainforests could disappear/could have disappeared by the early years of the next century.

● Students discuss the opinions expressed in the sentences. Monitor to check correct use of conditionals.

C ● Students look at the prompts and write sentences individually about themselves, which they then discuss in their groups.
● Check the sentences around the class, encouraging students to expand if possible on what they have written. Remind them that they do not have to keep repeating the *if*-clause when they are talking about more than one result.
● Answers will be according to the individual, but the following conditional forms are likely.

1 third conditional, or *if* + past perfect, *would* + infinitive, e.g. *If I had passed all my exams, I would have gone to university/I would be in a better job.*

2 first conditional, possibly with modal in the main clause to show uncertainty, e.g. *If I continue to study English, I'll/I might be able to take a teaching course in my own country.*

3 first or second conditionals, possibly mixed as above, e.g. *If I married my boyfriend next year, as he wants, I wouldn't be able to live near my parents./If I marry my boyfriend next year, I won't/might not be able to live near my parents.*

4 *if* + past perfect, *would* + infinitive, e.g. *If my family had moved to America when I was a child, I wouldn't be learning English now.*

D ● Read through the example consequence chain with the students and make sure that they know exactly what to do.
● Discuss which conditionals they think will be more likely (first and second).
● Divide the class into pairs. Each pairs chooses one or two of the topics and discusses the consequence chain, writing it up if you wish. They should use the outlines given but add in information if possible.
● After a set time, the pairs join up with other pairs to form groups. They discuss the consequence chains they have made.

Extensions

● Students could write up one or two other consequence chains for homework if you wish.
● Students could create third conditional consequence chains. In pairs or groups, they think of a series of connected events in the past, and then link them all together with a third conditional chain, e.g.:
John got up late on Thursday and had to rush to get to work for an important meeting. He ran out of the house and forgot to lock the door. His car wouldn't start so he ran to the bus stop and got a bus. He'd forgotten his wallet and the bus conductor called the police. He was taken to the police station, where the police phoned his office to check his identity. When he got to the office he'd missed the meeting. His director fired him because he was unreliable and had been mixed up with the police. When he got home he found that his house had been burgled, his spare car keys had been taken and his car had been stolen.
Students make as many third conditional sentences as possible, e.g.:
If John hadn't got up late he wouldn't have forgotten to lock the door. If his car had started, it wouldn't have been stolen.

Further practice: Workbook Unit 13, Exercises 6 and 7.

Pronunciation

13 Sentence stress

● Discuss with students which words usually carry sentence stress. (content words, such as nouns, verbs and adjectives, particularly those which carry the main meaning of the sentence)
● Students read through the examples and decide where the main stress is likely to be in each sentence.
● Play the extracts on tape for students to check.

Tapescript and answers

1 And if your pre'dictions are con'servative? If they 'are con'servative, then there'll 'certainly be more de'velopments.

2 'Should there be a con'siderable 'rise in 'sea level, 'many of these 'islands would 'clearly be in 'grave 'danger.

3 ... if the 'Arctic ice 'cap were to 'melt com'pletely by 2090, the en'tire 'weather pattern of the 'northern 'hemisphere would 'change.

● Ask students if they can find any exceptions to the description of sentence stress above.

Answers

In extract 1, the stress on *are* in the response: stressing the improbability of the predictions being conservative.
In extract 2, the stress on *should*: stressing the improbability again.

● Refer students to the work they did on stress in contradictions in Unit 1.
● Students read the conversation in pairs, preferably aloud so that they can try to 'feel' for the stressed syllables.
● Play the dialogue for them to check.

Tapescript and answers
(Underlining refers to the Extension below.)

A Do you be'lieve that 'sunbathing is really 'bad for you?

B Yes, I 'do. I've 'always been very 'careful about 'sunbathing, but now I 'won't go into the 'sun without a 'strong 'sun cream on.

A 'Don't you think you're being a 'bit, well, ex'cessive?

B   'No! 'You've read <u>a</u>bout the 'hole in the 'ozone lay<u>er</u>,
    'hav<u>en</u>'t you?
A   Well <u>of</u> 'course, but ...
B   So you 'have to ac'cept th<u>at</u> 'more <u>of</u> the 'sun's 'rays <u>are</u>
    getting 'through?
A   'Yes. B<u>ut</u> I sup'pose I've nev<u>er</u> tak<u>en</u> it 'really 'seri<u>ou</u>sly.
    I've been 'sunbathing through th<u>e</u> 'summer f<u>or</u> 'years
    now, <u>and</u> nothing's happ<u>en</u>ed t<u>o</u> me.
B   Nothing's happ<u>en</u>ed 'yet, y<u>ou</u> mean!

●   Students read the dialogue in pairs, paying attention to the
    stress. Monitor and correct stress where necessary.

Extension

●   To help students think about stress, it is often useful to get
    them to think about the weak forms in the sentences, i.e.
    the syllables which reduce to /ə/. (You could also look at
    the syllables which reduce to /ɪ/ – also a weak form.) They
    should read through the dialogue and try to pick out the
    unstressed syllables, e.g. the prepositions, weak syllables
    in words of more than one syllable. Play the tape again for
    them to check. Weak syllables are underlined on the
    tapescript above.

14   This exercise is a discussion based on the environmental issues
that individuals may be able to contribute to in various ways.

●   If your students are interested in the topics so far presented
    in the unit, they can discuss the moral and ethical issues
    here. If not, go straight on to the list of ways in which
    individuals may be able to protect the environment.
●   Students read through the list of things that can be done.
    Make sure that they understand them all.
●   Divide the class into small groups. The groups discuss
    whether they do any of the things in the list and why/why
    not. They discuss any other measures to help the
    environment that they can think of.
●   Open the discussion out to the class.

Writing skills

15   Hypothesising, expressing cause and effect

In this exercise the students work actively with the cause and
effect links.

A   ●   Read through the introduction with the students as far as
        the conditional sentence.
    ●   Students read through the table. Make sure they
        understand the cause and effect links.
    ●   They write two sentences for each relationship shown in
        the table, as instructed, one in the past, and one
        hypothetical. Students will have to decide for themselves
        whether they wish to write about the past or present for the
        conditionals, and how certain the effects are.

Suggested answers
(Many other combinations are possible.)
1   Because of the drop in winter temperatures, sales of double
    glazing have increased.
    If winter temperatures continue to drop, sales of double
    glazing will probably increase.
2   There is now less snow in the winter in some ski resorts. As
    a result, some of them have had to close.
    If more snow had fallen in the ski resorts, they wouldn't
    have had to close.
3   As more money is being spent on defence, so less is being
    spent on research.
    If more money were spent on defence, less would be
    spent on research.
4   Owing to a growing awareness of nutrition today, there are

fewer health problems in the population.
If people weren't becoming more aware of nutrition, there
wouldn't be fewer health problems.
5   Fewer jobs are available to people these days, therefore we
    have more leisure time.
    If fewer jobs become available, we will all have more
    leisure time.

B   ●   Students follow the framework given in order to write an
        essay of about 250 words.

Further practice: Workbook Unit 13, Exercise 9.

Final task

16   If only ...

A   **Background information:** The picture from a book cover shown
    is from *The Alteration*, by Kingsley Amis. Amis is an English
    writer, born in 1922, whose most famous book is *Lucky Jim*
    (1954), a satire on academic life. Amis writes amusing and
    highly satirical prose, and is a very popular contemporary
    writer in the UK. Information on *The Alteration* is given below.

    ●   Read the introduction with the students and encourage
        them to speculate about the event which didn't take place.
        They should use conditionals if possible.

Answer
The event which did not happen is the Reformation, i.e. the
movement in northern Europe in the sixteenth century away
from the Catholic Church, and in particular the creation of the
Church of England in 1534 by Henry VIII. *The Alteration* is
set in a strongly Catholic UK and it examines the day-to-day
life of the people.

B   This exercise now looks at events and inventions which did or did
    not happen and encourages students to speculate on the
    effects of these.

    ●   Make sure students understand what to do.
    ●   Play the dialogues on tape, stopping after each one and
        asking the students what the situation is. The students note
        down the situation for each one.

Answers
2   Electricity hasn't been invented.
3   Capital punishment hasn't been abolished. Britain is a
    republic (British presidential campaign), no longer a
    monarchy.
4   The sun's rays are considered very dangerous (hole in the
    ozone layer).
5   The steam engine is still in use; the diesel engine has not
    been invented.
6   Men can carry babies.

Tapescript
1   Oh no! I can't answer the phone now. I can't let him see me
    like this!
2   BOY   Mum, it's getting difficult to read. Can you pass me a
    candle?
    MUM   I can't right now. I've got my hands in a tub of
    water; I'm washing your school clothes.
3   RADIO NEWS   ... and those are the latest results. Back to
    today's headlines. The trial of Brian Dogherty was brought
    to a conclusion this afternoon with a verdict of guilty
    being returned. A sentence of capital punishment is
    expected tomorrow. Finally, the run-up to the British
    presidential campaign got under way today with a
    flamboyant parade ...
4   GIRL   Dad, I'm just going out now, OK?
    DAD   Yes, love, but wrap up warm – it's freezing out

there. And don't forget your skin guards and dark glasses.

5 A I'm getting more and more fed up with this journey to work.
   B Yes, it seems to get slower every day; the fares go up and the train's more crowded.
   A Mm. It's summer that gets me down – you either suffocate because of the lack of air or open the window and choke on the smoke.

6 WOMAN Hello, darling, I'm home. Is dinner ready?
   MAN Almost, but I've got something to tell you, wonderful news ...
   WOMAN You don't mean ... Oh, that's fantastic! When's it due?

- Students work in groups to discuss the effects of the situations in the dialogues.

C
- Divide the class into two teams.
- The students in each team work together to produce a few short dialogues like the ones on tape. The students could work in pairs in each team to produce one dialogue per pair.
- The teams read their dialogues to each other. This can be done as a competition, with points being awarded if the situation is guessed by the other team.
- The class choose one or two of the dialogues and speculate further.

 **Unit 14   The Secret of Life**

 Unit summary

Themes	Concepts of beauty; plastic surgery; genetics; physiognomy
Structures	Forms of comparison; comparison and contrast markers
Vocabulary	Parts of the body; categorising; vocabulary of medicine (in Workbook)
Skills	*Reading:* Matching headings; understanding methods of defining and explaining
	Listening: Listening for enjoyment
	Speaking: Describing people
	Writing: Writing an expository essay
Study skills	Dictionary work

 Teaching notes

Introduction

1 ● Use the photographs and questions to introduce the topic of different ideas of physical beauty.

Note: *Beauty is in the eye of the beholder* is a well-known proverb meaning that beauty cannot be measured objectively; whether an object is beautiful or not depends on the judgement of the person who is looking at it, not on the object itself.

● Introduce the questionnaire and divide the class into small groups.
● Students should complete the first line with their own opinion and then elicit the opinions of other group members, filling in the lines of the questionnaire to work out the most popular features in their group.
● Groups should compare their results and then report back to class to find the overall preferences for the class as a whole.

2 **Note:** You may wish to avoid the follow-up discussion questions at the end of this exercise if you have a sensitive or shy class.

● Read through the introduction and ask students to complete the prediction ranking task.
● Pre-teach:
chubby fat
acne medical condition which causes spots and sometimes scars on the skin, very common amongst teenagers
Caucasian people of European type appearance/racial background
● Students read the article and check if their prediction of the rank order is correct.

Answer
(Rank order according to the article.)
1 nose: *rhinoplasty* (*nose-jobs*)
2 ears: *ear-pinning*
3 chin: *chin augmentation*
4 facial skin: *dermabrasion* (removing acne scars from the skin)
5 eyes: *blepharoplasty* (for Asian teenagers – an eyelid operation)

● Students discuss the follow-up questions.

Extension
● The text raises a number of issues which your class may find interesting to discuss. Some suggestions:
Will artificial muscles for men become popular?
Is cosmetic surgery morally right?
Should adolescents be allowed to have it?
What do they think of eye operations for Asians wishing to look more Caucasian?
What are the psychological implications of cosmetic surgery?

Vocabulary

3 Parts of the body

● Students should try to complete the task without using a dictionary and then check each other's work in pairs.

Answers

1	crown	11	ribs
2	forehead	12	forearm
3	eyelid	13	wrist
4	earlobe	14	knuckle
5	cheekbone	15	palm
6	nostril	16	navel
7	jawbone	17	hip
8	Adam's apple	18	thigh
9	shoulder blade	19	calf
10	collar bone	20	toe

Note: *Ankle, elbow, armpit* and *biceps* are not needed. You may wish, however, to ask students to identify these parts of the human body.

4 Categorisation

A Students should be familiar with the technique of categorisation of vocabulary. (It was introduced in Unit 1.) It is a technique which they should be encouraged to use themselves as an aid to memory and understanding.

Answers

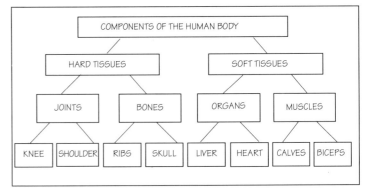

B ● Pairs should add as many words as they can to the word maps and then compare in small groups.

Extension
● Ask students it they can think of any alternative criteria for grouping this vocabulary. They should be able to suggest concepts such as function and location. To consolidate the vocabulary they could re-draw the maps using their own criteria.

Language work

5 Forms of comparison

A ● Elicit some of the following ways of comparing and write them on the board:
   age, colouring, sex, physique, social position, degree of fame, wealth, power.

Background information: The people in the photos are: (on the left from top to bottom) Diana Ross, King Juan Carlos of Spain, Arnold Schwarzenegger; (on the right from top to bottom) Elizabeth Taylor, Andie McDowell, Danny de Vito

   ● Ask each student to write two or three sentences comparing the people using some of the features on the board.

B ● Read through the instructions.
   ● Divide the class into groups of three and nominate A, B and C in each group.
   ● Allow a few minutes for students to exhange information and work out the matches.

Answers
A Diana Ross
B King Juan Carlos
C Andie McDowell
D Elizabeth Taylor
E Danny de Vito
F Arnold Schwarzenegger

C ● Students transfer examples from their information to the chart and add their own sentences from section A.

Answers
MAKING COMPARISONS
Metaphor
A sings like a bird.
C often dresses like a top model.
Simile
A is as thin as a rake.
F is as strong as an ox.
Comparative adjective
A is darker than the others.
Of E and F, E is the funnier.
C is better looking than E.
Comparative adverb
D has been married more often than the others.
E probably earns less than the others.
Superlative adjective
E is the least famous in this group.
B is treated with the most respect.
C is the youngest in this group.
D has the worst weight problem.
D is the oldest.
Superlative adverb
B ranks the highest.
F probably exercises the most frequently.
F is the most heavily built.
Expressing similarity
B is as tall as F.

D ● Explain the task and give an example if necessary.
   STUDENT A   X is the youngest.
   STUDENT B   Is X the attractive young woman in a white blouse?
   STUDENT A   Yes.

Further practice: Workbook Unit 14, Exercises 6, 7, 8 and 9.

Speaking skills

6 Describing people

A ● Go through the introduction and read the dialogue with a student.
   ● Students work in pairs to brainstorm 'describing' words and categories.
   ● Elicit examples and write on the board, students should explain the meaning of any words they give you which are unfamiliar to the rest of the class:

Suggested categories and examples
Height: *tall short medium average*
Age: *young old middle-aged teenager child infant in his/her early/late twenties/thirties/forties etc.*
Colouring: *dark fair Mediterranean-looking pale*
Physique: *slim overweight muscular shapely well-built lanky*
Characteristics: *big nose/ears wears ...*
Hair: *blond dark red mousey wavy straight long short curly*

B ● Students stay in their pairs to complete the task. They should aim to make a dialogue similar to that in section A.

C Game

This game works best with a large class of at least 12 – 15 students. If you have a smaller group you can change the category of described person from 'a member of the class' to 'someone famous in your country' (for monolingual groups) or 'an international film star, politician or musician' (for multilingual groups).

   ● Before introducing the game explain the use of the pronoun *they* in informal English to represent *he or she* when speaking generally or wishing to avoid referring to someone's sex.
   ● On a piece of paper, each student writes a short description of a member of the class without mentioning name, nationality, age, sex, and (if you want to make the game more challenging) what they are wearing at the moment.
   ● The papers are passed around the class. When they receive a paper each student should write the name of the person they think is described on the back.
   ● Students keep passing the papers and writing names until each paper arrives back at its original owner.
   ● Students report back to class, telling you who they had actually described, and the names that have been written on the back.

7 Listening

A ● In pairs, students discuss the factors a – e.
   ● Elicit and discuss their ideas, noting any interesting ones on the board.

Suggested answers
a Poor nutrition gives people bad skin, people tend to be short.
b Illnesses are more common if health care is not easily available, resulting in deformities, bad teeth.
c People have darker or fairer skin.
d Wealthy people can have a better diet resulting in healthier bodies.
e Open question.

   ● Explain the listening task and play the tape.

Answers
1 They illustrate the fact that people in the middle ages were much shorter than today.

2 It resulted in restricted growth of bones.
3 They have begun to increase in height as a result of eating more meat.
4 It showed that you had a high social standing because only the upper classes were able to avoid working outdoors in the sun.
5 That in England in the sixteenth century dental hygiene was non-existent.

Tapescript

RADIO ANNOUNCER ..and this will be followed by the weather report at nine-thirty. Now, *Pause for Thought*. The speaker this week is Dr Elizabeth Quintin, author of *Nutrition, Health and Physiognomy*.
(short pause)

DR QUINTIN People often ask me why I believe it is possible to change human appearance through environmental rather than surgical means. I generally find that the most effective answer is a consideration, not of the way we might change, but of the way we have changed. I am referring to the historical and anthropological evidence which is available to anyone who cares to look.

As a child I remember visiting medieval castles and houses and wondering why the doors and ceilings were so low. Did our ancestors really spend their lives stooping and crouching? Of course not, the explanation was an obvious one, they were much shorter than we are today. On average a good thirty centimetres shorter! A poor diet and inadequate nutrition in childhood meant that the Europeans of the middle ages never grew to their full height. A lack of calcium resulted in restricted growth of the bones. Conversely, in modern societies where protein-rich foods are commonplace – Western Europe and North America – we have seen an enormous increase in the average height of adults. Similarly the Japanese, traditionally regarded as of shorter stature than Europeans, have in recent years begun to increase markedly in height in response to a change from a predominantly non meat-eating diet to one in which imported meats have become increasingly important.

The appearance of human skin has also altered over time. For centuries smallpox was endemic in Europe. Those that suffered but survived were usually disfigured by unsightly scars. To be 'pock-marked' was considered unfortunate but not at all unusual. Now that smallpox has been eradicated by worldwide immunisation the possession of pock-marked skin has begun to be seen as a defect requiring surgical intervention.

In earlier centuries the colour of a European's skin was seen as an indicator of social position – the paler the skin the higher the social standing. No doubt due to the fact that only the upper classes were able to avoid working outdoors in the fields. Now the position is reversed, a darker skin is seen as indicating a person's ability to travel to warmer climates or to take long holidays, whereas a pale skin might show an inability to afford such expensive leisure pursuits. Nowhere can the impact of environmental factors on appearance be more obvious than in the area of dentistry. Although genetic susceptibility can be important, the most commonly recognised influences on our teeth are diet and health care. In England in the sixteenth century dental hygiene was non-existent and as a result by the age of forty Queen Elizabeth I was said to have had a mouth full of completely black teeth. On the other hand, the poorest peasants, unable to afford sweet foods and forced to eat vegetables and tough meat, often had remarkably good teeth. In the same way, people in the poorest countries today often need far less dental treatment than those of us subjected to the typical Western diet of processed and sweetened foods,

guaranteed to rot our teeth and thus require medical intervention.

Obesity is another problem which can be traced back to environmental rather than genetic causes. Here diet and exercise combine to dictate the degree to which our bodies shed or stockpile excess fat. In the age of mechanisation...

• Students should compare the answers with their ideas from the pre-listening stage.
• Discuss the follow-up questions. The class may like to vote on the question of whether genetic or environmental factors are most influential on our appearance.

Language work

8 Comparison and contrast markers (2)

A This exercise on markers of comparison and contrast builds on the work in Unit 6 Exercise 16 (connectives of contrast) and is developed further in Unit 13 Exercises 9 and 13 (cause and effect links).

• Elicit or remind students of the linkers they have already seen in Unit 6 and list these on the board.
  however   but   on the contrary   instead of   while yet   although   quite the opposite   in place of   if
• Read through the introduction and play the tape again for students to complete the matching task.

Answers
2 *conversely* 4
4 *similarly* 8
3 *whereas* 6
1 *on the other hand* 7
7 *in the same way* 5

• Ask the students to divide the markers into two groups and write them on the board.
  SIMILARITY: similarly   in the same way
  CONTRAST: conversely   whereas   on the other hand

B • Explain the task.

Suggested answers
1 + 6, 2 + 4, 3 + 8, 5 + 7
1 + 6 Excessive sunbathing can cause skin cancer, whereas/on the other hand/conversely, exposure to the sun stimulates the production of vitamin A and can make us appear more healthy.
2 + 4 In some traditional societies women developed deformed feet and legs because of the habit of tightly binding feet in childhood. Similarly/In the same way, in modern society women often suffer from foot and leg ailments due to the habit of wearing very high heels.
3 + 8 In the middle ages people often suffered from malnutrition and were therefore very slim whereas/Conversely/On the other hand, nowadays people eat too much and often suffer from obesity.
5 + 7 In the USA some wealthy women have collagen injected into their lips to make them appear fuller. Similarly/In the same way, in some African tribes women wear circular metal plates in their lips and earlobes to make them unnaturally large.

Reading skills

9 Matching headings

A • Elicit from the students anything they know about DNA and genetics.
   • Read through the introduction and check understanding.
   • Explain the matching task. Do not explain any vocabulary

at this stage, students will have the opportunity to go over vocabulary later.

Answers

1 Healing wounds	7 Lung Cancer
2 Pancreas	8 Diabetes
3 Arthritis	9 Superbabies
4 Bone Growth	10 Revolution
5 Heart Attack prevention	11 Drugs
6 Strokes	12 Understanding Disease

B   Answers

1 Diabetes	a	Arthritis
2 Arthritis	b	Heart attack
3 Stroke	c	Diabetes
4 Heart attack	d	Stroke

● Ask the class to brainstorm the names of other diseases in English and write these on the board with brief explanations.

Further practice: Workbook Unit 14, Exercise 5.

10 Understanding methods of defining/explaining

A ● Students complete the circling task.
 ● Ask the students to find five more ways of defining/explaining in the text.
 ● When they have found the examples ask them to think of a way to categorise them (including the two examples given in the Students' Book) and elicit the following.
There are seven ways of defining/explaining in the text. (Three of these have more than one example.)

Answers

1 Defining sentence
Pancreatic cancer is likely to be treated with magic bullets in ten years. These are antibodies which recognise the cancer cells and carry radioactive drugs to them. (para. 2)

2 Relative clause.
Insulin-like factor (IGF) an ingredient which makes bones start to grow again… (para. 4)
… using a special chemical protein called an enzyme which acts like a pair of scissors and snips off the unwanted DNA particles. (para. 12)

3 Reduced relative clause.
Atrial natriuretic peptide a newly discovered hormone … (para. 6)
genetic therapy the possibility of one human being physically … altering another. (para. 11)

4 Explanation between dashes
All cancers may be helped by magic bullets – antibodies which carry drugs to cancer cells – (para. 7)

5 Explanation in brackets
Scientists can actually take human strands of DNA (the chemical that stores information and contols all growth in our bodies) (para. 10)

6 Alternative word/phrase
he can clone or copy the DNA strands … (para. 10)
New nucleotides or particles then rush in to correct and repair the damage (para. 12)

7 Definition introduced by *means*
Genetic therapy means correcting inherited defects in the womb. (para. 11)

B ● Elicit that the journalist probably used a variety of reasons to avoid repetition.
 ● Read the 'alternative' method and discuss the questions. The alternative is too formal. It is the type of definition found in dictionaries, text books or academic essays, not in newspaper articles.

● Students can now go back to the text and look at the words they haven't understood. Rather than telling them the meanings encourage them to find the words in a dictionary and construct definitions and explanations following the models above.

Study skills

11 Dictionary work

Note: If you are short of time this exercise can be speeded up by asking students to work in pairs or small groups, dividing up the passage between them.

● Students should read through the passage, underlining all the words they feel need explanation.
● Students use dictionaries to find the meanings of the words.
● They re-write the passage beginning with the sentence given, inserting suitable explanations and definitions in their own words.

Model answer
DNA and its uses
DNA (deoxyribonucleic acid) is the basic genetic material present in most animate or living organisms. Molecules – the smallest units of a substance – of DNA are found in a cell's chromosomes, the parts of the cell which carry genes. Chromosomes occur in pairs: one from the mother and one from the father. The number of chromosomes differs from species to species: a normal human cell has 46.
DNA is made up of genes, linear sections (sections organised in lines) of a DNA molecule which contain the instructions for the development of particular characteristics that living things inherit from their forbears or parents and ancestors, such as eye colour. DNA molecules contain the genetic instructions needed for cells to organise and function. DNA is a large molecule made up of two separate strands wrapped around each other to form a double-helix, which means 'organised in two spirals'.
In 1985 Professor Alec Jeffreys discovered that the DNA of every living thing has its own unique genetic pattern – which means that every living thing has its own organisation of genes and that no two patterns are ever the same. This 'fingerprint' can be determined and used to identify criminals from biological materials left at the scene of a crime or to settle paternity disputes (questions of identifying a person's true biological parents) conclusively.

Writing

12 Writing an expository essay

This is the first of three exercises on the 'formal' or academic essay types in *Distinction*. The others are the comparative essay in Unit 15 and the discursive essay in Unit 18.

● At this level it is assumed that students are familiar with the conventions of essay writing. However, if you want to revise the basic features of essays elicit and write on the board the following key points.
Layout
Introductory paragraph which introduces the topic.
Main body (a number of paragraphs containing the main points).
Concluding paragraph summarising the points you have made.
Preparation
Work out your ideas and write out an outline or plan in note form before you begin the essay.
Style

Use formal vocabulary – avoid colloquialisms and slang
Avoid contractions and exclamations.
Use 'objective language' whenever possible – use passive forms, avoid extreme adjectives.
Do not use the personal pronoun 'I' unless the title specifically asks for your personal opinion/experience.
Always back up your points with reasons and examples.
● Read through the introduction and the essay outline with the class.
● Students can use one of the group writing methods outlined in the introduction or write the essay for homework.

Model answer

In the last few decades a new branch of science, genetic engineering, has opened up new possibilities for medicine and health. These new possibilities are the result of biotechnology, which allows scientists to interfere with and alter the biological processes of life itself. In genetic engineering, scientists can take strands of human DNA and copy and improve them before putting them back in the body. Doctors are hoping that this will lead to the ability to correct flaws and defects in the unborn child, a process known as genetic therapy.

Genetically engineered drugs are now becoming available and can be used to combat many serious diseases. One of the most exciting of these is an antibody which can be used to fight cancer. Known as 'magic bullets', these substances will be able to carry radioactive drugs to the cancerous cells. Biotechnology has also made it possible to use human insulin to treat diabetes, replacing the use of pigs as donors and thus reducing the risk of infection. Another example is IGF: within twenty years, doctors hope that this will be available to fight bone disease. One genetically engineered drug which is already on trial is Interferon, which is being tested for use against arthritis.

Scientists have also developed a technique of using chemical proteins called enzymes to cut out the unwanted parts of the DNA. These can then be repaired and put back into the body. This opens up the possibility of identifying faulty genes in unborn children and treating them while they are still in the womb. The children would then be born free of all genetic defects such as hereditary diseases, leading to a much healthier and longer life.

Of course, none of these treatments can change our susceptibility to environmental factors such as diet and nutrition, and these will continue to have a major effect on human health. What is more, although biotechnology has succeeded in producing new and effective drugs, the possibility of interfering with human genes is still the subject of ethical debate, and it may be many years before the techniques which are now theoretically possible become an everyday reality.

Further practice: Workbook Unit 14, Exercise 11.

Listening skills

13 Listening for enjoyment

Note: The aim of this exercise is enjoyment, there are no specific comprehension questions. Students who enjoy this kind of listening material and are studying in the UK may be interested in 'speaking books' – cassettes containing novels which are read aloud by actors. These are very popular in Britain and are available in bookshops, record shops and public libraries. Some international radio stations (e.g. BBC World Service) also broadcast this type of material.

A ● Read through the introduction and elicit any films/books

students are familiar with which deal with genetics and its possibilities.
● Students read the summary of the early chapters of *The Boys from Brazil*. Check that they understand everything in the summary and the general historical context before playing the tape.

Background information: Nazi-hunters are people who try to find and bring to justice the German soldiers and officials from World War II who committed war crimes but managed to escape and hide in foreign countries at the end of the war. Many of these criminals worked in concentration camps during the war and were involved in killing or conducting medical experiments on Jewish prisoners. Josef Mengele was a geneticist who worked in the concentration camp at Auschwitz and escaped to an unknown destination in 1945.

● Explain to the students that there are no questions to be answered, they should simply relax and enjoy the story.

B ● Students should discuss the questions in groups and then report back to the class.

Answers
1 (Let the students speculate about this. In the book the dogs attack and kill Mengele.)
2 Hitler's father died when he was thirteen. Mengele and the Nazis wanted to recreate Hitler's life as closely as possible, so they needed to kill the adopted fathers when the clones had reached this age.
3 Mengele hopes that at least one of the 94 clones will develop into a fascist dictator as Hitler did, and subsequently fulfil all the ambitions Hitler had before he was defeated in the Second World War.
4 The answer closest to the actual ending of the book is c.

Summary of the actual ending of *The Boys From Brazil*
After Mengele's death, Liebermann's colleagues want to kill all the 94 cloned children, in case any of them should develop into a second Hitler. Liebermann disagrees with this, arguing that such an act would make them as evil as Hitler had been. He destroys the list of 94 names. The novel ends with a scene in which Wheelock's son is drawing a picture of a Nazi rally, imagining himself standing on the podium with fanatical crowds around him. (It is left to the reader/viewer to imagine what will happen in the future.)

Tapescript
The Boys from Brazil
Wheelock looked concerned now. His fingertips were motionless on the album cover.
'There is a Nazi going about in this country,' Liebermann said, holding the briefcase on his lap, 'a former SS man, killing the fathers of the boys adopted through Frieda Maloney. Killing them in the same order as the adoptions, and the same time apart. You're the next one, Mr Wheelock.' He nodded. 'Soon. And there are many more after. This is why I go to the FBI, and this is why, while I go, you should be protected. And by more than your dogs.' He gestured at the door behind which the dogs were whining and barking.
Wheelock shook his head in amazement. 'Hmm!' he said. 'But this is so strange!' He looked wonderingly at Liebermann. 'The fathers of the boys are being killed?'
'Yes.'
'But why?'
'I don't know...'
'You don't know? All these killings are taking place and you don't know the reason?'
A gun came out from behind the album cover, aiming its muzzle at him. 'Then I must tell it to you,' the man holding the gun said. Liebermann looked at him; darkened and

lengthened his hair, gave him a thin moustache, filled him out and made him younger .... Yes, Mengele. Mengele! The hated, the so-long hunted; Angel of Death, child-killer! Sitting here. Smiling. Aiming a gun at him. 'Heaven forbid,' Mengele said, 'that you should die in ignorance. I want you to know exactly what's coming in twenty years or so. Is that ossified stare only for the gun, or have you recognised me?'

Liebermann blinked, took a breath. 'I recognise you,' he said. Mengele smiled. 'Listen, put the briefcase down very slowly and sit back with your hands on your head and relax; you have a good minute or so before I kill you.'

Liebermann put the briefcase down slowly, to the left of his feet, thinking that if he got a chance to go quickly to the right and open the door there, maybe the dogs whimpering on the other side would see Mengele with the gun and go for him before he could get off too many shots. Of course, maybe the dogs would go for him too, and maybe they wouldn't go for either of them without their master, Wheelock, who was presumably dead, giving a command. But he couldn't think of anything else to try.

'Listen closely now, dear Liebermann,' Mengele said. 'I'm going to tell you something that's going to sound totally incredible to you, but I swear to you on my mother's grave that it's the absolute truth. Would I bother to lie to a Jew? And a dead one? Do you know what I saw on television at one o'clock this morning? Films of Hitler. If that wasn't a sign from heaven, there's never been one. This album' – he pointed with his free hand, not taking his eyes or his gun off Liebermann – 'is full of pictures of him, ages one through thirteen. The boys are exact genetic duplicates of him. I'm not going to take the time to explain to you how I achieved this – I doubt whether you'd have the capacity to understand it if I did – but take my word for it, I did achieve it. Exact genetic duplicates. They were conceived in my laboratory, and carried to term by women of the Auiti tribe; healthy docile creatures with a businesslike chieftain. The boys bear no taint of them; they're pure Hitler, bred entirely from his cells. He allowed me to to take half a liter of his blood and a cutting of skin from his ribs – we were in a Biblical frame of mind – on the sixth of January, 1943, at Wolf's Lair. He had denied himself children because he knew that no son could flourish in the shadow of so godlike a father; so when he

heard what was theoretically possible, that I could create some day not his son but another himself, not even a carbon copy but another original, he was as thrilled by the idea as I was. It was then that he gave me the position and facilities I required to begin the pursuit of my goal. Did you really think my work at Auschwitz was aimless insanity? How simple-minded you people are! You see? I'm giving you more than one minute ...' He looked at the clock – Liebermann got up and – a gunshot roared – stepped around the sofa end, reaching. A gunshot roared, a gunshot roared; pain flung him against hard wall, pain in his chest, pain further down. Dogs barked loud in his wall-pressing ear. The brown door thumped and quivered; he reached across it for its glass diamond knob. A gunshot roared; the knob burst apart as he caught it, a small hole in the back of his hand filling with blood. He clutched a sharp part of knob – a gunshot roared; the dogs barked wildly – and wincing in pain, eyes tight shut, he twisted the part-knob, pulled. The door threw itself open against his arm and shoulder, dogs howling, big Dobermans, teeth bared, eyes wild, sharp ears back ...

Final task

14 The human body of the future

A
- Read through the introduction and ask students to describe and react to the illustration of the human body of the future.
- Remind students of the information on evolution in Unit 12. Ask them if they think human evolution has stopped or will continue to develop, and if so, over what kind of time period.
- Explain the chart and go through the first example. Divide the class into pairs to complete the chart.

B
- Pairs combine to compare their ideas, then turn to the suggestions on page 161 of the Students' Book to check.

C
- Students should decide which of the changes are most likely to take place, explaining their reasons. List these on the board.
- Close the lesson with a class discussion of how the changes might affect everyday human life.

Unit summary

Themes	Language awareness unit covering the Initial Teaching Alphabet; linguistic development; children's books
Structures	The definite article; participle clauses
Vocabulary	Matching words with definitions; multi-word verbs with particle *down* (in WB)
Language skills	*Reading:* reading to infer attitude and tone; analysing style *Listening:* understanding anecdotes *Speaking:* comparing and contrasting *Writing:* comparison and contrast (2); writing a comparative essay
Pronunciation	Sound-spelling correspondences (1), full vowels

 Teaching notes

Introduction

1 This is the third of the language awareness units. It looks at linguistic development in children, and writing books for them.

- Introduce the topic by asking around the class if any students have young brothers or sisters, or, if appropriate, young children of their own. Ask them if they remember anything about the way that these children acquired language and discuss any points or anecdotes they raise.
- Focus attention on the first cartoon. Students read the questions and discuss them in pairs, before opening the discussion up to the whole class.

Answers
Students' opinions may vary on these, but the main impression of the cartoon should be that children's grasp of language is more sophisticated than adults believe, and that adults speak to children in a way that trivialises their language.

2 This exercise looks at the stages in the linguistic development of an English-speaking child. It may also remind students of some of the problems they had when they were first learning English, and help them to appreciate that the mistakes made were a normal part of the learning process.

- The students work in pairs to read through the cartoons and decide what the child is trying to say in each one.

Answers
1 Dog.
2 Stop, stop!
3 The milk has all gone.
4 The baby's crying.
5 I want my toy.
6 Don't sit there!
7 Look! Lots of sheep.
8 Mummy's sitting in the chair.
9 I hid my teddy.
10 This isn't my teddy.

- Students try to work out what the linguistic rules are that the child is breaking. In some cases, e.g. 9, this should be quite easy.

- The students turn to the relevant pages (166 and 175) at the back of the book and match the rules with the cartoons. Then they discuss them together to ensure they understand which rule is being broken in each cartoon.

Answers
1 c   2 g   3 j   4 d   5 b   6 h   7 f   8 e
9 a   10 i

- Ask students to discuss the stages of learning for children in their language. Do not spend long on this if it is not really appropriate to the class.

Reading skills

3 Inferring attitude and tone

A This text is very sarcastic in tone and quite amusing for the native speaker. Better classes should be able to appreciate the tone and humour, but certain concepts will need to be discussed with the group first.

- Focus students' attention on the questions. Encourage them to discuss what they think makes English spelling difficult. (Probably the lack of one-to-one sound and letter correspondence.) Ask if they think English-speaking children have difficulty when learning to spell and how they might be taught.
- Write the phrase *Initial Teaching Alphabet (ITA)* on the board and explain that it was a system of teaching English-speaking children how to spell, and that it did so by simplifying the language. Ask students how it might have simplified the language. (By setting up one-to-one sound and letter correspondences.)
- Make sure students understand that *the Guardian* is a quality newspaper, and that *Teletext* is the text-based news and information service broadcast with television signals.

Note: there is a lot of difficult vocabulary in this text. Encourage students to try to understand the gist and not to worry about unfamiliar words.

- Students read the text to find out how the language was simplified.

Answer
It was a phonetically-based system with one letter per English sound.

B These questions help students to understand the ironic tone of the article.

- Students read the text more carefully to answer the questions.

Answers
1 They are very sceptical towards the ITA, as many of the adjectives and phrases show: *hastily developed, badly researched, pernicious nue speling, catastrophe* etc.
2 That it was a misconceived, complicated way of simplifying the language, and that it was useless anyway as children eventually had to learn the conventional alphabet.
3 Again, they are very sceptical and negative: *Sir James Pitman and his crazed evangelical lackeys.*
4 That they cannot spell: *... niches where the lexicologically crippled could be usefully and gainfully employed.*
5 No, it is rather ironic. This is indicated by the metaphors given, e.g. that adults always lie to children, the

comparison ofthe alphabet with upside-down Serbo-Croat, and the references to *the Guardian* and *Teletext* etc.

6 This paragraph suggests that British parents purposely deceive their children, and are therefore cruel, but the examples cited are fairly common, innocent 'lies' told so children can enjoy themselves (*Santa Claus/the tooth fairy*) or in order not to hurt their feelings (*that their pet doggie hasn't been put down*).

C This task focusses on some of the more difficult words in the text.

● Students find the words in the text and match them with their definitions.

Answers
1 d   2 f   3 b   4 g   5 h   6 a   7 c   8 e

● Some other words from the text you may wish to discuss:
credulous of a person: believing without question
crazed mad
evangelical spreading an idea or faith
lexicologically from lexicology – the study of words

Background information: *Santa Claus.* Another form of St Nicholas, but today seen as a traditional Christmas figure who brings presents on Christmas Eve. He is depicted as a fat, jolly man dressed in red with a long white beard.
The tooth fairy When a child loses a milk tooth, he or she places it under the pillow on going to bed. During the night it is 'transformed' into a small coin by the parents.
Sixpence A coin in pre-decimal sterling, with the value of 2.5 pence in decimal currency.
The references to *the Guardian* and *Teletext* page-setters reflect common feeling in the UK that there are too many spelling errors in both the newspaper and *Teletext*.

D Focus students' attention on the two essays above the reading text. They should read through them and work out what has been written.

Answers
Blue letter
I like stories, I like Goldilocks and I like The Three Pigs when the wolf chases them.
Pink letter
Dear Mister Sir James Pitman
Thank you for the books and I like the books and I like all the book [books] you have give [given] us and ...

● Ask whether students feel they are good examples of children's writing in English. (They're not, and have been chosen for that reason.)
● Ask students to see if they can work out any of the spelling 'rules' in the ITA from the two essays.

Answers
1 The following sounds are given one written version only:
/ʌ/ = u   /aɪ/ = ie
/ʊ/ = w   /ɪə/ = ee
/eɪ/ = ae   /ɔː/ = au
2 Silent letters are left out: the *-e* in *James* and *like*, the *-c* in *Goldilocks*, the *-h* in *when*.

Language work

4   Participle clauses

A Students look at the example and answer the questions about the participle.

Answers
Its subject is *adults*, and it is active.

● Students read the sentences and underline the participle clauses (the ones starting with a present or past participle). They then answer the questions below.

Answers
1 active, past
2 passive, past
3 passive, present
4 active, present

● Discuss the use of the participles – the past participle is used in passive clauses only. The time is made clear either by the tense in the main clause or by a time adverbial.

B Students combine the sentences, using participle clauses.

Answers
1 She stayed at the school for ten years, hating every minute of it.
2 The London Book Fair, held once a year in the city, is a huge trade fair.
3 Aidan Burrow's new book, voted 'Book of the Year' in 1992, will be loved by children evrywhere.
4 These books, nominated for the same prize, are all also worth reading.
5 John, being a rather disruptive child, is often sent out of his class.
6 The school I attended was very well-respected, getting excellent exam results every year.

See also: Participles in adverbial clauses, Unit 18, Exercise 8.

Further practice: Workbook Unit 15, Exercise 5.

5   The definite article

A This exercise helps students to understand the rules governing the usage of the definite article.

● Students read through the six examples from the text and discuss in pairs why the article is used in each one. (In 6 they should look at the first definite article only.)
● Students match the examples to six of the rules beneath them. Encourage them to do the obvious ones first, as they will be able to do some by elimination.

Answers
1 a   2 c   3 f   4 e   5 h   6 d

● Check these answers. Then students match the next three sentences. (In 8 they should concentrate on the non-use of the article before *school*.)

Answers
7 g   8 i   9 b

B Make sure students understand these uses. Then ask them to correct the text.

Of course, one of the best ways for children to learn ✔
how to spell is by introducing children to ~~the~~ books at a
very young age. Initially, young children can learn ✔
∧ alphabet by reading some very simple alphabet- and ∧ the
letter-based books, for example, ∧ type of book which ∧ the
presents a simple story focussing on one letter of the ✔
alphabet. ~~The~~ books can usually be read either at school,
in ∧ classroom, with the help of ∧ teacher, or at home, with ∧ the x2
the help of one or both parents. While ∧ very young need
this help from adults, older children should be ✔
encouraged to select their own reading material, ✔
especially if there is a good library in the school they ✔
attend, and to read at ∧ times which suit them. In this age ∧ the

of watching TV for ~~the~~ pleasure, rather than ~~the~~ reading
for pleasure, it is often useful to give children a purpose ✔
for reading. In fact, some of ∧ most widely read books ∧ the
these days do exactly that. ~~The~~ reading is a pleasure as
well as an educational tool, and it is part of our ✔
responsibility as adults and parents to educate children ✔
to appreciate ∧ pleasure of reading. ∧ the

Note: In line 7 of the text, *The* has been deleted on the
assumption that this is a general statement about all books. It
would also be possible to leave *The* in the sentence and tick
this line as correct, assuming that *The books* refers only to the
type of book specified in the previous sentence. In lines 7 and
17, the deletion of *The* necessitates a capital letter at the
beginning of the next word, Books and Reading respectively,
but students have not been asked to do this.

Further practice: Workbook Unit 15, Exercise 4.

Listening skills

6   Understanding anecdotes

A   • Students read the introduction. Ask them what kind of
things they think authors must bear in mind when writing
children's books.
   • Pre-teach: *toddler* (child who is just starting to walk) and
recorder (wind instrument often played by children).
   • Play the interview through once only. Ask students what Jill
Murphy says she must think about. Is it the same as their
suggestions?

Answers
She often makes her books sound rather jolly.
She is careful not to write down to children (i.e. not to be
condescending).
She tries to make the language as simple as possible.
She shows as much as possible in the pictures.
She is careful not to try to create her childrens' books as
children themselves would write, speak (or illustrate).

Tapescript
INTERVIEWER   Right. Erm, what would you say is the main
difference between writing for the ... the younger children
and writing for thirteen year olds, erm, do you feel that you
have to adapt your language drastically?
JILL   Just the difference in the way that you would speak, I
suppose, to, er, you probably don't even notice that you do
it, but if you, er, say, speak to a small child, a little toddler for
example, you tend to sound slightly sort of mad in fact and
over-jolly when you're trying to explain things to them
because they respond very well to that, and as they get more
language you tend to ... , I mean, funny but I really don't
write down very much at all. I mean, *The Worst Witch*, which
is for quite a young age group, is written in a very
old-fashioned, straightforward style. So I don't really alter it
very much, once you're past the toddler stage, I suppose in
the way that with children, once they get out of the toddler
stage and can really speak to you and have a very good grasp
of language, I don't really speak to children any differently
than I would speak to an adult, except that you don't talk
about things that they don't understand you know.
INTERVIEWER   Mm. Do you find, though, that with writing for
the younger ones you would use shorter sentences or do you
simplify ...?
JILL   Well, yes, with picture books you try and make it as
simple as possible because the pictures tell you a lot as well,
so you tend to ... I mean, a good example was in *Five
Minutes' Peace*, if you look at that one, em, it has a bit when
they, ... one of the children comes in and plays a tune on his

recorder, and the original script said, I think, *'Can I ...'* (that's
the other thing, it should be *'May I ...'* but children never say
'May I'; it sounds too sort of prissy) so in fact it says *'Can I
play you my tune on the recorder, Mum?' said Lester*, or
something like that. And, in fact, my editor pointed out that
you don't need *on the recorder* because there he is in the
picture playing the recorder, and it sounds much more
concise to say *'Can I play you my tune,' asked Lester* ...
INTERVIEWER   Mm, that's interesting.
JILL   because that's the sort of thing Lester would say and
it's a much more attractive sentence. It's a good editor I've got
there ... Walker Books ... have to say this.
INTERVIEWER   Uh – uh. Do you feel that you would use certain
language that is specifically language children would ...
children would use, erm, for example, do kids use adjectives
to describe something that's really good, which an adult
might not use, and therefore do you put them into your
writing?
JILL   Well, I don't know because they use such extraordinary
adjectives. I mean they have all the street stuff now, don't
they, like *wicked* for example, they were all saying for quite a
long time, meaning something was wonderful, whereas we
would say, well, as a fogey I would say that *wicked* means
that somebody was absolutely dreadful, and you know,
appalling behaviour and possibly verging on evil ...
INTERVIEWER   Yes.
JILL   ... whereas a child would say 'Oh, that's wicked,' and
mean, ... I've even had letters saying that my books were
wicked and I thought 'What do they mean, they're wicked?'
only to find out they mean they're *really brilliant, brill*, all
sorts of things like this, so, you can't really. I just stick to what
I know is the King's English and – Queen's English, rather –
and they have to make what they will of it, and they don't
seem to mind at all.
INTERVIEWER   Mm. I think they probably expect something
adult in books anyway.
JILL   Yes, they do. I think the other thing is it's a slight mistake
to do any grovelling to them. I mean, I remember ages ago
when I worked in a children's home I used to draw them lots
of pictures, and one evening I drew a – I'd been looking at
their pictures and this little girl did a wonderful drawing of
me putting a vase of flowers on the table, where I appeared
to be floating through the air and the table had all the legs
dangling out of the bottom like they do. So when I next did a
picture for them, I did a table with all of the legs sticking out
of the bottom because I thought it rather attractive the way
she'd drawn it, and I remember her saying to me 'Don't draw
it like that, Auntie. Draw it the way you do, you know,
properly, like you can do.' And she, although she drew it like
that it was because she hadn't got the mental equipment to
do it properly yet, you know, she couldn't work out how to
do it, and she liked to see a table in perspective, the way I'd
do it, because it looked like the real thing and she was rather
cross with me for trying to be like her and I thought I learned
a lesson from that.

B   This task looks at understanding anecdotes. This can be quite
difficult, especially in relaxed circumstances, as in telling
anecdotes people tend to take a lot of knowledge for granted
and to use more colloquial expressions.

   • Ask students if they can remember anything about the two
anecdotes. (The first is about a boy playing a recorder and
the second is about the little girl who drew a picture of Jill.)
   • Play the interview again, and again play it once only. You
can indicate to the students when the two anecdotes start,
to help them. (*Well, yes, with picture books you try ...*, and *I
remember ages ago when I worked in a children's home ...*)
   • Students listen, make notes and then discuss the anecdotes

in groups. Ask two students to relate the anecdotes to the class.

C
- Students read the gapped text about Jill's second anecdote. They try to complete it from memory.
- Students compare their answers in pairs or groups. If there is any disagreement, play the anecdote again.

Answers
1   write down/grovel   2   children's home   3   done a drawing/drawn a picture   4   unrealistic/out of perspective
5   copy/mimic/reproduce   6   unexpected   7   learnt a lesson/learnt something   8   mental equipment/ability
9   find it/think it is

Writing skills

7   Comparing and contrasting (3)

This exercise continues presenting connectives of comparison and contrast and builds on work done in Units 6 and 14.

A
- Students read the short extract about the word *wicked*. They find the connective of contrast – *whereas*.
- Students read the example sentence and think of as many different ways to compare the two ideas as possible. They can look back at Units 14 and 6. Get some suggestions from the students and write the connectives on the board.

B
- Read through the new connectives with the students. If they are unsure of any of them, they can use them to join one of the two example sentences.

Note: There is a description in the Grammar Reference at the back of the Students' Book of the use of all the connectives of comparison and contrast presented.

- Students rewrite the pairs of sentences, using the connectives. Make students aware that they may have to change the wording in the sentences, especially when using *It's the same for ...* and *It's also equally true of ...* . They may also need to change *it* to *this* in these two constructions.

Answers
(The suggested answers given here use only the connectives in this exercise. Accept any correct answers using connectives from earlier units.)
1   Children learn their language by listening to it, whereas/while most adults learn a foreign language by learning rules.
2   While children like trying out new sounds, adults feel inhibited and embarrassed.
3   Children formulate their own rules and try them out. This is equally true of adults when they are learning a foreign language.
4   Children do not know they are doing this. Adults, on the contrary, are very aware that they are doing it.
5   Children learn more quickly if they enjoy themselves. But by the same token, adults also learn more quickly if they enjoy it.

Extension
- If your students need more practice in these connectives, ask them to write a few more sentences comparing and contrasting adults and children.

Reading skills

8   Analysing written style

A   The text is a children's story by Roald Dahl. (There is a reading text about Roald Dahl in the Workbook Unit 15, page 60.)

- Students look at the picture and discuss the questions. They should recognise that the story is likely to be humorous.
- Tell the students that the word *twit* (the name of the story) is a colloquial way of saying *idiot*. From this they should be able to predict something about the story.
- Students read the story. Ask a student to summarise it for the class. (There should be no problems with comprehension – it is quite simple.)

B
- Ask students how old they think the intended readers of the story might be. (Probably children of 7 or 8.)
- They read through the questions, then go back through the text and try to answer them. These questions are quite difficult so students may prefer to work in pairs.
- Discuss the answers in open class.

Answers
1   Yes, it's jolly in tone: *pop it back in, plotting away like mad*, it also keeps everything simple. (See 2 below.)
2   It's an easy style, characterised by short sentences, direct speech, simple conjunctions (*and, because, so*), not much subordination. The grammar is natural but quite simple, not expressing concepts that may be beyond the children's understanding, such as conditionals. There is a lot of repetition: *You can play a lot of tricks because you can ... and you can ...; He wiped the white froth onto his sleeve and wiped his sleeve ... .*
3   The vocabulary is quite colourful (*nasty, like a wombat, you old hag*) but there is nothing there which would not be used in adult books. This is what Jill Murphy means by 'not writing down' – using real language but in such a way that children understand it.
4   The story is unlikely to be in a book for adults as the humour is rather too obvious. However, there is something slightly wicked about Dahl's humour, and for that reason his books could be enjoyed by adults more than those of many children's writers. Dahl is also very well-known as a writer of books for adults, especially short stories.

Extension
- If students are interested in reading any of Dahl's work, they should look for a collection of his short stories.

Writing skills

9   This is an opportunity for students to discuss some of the ideas from this unit and to compare what they know and have learnt about children in the UK to their own experience.

- Students read through the quotes and facts and discuss in pairs what they tell them about children in the UK.
- Discuss this in open class.
- In pairs or small groups the students compare this to attitudes in their country/countries. They should make notes of some of the similarities and differences as they are talking.
- Open the discussion to the class, and ask students to offer comparisons, using the language of comparison and contrast.

10   This exercise puts into written practice the ways of comparing that students have learnt in this and the last unit. It is the second of the academic essay types. In written exams students will be able to recognise an essay title referring to comparison because of the use of the word *compare* (*the advantages and disadvantages*), or a phrase such as *examine the similarities and differences between …* .

Comparison essays can be tackled in two ways, either by writing one paragraph about the first item of comparison and a second paragraph about the other item, or by taking each area of comparison and tackling it in a different paragraph. For example, for the essay suggested here, students could either write one paragraph about their country, one about the UK, and one comparing the two; or they could find areas of comparison, e.g. education, discipline, the law and write a comparative paragraph about each.

- Read through the introduction and instructions with the students.
- Discuss with them how to organise their article. Remind them of the need for an introduction and a conclusion, and discuss the possible ways of organising suggested above.
- If necessary, discuss some of the ideas to go in the article. (This should have been covered in Exercise 9.)
- Students write the article, either in the class or for homework.

Further practice: Workbook Unit 15, Exercises 7 and 8.

Pronunciation

11 Sound-spelling correspondences (1)

This is the first of two exercises looking at the way that vowel sounds are represented in written English. This exercise looks at the eleven full (long and short) vowels; Exercise 8 in Unit 20 looks at diphthongs.

- Introduce the topic by discussing the possible confusions in English spelling.
- Give students a couple of minutes to work in pairs to find different ways of spelling the phoneme /ɑː/. They should find some of the following: *ar – park, a – path, ea – heart, au – laugh, al – calm*

A
- To make sure that students are aware of the eleven full vowel sounds, play the tape for them to listen and practise the sounds. Only spend time practising those sounds which cause your students difficulties.

B
- Students work in pairs to work out which sound each of the words in the list represents. When they are sure, they should add them to the chart.
- As each pair finishes, they should check their charts with another pair. Then check answers around the class.

Answers

/iː/ sleep: key, leaf, police, seize, these, thief
/ɪ/ slip: build, cities, pretty, private (can also be /ə/), symbol
/e/ slept: many, read
/æ/ slap: plait
/ɑː/ sharp: bath*, clerk#, heart, laugh*, palm
* = /æ/ in many varieties of English
# = /ɜː/ in American English
/ɒ/ shop: cough, sausage, watch
/ɔː/ short: bought, lawn, salt, taught
/ʌ/ shut: blood, son, young
/ɜː/ shirt: church, heard, journey, serve, worse
/ʊ/ shook: could, put, wolf
/uː/ shoot: lose, rude, you

C
- Divide the class into pairs. Students look at the relevant pages.
- Explain the task: each student has a chart like the one in B, with three words under each phoneme. They have to read the words out to their partners in random order, ensuring clear pronunciation of the vowel. As they listen to their partners, students have to decide which vowel they hear and write the word in their chart, using the words form the chart in B to predict the spelling of the word, if they do not know it. (Student B will have to continue the chart in an exercise book.)
- Set a time limit for students to do the task (about 10 – 12 minutes) and monitor as they are doing it. Deal with any problems afterwards.

Further practice: Workbook Unit 15, Exercise 6.

Final task

12 Writing a children's story

This writing task is intended to get students thinking about the style of what they are writing, as well as the language and the content. Writing something for children is one of the easiest ways of starting to think about style, because the language can (and should) be kept very simple. (There is more work on writing in particular styles in Unit 20.)

- Discuss the task with the students. It is divided into simple steps so the students should have no difficulty in working out what to do.
- Students read the start of the story (stage 1).
- Help if necessary with vocabulary. The pictures will help with some (e.g. *barley*). Other words they may not know but may be useful are:
  gawky awkward, suggesting long legs and clumsiness
  stumpy-legged short-legged
  bristling starting to feel angry
  scoffed mocked, expressed scornfully
- Divide the class into groups. Each group decides the development of the story by looking at the pictures and reading the captions (stage 2). It doesn't matter if groups interpret them slightly differently.
- Groups list the events and discuss the paragraphs (stage 3).
- They look back to Exercises 6 and 7 and decide what kind of language they need to use (stage 4). You could discuss this as a class if you feel it necessary.
- Groups divide the story into parts to match the number of students in the group. Each student writes his/her part (stage 5). This could be done at home with some time allowed in the next lesson for them to put the stories together.
- Students should check each other's work for errors: each section of the story is passed to another student in the group so that no one is looking at his/her own work. (This is best done in pairs if possible.)

Note: There is a formal exercise on editing and correcting one's own work in Unit 16.

- Groups put the sections together to make the complete story (stage 6). Either collect the stories in for a final check, or let students display them on the walls. You can then discuss any errors with the relevant groups/students.

Note: You might like to make this into a full poster display by giving students large sheets of coloured paper to mount their stories on. In this case, the groups may want to write their stories out neatly before displaying them.

Unit 16   The Written Word

 ## Unit summary

Themes	Literature; publishing and book buying; contemporary novels; poetry
Structures	Sentence adverbials and adverbs; forms of adjectives and adverbs; order of adverbs (in Workbook)
Vocabulary	Gap filling; literature (in Workbook)
Pronunciation	Rhythm and stress in poetry
Skills	*Reading:* recognising literary styles and genres
	Listening: listening and summarising
	Speaking: reciting poetry
	Writing: editing and error correction

 ## Teaching notes

Introduction

1
- Read through the introduction and focus on the advertisement. Ask students to give reasons why people might use book clubs and elicit some of the following: cheap prices; convenient for people who live in remote places; can cater for specialised interests; easier to select from a catalogue than spend hours in bookshops
- Students individually choose five books from the advertisement.
- Students complete the matching task and choose their favourite type of book.

Answers
Mary Queen of Scots historical biography
Pirates of the Asteroids science fiction
Hutchinson Factfinder reference book
The Looking-Glass War thriller
Top One Hundred Italian Dishes cookery book
Tess of the D'Urbervilles classic novel
New England travel guide
It Shouldn't Happen to a Vet humorous novel

- Ask students to give one or two further examples of each category of book to check that they understand the descriptions. These could be books written in English or books in their own language.
- Elicit from the class any other types of book they know of, such as those below, and write them on the board.
romance   spy novel   poetry   anthology
short stories   autobiography   memoirs
manual   annual   text book
- Form the students into small groups to discuss questions **a** and **b**.
- Groups report back to class and work out overall preferences for the whole class.

Reading skills

2 Recognising literary styles and genres
A Students should have no difficulty matching the extracts to the categories in the chart.

Answers
A Thriller (*The Looking-Glass War* by John le Carré)
B Historical biography (*Mary Queen of Scots* by Antonia Fraser)
C Classic novel (*Tess of the D'Urbervilles* by Thomas Hardy)
D Science fiction (*Pirates of the Asteroids* by Isaac Asimov)

B
- Read through the instructions and the list a – l, checking that the students understand the terms.
- For classes which are unfamiliar with this type of material and task, the exercise will be more successful if you allow students to work in pairs or small groups.

Suggested answers
classic novel: c f k
thriller: d h l
historical biography: a e g
science fiction: b i j

C Some classes may need help with this section. If so, give the students one example of each feature to get them started.

- Point out that archaic words cause difficulty even for native speakers of English – they shouldn't feel discouraged if they find extract C difficult, as it was written over a hundred years ago and is in a rather literary style.

Note: Some students may wish to know the meaning of the archaic words. They are given beside each word in the answer below.

Answers
archaic words (from text C)
integument skin
nap surface with short smooth hair or fibres
rind hard skin of meat or fruit
a staring sketch a conspicuous outline
white worsted traditional woollen cloth

metaphors (from text C)
like the moves of a chess player...;
a white nap as of fur grown from the rind...;
forming a staring sketch...
like loops of white worsted...

scientific terms (from extract D)
air-lock   vacuum   cylinder of liquid oxygen

invented terms (from extract D)
micro-heatgun   semi-space-suit

D Use the questions to generate a brief class discussion.

3 This exercise requires the students to use a lot of imagination. If your class find this type of activity difficult, you should go through the four extracts with the whole class first, eliciting and suggesting ideas about the 'Secondary World' each of them creates.

- Read through the introduction, pointing out if you wish that Tolkien wrote *The Hobbit* and is famous for his highly imaginative children's books.
- Students work individually to make notes about their selected extract.
- Students get together with others who chose the same extract and compare their ideas.
- Groups report back to class. There are no correct answers – students should be encouraged to be as imaginative as possible.

4
- Elicit answers to the warm-up questions.
- Students read the article and answer questions 1 – 4.

Answers
1 The average Briton reads 9.2 books a year.
2 The discrepancy is that some people read books but do not buy them and others buy books but do not read them.
3 *A Brief History of Time* by Stephen Hawking.
4 It is difficult to keep up with trends because so many books are published, they are very varied and often very long.

- Elicit answers to the follow-up questions.

Answers
a Buying books to give as presents.
b Buying books in order to keep up with other people rather than out of genuine interest.

5
- Students work in small groups to discuss the reasons and together agree on a rank order for column **a**.

Note: In a mixed nationality class the order in column **b** may not be the same for everyone in the group.

- Groups report back to class and work out the rank order for the class as a whole.
- If you have a mixed nationality class, you might like to focus on how the rank order differs from country to country, asking students to suggest reasons for the differences such as education, culture and the relative cost of books.

Vocabulary

6 Gap-filling
- Students who need help will find clues on page 161 of the Students' Book.

Answers
1 voracious   2 numerous   3 discrepancy
4 recipients   5 bestseller   6 digest   7 cursory
8 hardened

Language work

7 Sentence adverbials and adverbs

A
- Read through the introduction and ask the students to study the extracts.
- Elicit answers to the questions.

Answers
Differences
In **1a** *clearly* is a sentence adverbial and indicates the writer's attitude to the statement as a whole. (In other words, the writer feels that the discrepancy is obvious to the reader and cannot be disputed.)
In **1b**, *clearly* is an adverb of manner describing only the way in which the books were (not) written.
In **2a**, *yet* is a sentence adverbial and indicates the writer's attitude to the statement as a whole. (In other words, the writer feels that this statement is surprising in view of what has already been written.)
In **2b**, *yet* is an adverb modifying the verb, indicating that this has not happened up to this time.

Position
The importance of the position is that the sentence adverbials are placed at the beginning (or end) of the sentence, whereas the adverbs are placed next to the verb they describe.

B
- Students can do this section in pairs.

Answers
Examples from the text:
understandably (paragraph 3)
similarly (paragraph 4)

Sample sentences using the words as adverbs:
The students were understandably annoyed at failing the test.
All the students in this class are similarly dressed.

- Elicit the answers and write two or three example sentences on the board.

C
- Students will find this task easier if they put the adverbials into context sentences. Give them one or two on the board to start them off.
Personally, I have never enjoyed reading science fiction.
Frankly, I think that book is absolute rubbish.
- Pairs should get together to compare answers.

Answers
a ideally   b superficially   c personally   d certainly
e frankly   f admittedly   g naturally   h incidentally
i apparently

D
- Students can do this in pairs. If they have difficulty, give them the answer to item 1 on the board as an example.

Answers
1 *Honestly*, I don't think he can express himself.
   I don't think he can express himself *honestly*.
2 *Clearly* the exercise hasn't been explained.
   The exercise hasn't been explained *clearly*.
3 *Naturally* she is a gifted writer.
   She is a *naturally* gifted writer.
4 *Yet* I haven't seen him read a serious book.
   I haven't seen him read a serious book *yet*/I haven't *yet* seen him read a serious book.
5 *Personally*, I don't think he will apologise.
   I don't think he will apologise *personally*.
6 *Frankly*, she finds it impossible to write.
   She finds it impossible to write *frankly*.

- To check that students have fully understood the different meanings of the sentences they have written, ask them to explain the sentences to you using different words, as below.
Honestly, I don't think he can express himself. (My true opinion is that he cannot express himself.)
I don't think he can express himself honestly. (That man cannot express himself without lying.)

Further practice: Workbook Unit 16, Exercise 6.

Listening skills

8 Listening and summarising

Background information: Jon Elkon was born in South Africa and now lives in London. *Umfaan's Heroes* (published 1989) is set in South Africa and tells the story of a young man growing up and reacting against the apartheid system in the 1960s. *Laszlo's Millions* (published 1991) is a sequel to *Umfaan's Heroes* and is a satirical novel set in the London of the 1970s.

A
- Ask the students to describe the book covers and predict what the books are about.
- Explain the ordering task and play the tape.

Answers
4 what makes a bestseller
7 political issues
6 the computer novel
2 faction

1 what a novel is
5 escapism
3 where characters come from

B ● Read through the instructions and the eight items.
   ● Point out that the students should not try to express everything Elkon says. They must condense what Elkon says to fit into one sentence. This involves distinguishing the key points from the supporting information and then expressing the key points in their own words.
   ● Play the tape several times if necessary and allow students to work together on their summaries.

Suggested answers

2 Elkon explains the meaning of *faction* as *lying about people who are still in existence.*
3 Elkon explains that he collects his characters from real life, based on people he has met.
4 Elkon describes the most important factor in a bestseller as empathy, so that the reader knows how the character feels.
5 Elkon describes the plot of a typical bestseller as a female main character who will lose and then regain the man of her dreams and end up rich.
6 Elkon sees the novel developing in the future into the computer novel with pictures on screen.
7 Elkon explains that the traditional novel will survive because it is like a close friend, and because you can be alone with the fantasy.
8 Elkon doesn't think that novelists have a duty to investigate political issues but says that politics will come into a novel because politics is a part of life.

C ● Students should discuss the statements a – d in small groups.
   ● Monitor and check that students are giving reasons for their opinions and using examples to explain their points.
   ● After a few minutes ask the groups to report back with their opinions. A quick way to do this is to take a vote on who agrees and disagrees with each of the statements.

Tapescript

INTERVIEWER Jon, you've written two novels and a text book, and you're working on a third novel now. What is it that makes a novel a novel?

JOHN ELKON Um, well, that's a very interesting question – a novel is, well, the word *novel* means *new*, doesn't it? [Mm] And the word *fiction* means *lie*, so a novel is a new lie [Right] right, and I like lying and I'm paid to do it.

INTERVIEWER Sounds a good ... as good a reason as any. But is that what makes a novel a novel, the fact that it's not true, that it's made up?

JOHN ELKON Well, nowadays there ... there's a new strain of novels which are about real people. They're about historical characters – there's always been the historical novel – but there are novels about people who are still alive, for example.

INTERVIEWER Oh, is that what's called *faction*?

JOHN ELKON Faction – or lying about people who are still in existence – but the thing about the novel is it's, um, it's really fables, it's story-telling. Everybody loves to tell stories, [Mm] it's a way of um, relaxing and entertaining people.

INTERVIEWER Actually, curiously saying ... your saying that faction is based on ... on real people who are living – are any of your characters based on real people or ... where do they come from, the characters?

JOHN ELKON Well what happens is that one, of course, collects characters, one collects people, and you go through life and you meet people who you find particularly interesting and you think 'Oh I'll put that one in my bag,' and sooner or later they'll emerge. But they'll be completely changed and completely altered, because my character in my novel will be the sort of um ... very very loosely based on somebody – but they're going to be ... they'll have different colour hair or they'll have different colour ideas, or different sorts of ideas. So what'll happen is that you'll have to make them fit in to what's happening in the book, what's happening in the plot.

INTERVIEWER So what is it that ma ... I mean, in your opinion, what is it that makes a book one of those very small number of bestsellers?

JOHN ELKON I think that there is a formula. I think that the form ... the main formula and the most important thing about writing bestsellers is firstly, empathy, right? Empathy is that when you – writing about a character in a certain situation, the reader – must think 'I know exactly how that character feels,' and when they ... the character does and performs certain things the reader must think 'Oh, I'd like to do that,' or, 'Oh, I could do that.' And that is why the novelists who sell the most are novelists who will approach, um, their book as if they were selling a chocolate bar. [Mm] They will identify what their market is and they will write specifically for that market.

INTERVIEWER So do you mean in the sense of catering to people's fantasies?

JOHN ELKON Very very much so. That's what the job is.

INTERVIEWER Or escapism?

JOHN ELKON People love to escape, and if you can make them escape to a place they really want to escape to ... for example, the most successful novelists, if you look at those who've really made a lot of money: they have a female male ... main character and this female main character will lose, and then re-gain the man of her dreams, [Yes] and will end up rich – if she didn't start rich – so this is obviously fulfilling the fantasy of many people who would like to do just that.

INTERVIEWER What about contemporary literar ... literature generally? Do you feel that it's relevant to modern life? A lot of people say that it's a past art form and, you know, the mass media of television, films, video are really the way that people express themselves nowadays.

JOHN ELKON Well, this is very very largely true. And also I think we're going to see the computer novel in the very, very near future [Yep] we're going to see a novel which will appear on a computer screen and possibly, possibly you'll be able to hear it as well and there'll be pictures. So it'll be a multi-media thing soon and I think that novelists are going to have to do this, they're going to have to take this on board and realise it's going to be a multi-media field um, but there will always be a market for a book because a book is like a close friend: if you go to bed with a book you're alone with the author, you're alone with the dream, you're alone with the fantasy and that's a very very special thing [Mm] and there'll always be people who want to do that.

INTERVIEWER Now, of course, you are originally from South Africa ...

JOHN ELKON Yeah.

INTERVIEWER ... and that certainly featured in your first novel, that background. Do you feel any sort of, er, duty of the novelist to investigate political issues or social issues, in their work?

JOHN ELKON I don't think it's a duty but I think that sometimes the novelist can't help these things creeping into their work. It is important that a novelist does not necessarily see him or herself as a force to change society. The novelist should really see themselves as a force to improve their own writing and to communicate much, much better with the reader. And if politics comes into that it is because politics comes into life: you can't actually avoid politics – it is part of life. But I don't think that one should ever preach.

Writing skills

9 Editing and error correction

A   • Ask the students if they think editing and correction are important and elicit their reasons.
   • Students should correct the extracts 1 – 6.

Answers

1   Shakespeare wrote *Hamlet* when he was living in London.
2   Poetry is my favourite form of literature.
3   I read that book because it was recommended by my teacher.
4   Critics agree that this book is of very poor quality/weak.
5   Charles Dickens was born in 1812. He wrote *Pickwick Papers* in 1836. This was followed by *Oliver Twist*, *Nicholas Nickleby*, *Great Expectations* and others. He died in 1870.
6   *Macbeth* is a tragedy whereas *Twelfth Night* is a comedy.

B   • Read through the Editing/Correcting Checklist with the class and check understanding of the categories and examples.
   • Divide the students into pairs to complete the error analysis and matching tasks.

Answers (types of error already in the checklist)

1   c (capital letter needed for *hamlet* and *london*)
    e (no definite article needed in *in the London*)
2   e (no definite article needed with *poetry*)
    e (wrong subject/verb agreement in *poetry are*)
    f (wrong spelling *faverite*), e (uncountable noun with no plural from *literatures*)
3   d (incorrect linking structure in *I read that book the reason is*)
    f (wrong spelling *recomended*)
4   c (no colon needed)
    a (inappropriate use of colloquialism *a load of rubbish*)
5   f (repetition of linkers *and*, *and then* and *then*)
    c (far too long a sentence)
6   f (incorrectly used and spelt adjective *tragic* where noun needed; either misuse of noun *comic* – a children's magazine with strip cartoons in – or misuse of adjective *comic*)

   • Ask the pairs to add these types of mistakes to the appropriate sections of the checklist, with any more they can think of.

Suggested answers (additional types of error)

a   *Layout and appropriacy*
    Is the handwriting neat and legible?
b   *Paragraphs*
    Is the sequence within the paragraph clearly marked and constructed?
c   *Punctuation*
    Have colons and other punctuation marks been used correctly?
d   *Linkers*
    Has a variety of (time) linkers been used?
e   *Grammar*
    Have (countable and) uncountable nouns i.e. singular and plural been used correctly?
f   *Vocabulary*
    Has the right part of speech/type of word been used?

   • Bring the class together and list all the types of mistakes they have thought of on the board. Add any more if they arise.

C   • Explain the task. Students should first find the errors in the essay, checking with each other that they have found them all. Then they can re-write it correctly.

Suggested answer

Jon Elkon has written two novels and he is working on a third. He comes from South Africa and he describes the novel as 'a new lie', and contrasts fiction with 'faction', which is based on people who really exist. The characters in Elkon's novels are loosely based on real people, but they are changed to fit in with the book. For instance, they might have different colour hair or different ideas.

According to Elkon, best-selling novels are written to a formula, the most important part of which is empathy, so that the reader knows how the character will feel in certain situations. People love escapism and the most successful bestsellers are the ones which allow people to escape to a place they really want to escape to. Successful novels often fulfill people's fantasies. For example, a typical plot is one in which a female character loses the man of her dreams, then regains him and ends up rich.

Elkon predicts that in the near future we are going to see the computer novel. The computer novel will appear on a computer screen with sounds and possibly also with pictures. But he believes the traditional book will always have a market because it has a special relationship with the reader. When you read a book, you are alone with the author and the fantasy, and there will always be people who want to do that.

Jon Elkon doesn't believe that a novelist has a duty to investigate social or political issues. He does not think novelists are a force to change society. Politics always comes into a novel because it is part of life, but novelists should never preach.

Language work

10 Forms of adjectives and adverbs

A   • With a weak class you should go through the questions with the students. With a strong class students can study the extracts and answer the questions in pairs.
   • If students find it difficult to answer the questions, refer them to the Grammar Reference section at the back of the Students' Book.

Answers

1   a adjective   b adverb   c adverb
2   a *High* is used as an adjective describing the noun *standard*; it means *a good* or *superior standard*.
    b *Highly* is an adverb describing the adjective *imaginative*; it means *extremely* or *very imaginative*.
    c *High* is an adverb describing the verb *aim*; here it means *aiming at a high level* or *standard*.
3   The usual form of an adverb is a word ending in *-ly*.
4   *slowly* adverb *Old people walk slowly.*
    lovely adjective *What a lovely dress.*
    pretty adjective *She's a pretty child.*
    pretty adverb *It's pretty expensive, I'm afraid.*
    early adjective *I'm catching the early train.*
    early adverb *He arrived early.*
    fast adjective *She drives a fast car.*
    fast adverb *Sprinters can run fast.*

   • Ask students to tell you any more adverbs they know which look like adjectives and write them on the board. If necessary, elicit those below.
    close   dead   direct   fine   hard   high   just   late   long   low   pretty   short   short   slow   wide   wrong
   • Point out that there are several adverbs which have two forms and a difference in meaning, such as *high* and *highly* in the introductory example in section A of the exercise.

Elicit some more examples and write them on the board.
*fine   finely   hard   hardly   just   justly   late
lately*

B Students may need to use a dictionary for this task.
1 highly; high   2 free; widely   3 direct
4 most; mostly   5 short   6 late   7 close
8 wrongly   9 fine   10 justly

Further practice: Workbook Unit 16, Exercise 8.

Pronunciation

11 Rhythm and stress in poetry

A ● Discuss the introductory questions and encourage the
students to talk about their views on poetry.
● Elicit the main differences between poetry and other forms
of literature and write these on the board.
1 Poetry is meant to be spoken and listened to, not read.
2 Poetry often uses literary devices such as metaphors and
personification.
3 Poetry often uses special stress patterns and rhyming
sequences.
● Students read the poem and answer the questions.

Answers
1 The poem tells a story of a young girl. She is not
conventionally attractive, but when she smiled at the
writer she appeared beautiful in his eyes, and he thought
she might love him. Now she has rejected the writer, but
even when she frowns she seems, to him, to be more
attractive than other girls.
2 She is not beautiful.
3 It is usually spelt *never*.
4 Metaphors: *her eye was ... a well of love, a spring of light.*
Personification: *her looks are coy and cold.*

B ● Read through the instructions and ask the students to
complete the rhyming sequence and syllables.

Answer
She is not fair to outward view   A (8 syllables)
As many maidens be;   B (6 syllables)
Her loveliness I never knew   A (8 syllables)
Until she smiled on me.   B (6 syllables)
O then I saw her eye was bright,   C (8 syllables)
A well of love, a spring of light.   C (8 syllables)

But now her looks are coy and cold,   A (8 syllables)
To mine they ne'er reply,   B (6 syllables)
And yet I cease not to behold   A (8 syllables)
The love-light in her eye: B (6 syllables)
Her very frowns are fairer far   C (8 syllables)
Than smiles of other maidens are.   C (8 syllables)

● Ask students to discuss the construction of the poem and
predict how it should be spoken. They should notice that it
is constructed with a regular pattern of syllables and
stresses. It should therefore be spoken with a very regular
rhythm.
● If students are unsure about how the lines should be
spoken they can turn to the marked-up example on page
161 of the Students' Book.
● Ask students to try reading the poem aloud to a partner or
to the whole class.

C ● Play the poem on tape so that the students can compare
the actor's interpretation of the rhythm with their version.
● Students should try to reproduce the rhythm and stress
pattern from the tape. They should practice reading it
aloud to a partner.

Speaking skills

12 Reciting poetry

A ● Ask the students to read the first four lines of the poem.
They should notice that the rhythm is very regular, similar
to that of the previous poem.
● The students should notice that each pair of lines rhymes.
Point out that this is known as rhyming couplets and that
the whole poem is constructed in this way.

B ● Explain the task and divide the class into groups of three to
complete the activity.

Answer
(The completed poem is on page 162 of the Students' Book.)

C ● Students can check their answers and then practise reading
the poem.

Final activity

13 The literature game

Note: This game is based on *Noughts and Crosses* (*Tic-tac-toe*
in American English). Most students are familiar with this
game, the difference here is that each box contains a question
which must be answered. The first game is suitable for most
students. The second game is more challenging and may be
more suitable for students studying in the UK or those students
with a good knowledge of literature. It can also be used as a
lesson 'filler'.

● Draw this grid on the board and write the key alongside.
Each box in the grid has a question. (See below).

	A	B	C	D	E
1					
2					
3					
4					
5					

A International Literature
B British Writers
C Quotations
D American Literature
E Famous Characters from
Literature

● Divide the class into two equally sized teams, the Noughts
(represented by 0) and the Crosses (represented by X).
Appoint a captain for each team, who will be responsible
for calling out the answers once he/she has conferred with
the rest of the team.
● Explain that the aim of each team should be to make a
horizontal, vertical or diagonal line of their symbols across
the board.
● Read the following and explain the rules to the class in your
own words.

Playing the Game
● Toss a coin to decide which team starts.
● Teams take it in turns to choose boxes.
● The team calls out the number of a box. (e.g. A1). Read out
the question to the class. If the team answers correctly, put
their symbol in the box. If they answer incorrectly, allow the
other team to try and answer. If they succeed, put their
symbol in the box instead. If neither team answers
correctly, draw a question mark in the box to indicate that
it has already been 'played'.
● Then ask the other team to choose a box and repeat the
process either until one team successfully completes a line
OR all the questions have been answered. If neither team

manages to complete a line the winner is the team with the most symbols on the grid at the end.

THE LITERATURE GAME: GAME 1

A International Literature

1 Who wrote *Don Quixote*?   Miguel de Cervantes
2 What nationality was Victor Hugo?   French
3 Which war was *War and Peace* about?   Napoleonic War against Russia
4 Who wrote *The Iliad* and *The Odyssey*?   Homer
5 Which European playright became president of his own country?   Vaclev Havel

B British Writers

1 What was Dickens' first name?   Charles
2 Who wrote *The Importance of Being Earnest*?   Oscar Wilde
3 Why is Ian Fleming famous?   He wrote the James Bond books
4 What was the surname of three sisters named Anne, Emily and Charlotte, who were all famous novelists?   Brontë
5 In which country is Shakespeare's *Macbeth* set?   Scotland

C Quotations

1 Finish this line from *Hamlet*: *To be or not to be, that ...*   ... is the question.
2 How does the title of this famous science fiction book end? *2001, A Space ...*   2001, A Space Odyssey
3 In which fairy story does a witch say, 'Mirror, mirror, on the wall, who is the fairest of them all?'   Snow White
4 What number is missing in the title of this book by Gabriel Garcia Marquez: *... Years of Solitude* (*... años de Soledad*)?   One hundred
5 Complete this quotation from Oscar Wilde: *The only thing worse than being talked about is ...*   ... not being talked about.

D American Literature

1 Which famous film star was married to the author Arthur Miller?   Marilyn Monroe
2 Who or what was Moby Dick?   It was a whale.
3 What was the name of the bestselling novel about the American Civil War which was made into one of Hollywood's most famous films?   Gone With the Wind
4 What famous scandal did the writers Woodward and Bernstein discover in Washington in the 1970s?   Watergate
5 What was the name of the famous book about the Mafia written by Mario Puzo which was made into a film with the same name starring Al Pacino and Marlon Brando?   The Godfather

E Famous characters in literature

1 Which country was Hamlet a prince of?   Denmark
2 What character was shipwrecked on an island in a book of the same name by Robert Louis Stevenson?   Robinson Crusoe
3 What was the name of the scientist who made a monster from parts of dead bodies in a book which has been filmed many times?   Baron Frankenstein
4 What was the name of the English boy in a book by J M Barrie who learnt how to fly and went to Never Never land with a fairy called Tinkerbell?   Peter Pan
5 Who did the Roman Mark Antony fall in love with in a famous play by Shakespeare?   Cleopatra

THE LITERATURE GAME: GAME 2

A International Literature

1 What moral philosophy did Jean-Paul Sartre expound?   Existentialism
2 Who wrote *The Brothers Karamazov*?   Dostoyevsky
3 Which French woman wrote *The Second Sex*?   Simone de Beauvoir
4 What seven-volume masterpiece by Marcel Proust is about memory?   *A La Recherche du Temps Perdu*
5 Of which country is Luis de Camoes the national poet?   Portugal

B British Writers

1 To which country did E M Forster take 'a passage'?   India
2 To aid which nation's struggle for independence did Lord Byron fight and die?   Greece
3 Who wrote *A Room of One's Own*?   Virginia Woolf
4 Which novel by Charles Dickens is set during the French Revolution?   *A Tale of Two Cities*
5 Who wrote *The Canterbury Tales*?   Geoffrey Chaucer

C Quotations

1 Who said, 'Veni vidi vici'?   Julius Caesar
2 Finish this quote by President Franklin D. Roosevelt: *The only thing we have to fear is...*   ... fear itself
3 Complete the following quote by Jean-Jacques Rousseau: *Man was born free and everywhere he ...*   ... is in chains.
4 Who said, 'From each according to his abilities, to each according to his needs'?   Karl Marx
5 Which Shakespearean character says the line 'Is this a dagger I see before me?'   Macbeth

D American Literature

1 In which novel did F Scott Fitzgerald depict the fragility of the American Dream?   The Great Gatsby
2 Which city is the setting of *The Bonfire of the Vanities*?   New York
3 Who wrote the Declaration of Independence?   Thomas Jefferson
4 Who wrote *The Colour Purple*?   Alice Walker
5 Complete the title of this novel by Ernest Hemingway: *The Old Man and ...*   ... the Sea

E Famous characters in literature

1 Who was *The Once and Future King* in the book of the same name by T H White?   King Arthur
2 Who was Sherlock Holmes' assistant?   Dr Watson
3 Who did Tom Sawyer meet rafting down the Mississippi river in the book by Mark Twain?   Huckleberry Finn
4 Which Belgian detective was invented by Agatha Christie?   Hercule Poirot
5 Which mythological Greek king turned everything he touched into gold?   King Midas

Unit summary

Themes	Popular culture: fashion; pop music; humour
Structures	Order of adjectives; introductory/impersonal *it*
Vocabulary	Fashion; fabrics; patterns and colours; vocabulary of clothing (in Workbook); idioms of fashion/lifestyles (in Workbook)
Skills	*Reading:* identifying supporting statements
	Listening: predicting and checking information
	Speaking: telling jokes
	Writing: writing a song review

Teaching notes

Introduction

1
- Use the pictures of magazines and the questions to introduce the theme of popular culture. Elicit that popular culture includes such things as pop music, fashion, theatre, films and television, humour and magazines.
- Divide the class into groups of four and nominate Students A, B, C and D in each group. (If you have an odd number in the class, one or two groups can have two Student Ds.)
- Read through the introduction to the quiz, pointing out that students must only exchange information orally, and explain to the class that the winner will be the group which finishes the quiz correctly first.

Answers
1 Abba   2 Jean Paul Gaultier   3 Pedro Almodovar
4 Woody Allen   5 *Dallas*   6 U2   7 Calvin Klein
8 *The Wall*   9 *The Cosby Show*   10 Bryan Adams
11 *Monty Python's Flying Circus*   12 *Star Trek*
13 Madonna   14 The Sex Pistols   15 Gerard Depardieu
16 Arnold Schwarzenegger   17 Bette Midler
18 Phil Collins   19 Steven Spielberg   20 Reebok
Incorrect names: Luciano Pavarotti, Guns'n'Roses, Yves Saint Laurent, *Twin Peaks*

2
- Use the photograph and the questions to introduce the topic of fashion and fashion magazines/journalism. Ask the students to name any magazines in which they read about fashion and suggest reasons why fashion is such a popular subject with many people.
- Read the introduction to the short fashion article and explain the chart completion task.
- Pre-teach the following:
   couture (as in *haute couture*) high fashion, i.e. fashioning of exclusive clothes for wealthy clients by top designers
   yuppies young urban professionals (a term created by British and American journalists to describe the young British businessmen and women who made money in the economic boom of the 1980s; often used perjoratively to describe young people whose desire to make money outweighs other values or interests)

Answers

	WOMEN		MEN	
	in fashion	out of fashion	in fashion	out of fashion
shapes	curvaceous line, tight-waisted	boxy shoulder-padded shape	figure-hugging, narrow shoulders	box jacket
colours	pastels, brown and mustard	primary colours	ochre and fawn	blues and grey

- Students should discuss the follow-up questions in small groups and report back to class.

Reading skills

3 Identifying supporting statements

A Ask students how much popular culture influences their lives – the clothes they buy, the films they see, the music they listen to etc.
- Discuss whether this influence is positive or negative.
- Explain the reading task.

Answers
1 *Looking at a representative sample in any street I can see a uniform just as anonymous as the green jacket of the Chinese peasants; it is the uniform of fashion.* (para. 2)
Ask teenagers what music they listen to or which TV shows or movies they watch and you will hear much the same short list of whatever is 'in' that month. Yet each and every one of them believes that he or she is a true individual. (para. 3)
2 *The individuality which we think we are expressing through our choice of clothes, music and entertainment is in reality a way of conforming to the fashions which are dictated to us by the small group of people who control the media and manufacturing companies.* (para. 4)
3 *Teenagers are the most willing victims of all. Go to any youth club or discotheque in Britain or the United States and you will see an army of blue jeans, trainers, sweat shirts and baseball caps. Ask teenagers what music they listen to or which TV shows or movies they watch and you will hear much the same short list of whatever is 'in' that month.* (para. 3)
4 *When we buy a new pair of jeans we think we are exercising an individual choice, but we are subconsciously aware that this year straight legs are in and flares are out, this year black is fashionable but yellow is not; and so our choice is not free at all, because nobody wants to look ridiculous by wearing something which is 'out-of-fashion'.* (para. 3)
5 *Fashion, music, TV, newspapers, movies ... all have one thing in common – the message that to be fashionable we must buy things. A record by a new group, a new style of jacket, a new video, a new magazine. Every time something goes out of fashion and something new comes in it is time to get out the credit cards and cheque book.* (para. 4)

B
- Students work in pairs to discuss the writer's points. Each pair should think of further examples for the points they

agree with.
- If students do not agree with the writer they should think of counter arguments.
- Pairs report back to class to compare their opinions and further points or counter arguments.
- If students find the topic stimulating you may wish to expand the exercise into a whole class discussion on the influence of popular consumer culture.

Vocabulary

4   Fashion: fabrics, patterns and colours

A   • Students use words from the short fashion article to complete the word maps.

Answers

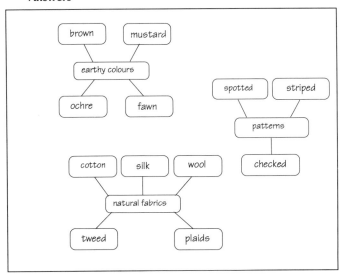

- Ask students if they can think of any further words to add to the word maps.
- Students use words from the maps (and any other words they can think of) to describe the photograph on page 125.

Suggested answer
The man is wearing a brown tweed suit, a striped shirt and a spotted tie. He is carrying a dark, rolled umbrella.

B   • Students should complete the vocabulary matching task and then compare their answers with a partner.

Answers
1   totalitarian regimes   2   pundits   3   grey-clad
4   much-vaunted   5   coined the phrase
6   regardless of   7   trainers   8   flares
9   ridiculous   10   conforming

Language work

5   Order of adjectives

A   • Point out that between them the extracts contain all the types of adjectives students are likely to encounter.
- Students should complete the list with all the adjectives from the extracts.

Answers
1   Quantity or determiner: *a range   several*
2   Origin: *Victorian   Scottish*
3   Opinion: *nostalgic   traditional   old-fashioned*
4   Colour: *pastel   brown and mustard   dark*
5   Material: *silk   tweed   wool*

6   Size: *large*
7   Shape: *tight-waisted   pointed*
8   Age: *1950s*
9   Defining adjective/noun: *riding*
10   Noun: *suits   outfits   suits   lapels*

- Explain that by cross-referencing the adjectives in the list with their relative positions in the extracts they will be able to work out the sequence and transfer this to the diagram at the bottom of the page.

Answers
A   Opinion   B   Size   C   Age   D   Shape   E   Colour
F   Origin   G   Material

- Students should use the words given to describe the picture on page 125.

Answer
An elegant new dark brown English tweed suit.

B   • Elicit from the students that sentences **b** and **c** sound more natural than sentence **a**. Elicit that sentence **a** has too many adjectives following each other to sound natural.
- Explain that it is unusual to find more than two or three adjectives together in one sentence. In English it is more usual to give the information in additional clauses (as in sentences **b** and **c**) or in additional sentences.
- Explain the re-writing task.

Answers
Theoretically correct order
1   A range of inexpensive, tight-fitting, dark blue American cotton jeans.
2   Some unattractive, large, old grey polyester bedspreads.
3   Stephen's expensive, new, black Japanese Yamaha motorbike.
More natural order
1   A range of inexpensive, tight-fitting American jeans in dark blue cotton.
2   Some unattractive old bedspreads in grey polyester.
3   Stephen's expensive, new, black Yamaha motorbike from Japan.

C   • Each student should look around the classroom and choose an item of clothing. Ask each student in turn to describe the item they have chosen using at least three or four adjectives. The rest of the class guess which item is being described and call out the name of its owner.

Further practice: Workbook Unit 17, Exercise 6.

Language work

6   Impersonal/Introductory *it*

A   **Note:** The use of introductory *it* (as one of a number of passive constructions) is previewed in Unit 6 Exercise 9.

- Ask students to study the extract and elicit answers to the questions.

Answers
… *it was said*… means *some people* (we don't know exactly who) *said*.
The passive has been used because we don't know who said this. It was a general view rather than something said by a specific person.
The first *it* has a purely grammatical purpose (it acts as a 'preparatory subject') whereas the second *its* is a possessive adjective used in conjunction with *respect* but referring back to *the free world*.

- Explain that the first underlined example is known as an

introductory *it* construction and is used where the subject of a sentence is an infinitive or *that* clause.

B ● Ask students to re-write the underlined phrases. Point out that they should use the same tense as the original phrase.

Answers
1 It is often said ...
2 It has been said ...
3 It was announced ...
4 It has been claimed ...
5 It is argued ...

● Write the following sentence on the board:
Many Americans say that New York is the most exciting city in the world.
● Ask the students to re-write the sentence using an introductory *it* construction. Elicit this sentence and put it on the board.
It is said in America that New York is the most exciting city in the world / In America it is said that ...
● Now ask the students to write similar sentences about views in their countries.

C ● Elicit that the two sentences, while grammatically correct, are rather unusual in spoken English. They are more appropriate for formal written English.
● Ask the students to re-write the sentences using an introductory *it* construction and elicit the following.
It is a commonly held belief that fashion is an effective way to express one's individuality.
It can be extremely expensive to follow fashion slavishly.
● Students complete the sentence transformation task.

Answers
1 It is more entertaining to watch movies than to read books.
2 It is the article's conclusion that fashion is a conspiracy by big business.
3 It is an inescapable fact that pop music is an important influence on young people.
4 It is of crucial importance to understand the mass media in today's society.
5 It is a sad fact of modern life that more people watch a single episode of Dallas than have ever seen a Shakespeare play.

Note: Students will find further uses of introductory *it* constructions described in the Grammar Reference section at the back of the Student's Book.

Further practice: Workbook Unit 17, Exercise 9.

Listening skills

7 Predicting and checking information

● Read through the introduction and the pre-questions.
● Ask students to match two of the artists in the list with their photographs in the collage. Illustrated are Eric Clapton and Bryan Adams. If you and your students wish, they can identify other stars illustrated such as Paul McCartney, The Beatles, Mick Jagger, Frank Sinatra and Elton John.
● In pairs, students predict the order of popularity and number the songs 1 – 10.
● Play the tape for students to check their predictions, write in the correct order and the dates of release.
● Students check their answers with their partner.

Answers

	Song title	Artist	Date
5	*Against All Odds*	Phil Collins	1984
3	*Bohemian Rhapsody*	Queen	1975
2	*Careless Whisper*	George Michael	1984
1	*(Everything I do) I do it for you*	Bryan Adams	1991
8	*One of these nights*	Eagles	1975
4	*Stairway to Heaven*	Led Zeppelin	1971
9	*The Boys of Summer*	Don Henley	1985
10	*True*	Spandau Ballet	1983
6	*Unchained Melody*	Righteous Brothers	1966
7	*Wonderful Tonight*	Eric Clapton	1977

Tapescript
... and so here it is, the Capital Radio all time Hall of Fame, and we're down to the last 10 songs starting off with, at number 10 Spandau Ballet's '83 hit *True*, from 1985 Don Henley's *The Boys of Summer* at 9. The Eagles get in at number 8 with *One of These Nights* from '75, and another oldie from '77, Eric Clapton's *Wonderful Tonight* is in at 7. At number 6 is the oldest song in the top ten, from 1965 The Righteous Brothers and *Unchained Melody*. Multi-talented Phil Collins' song from the '84 film *Against All Odds* is at 5 and Led Zeppelin's classic heavy metal anthem from '71, *Stairway to Heaven* is in at number 4. Queen's operatic *Bohemian Rhapsody* from 1975 comes in at 3 and number 2 is the tear-jerking *Careless Whisper*, a hit for George Michael in '84. So, here it is, the all-time greatest pop song according to your votes, already immortalised by its record-breaking 16 weeks at number 1 in the British charts back in 1991, Bryan Adams and *Everything I do, I do it for you*, the theme from the movie *Robin Hood, Prince of Thieves* and ...*(fade out)*

Writing skills

8 Writing a song review

Note: This is the second review writing task in *Distinction*. In Exercise B, students compare the song review with the film review in Unit 11.

A ● Students should read the song review and complete the labelling task.

Answer

BRYAN ADAMS
(Everything I do) I do it for you   (single)

Originally written as the theme song for the film 'Robin Hood, Prince of Thieves', *(Everything I do) I do it for you* was recorded by Bryan Adams in 1991. It was an immediate success and became the best-selling single in the British charts for a record-breaking sixteen weeks, longer than any other song since the chart began. Although the lyrics are simple and similar to many other love songs, the song has a powerful emotional impact because of its extremely strong melody and the haunting quality of Bryan Adams' singing. The song has a classic structure with three verses and a chorus which is repeated after each verse.

The production is extremely clever as the song gradually builds up from a slow and quiet beginning, getting louder and faster with the introduction of more instruments, as Bryan Adams' voice gets higher and more strained. As a clever touch, at the end the instruments die away and the last line is sung slowly and quietly, fading into silence.

Although it is a traditional ballad with little new to offer in lyrics or instrumentation, it is a masterpiece of its kind: melodic, emotionally sung and beautifully produced.

b, f, d, f, e, c, a

- Elicit that the background information is used as the introduction and the reviewer's overall opinion is used as the conclusion.

B
- Ask students to turn to page 84 (Unit 11 Exercise 6) and to compare the song review with the film review.
- Elicit the following:
  Similarities
  Both reviews include some background information (dates and origin), comments on performance (the actors' and the singer's), the structure and the reviewer's opinion.
  Both reviews use the present tense to describe the film/song.
  Both reviews use a lot of adjectives.
  Differences
  The film review concentrates on the plot of the film.
  The song review describes the production.
  The film review mentions other opinions apart from the reviewer's.

- Ask the students to suggest reasons for the differences. For example, films have a plot but songs do not.

C
- Explain the task to the students. They can choose any song they like but they should follow the style and include the same categories of information as the model.
- Students should use the headings a – f to write notes about their chosen song. Students who choose the same song can work together in pairs or small groups.
- The final review can be written up as homework.

Speaking skills

9 Telling jokes

Note: Humour is notoriously difficult to appreciate in a foreign language and is often culturally specific. Point this out to your students and explain that they should not feel disappointed if they do not find the cartoons and jokes in this section amusing.

A
- Ask the students to look at the two cartoons on the left. Encourage them to explain why the cartoons are funny. If necessary, point out that a slimmer is a person who feels fat and deliberately tries to lose weight by dieting.
- Point out that this type of humour (laughing at other people's misfortunes) is called *Black humour* in English.

B Ask students to look at the two pictures on the right and predict the jokes they illustrate.

C Ask the students to listen to the tape and match two of the jokes they will hear with the pictures.

Answers
Joke F: top picture
Joke D: bottom picture

- Now play the tape again and ask the students to answer questions 1 and 2. Check that they understand the meaning of *stereotype* (a fixed and often false image or belief, usually referring to a particular group of people).

Answers
1 Jokes C (change) and G (pull yourself together)
2 Jokes B (psychiatrists) and F (accountants)

- Now ask the students to explain the puns and the stereotypes. Play the tape again if necessary.

Answers
Puns
C The phrase *No change* means that his condition is the same as before; it also refers to a machine which you put money

in but will not give you any back if you put in too much (e.g. £1 for a 75p charge).
G The phrase *pull yourself together* means *stop being silly*; it also refers to closing/pulling a pair of curtains.
Stereotypes
B The stereotype is that psychiatrists never make people do things they don't want to do.
F The stereotype is that accountants are very mean with money.

Tapescript
A After a long course of psychiatric treatment the patient was cured. 'Well,' said the psychiatrist, 'Your life's in front of you now. What are you going to do with it?'
'Well,' said the patient, 'I've got high academic qualifications, so I can really take my pick of jobs. I might try the law, politics, advertising, public relations, management, broadcasting, writing maybe. On the other hand I might go back to being a teapot.'
B How many psychiatrists does it take to change a light bulb? – Only one. But the light bulb really has to want to be changed.
C 'Doctor, Doctor, my son's just swallowed seventeen and a half pence.'
'How is he?'
'No change yet.'
D Two fortune tellers met on the sea-front.
'Ah,' said one, 'Lovely day, isn't it?'
'Yes,' said the other. 'Reminds me of the summer of 2036.'
E There was a man sitting in a railway compartment and he kept snapping his fingers. Snap, snap, snap, with monotonous regularity. It was getting on everyone's nerves and eventually the man opposite could not keep quiet any longer.
'Look, do you have to keep snapping your fingers?'
'Oh, yes,' said the man, 'it keeps the tigers away.'
'But really,' blustered the irate commuter, 'there aren't any tigers in England!'
'See,' said the man, 'it works!'
F An accountant and his wife were shipwrecked on a desert island. After a week their clothes were torn to shreds, their provisions had run out and they were exhausted. 'Oh, Jeremy,' said the wife, 'Things just couldn't be worse.'
'Oh, but they could,' said Jeremy. 'We might have bought return tickets!'
G 'Doctor, Doctor, I feel like a pair of curtains.'
'Oh, pull yourself together, man.'

D
- Read through the introduction and the two jokes. Point out that *Pete* is the abbreviation for Peter, and *Doug* is the abbreviation for Douglas, both common English names.
- Explain that the puns are based on the fact that the two names are homophones and point out that the pronunciation of the two names is Pete /piːt/ and Doug /dʌg/.
- Students may need to use dictionaries which include phonetic transcriptions in order to work out the puns.
- Elicit the following explanation:
  Pete sounds like *peat*, plant material which has been buried in the ground for many years and decomposes
  Doug sounds like *dug*, the past tense of *dig*, meaning to work the ground with a spade
- Ask students if they can make puns in their language(s) and elicit examples.
- Focus attention on the cartoon of the British airforce and ask the class to explain the stereotype.

Answer

The stereotype is that the British always refuse to accept unpleasant realities and have an over-optimistic, 'stiff upper lip' approach to problems, however ridiculous the results.

● Elicit any other stereotypes of the British which students are aware of.
● Students discuss stereotypes used in their country.

Note: You may wish to use this opportunity to discuss the role of stereotyping more generally. Students often find this a fascinating subject to discuss.

● Before going on to the next section you may wish to put the following vocabulary chart on the board.

NOUN	ADJECTIVE	VERB
stereotype	stereotypical	stereotype
satire/satirist	satirical	satirise
sarcasm	sarcastic	–
irony	ironic	–

Note: A *satirist* writes satirical comedy.

● Discuss these other forms of humour with the students. Elicit the following explanations and further examples.
Satire humour which ridicules something by presenting it in an extreme form, often referring to social groups or politics. (Jokes B, F and airforce cartoon)
Sarcasm humour which is bitter and intended to hurt someone's feelings. (Note the well-known English saying *Sarcasm is the lowest form of wit.*)
Irony humour based on saying the opposite of what one actually means.
Strange unexpected logic humour based on something which appears logical but is not, or vice versa. (Jokes D and E)

10 ● Play the 'knock knock' joke on the tape and elicit answers to the questions.

Answer

The joke is based on a pun: the word *May* is both a woman's name and a modal verb.

● Explain that this type of joke always follows a set sequence and makes use of the fact that many English names sound like other words or parts of words/phrases (although the spelling may, of course, be different).
● Divide students into pairs to practise making jokes using the prompts. Go through the first one as an example:
  A Knock, knock.
  B Who's there?
  C Ivor.
  B Ivor who?
  A I've a present for you.
● Monitor the pairs and check that they have learnt the standard sequence.
● Ask the pairs to make 'knock knock' jokes using the name prompts. They should try to work these out themselves. If they are stuck they can turn to the clues on page 162 of the Students' Book.

Answers

ANN And what makes you think I want to come in?
CARRIE Carry my bags in please.
SHIRLEY Surely you're not serious?
HAROLD How old are you?
ISABEL Is a bell better than knocking?

● Ask students if they can make 'knock knock' jokes in their language(s) and elicit examples.

Tapescript
A Knock, Knock.
B Who's there?
A May.
B May who?
A May I come in?

Final task

11 The popularity questionnaire

● Explain that the purpose of the questionnaire is to find out the different preferences of the class.
● Students should work in pairs. Each member of the pair should make a copy of the blank questionnaire on a piece of paper. There should be half as many horizontal lines as there are students in the class. In other words, if there are 20 students in the class each member of the pair should have 10 lines.
● Each pair chooses five categories from the list and writes these into the boxes 1 – 5 at the top of the chart.

Note: The questionnaire will be more interesting if you encourage different pairs to choose different categories.

● Pairs then fill in the first line with their prediction of what will be most popular in each of their categories.
● Pairs take their questionnaires around the class, asking their classmates for their preferences and filling in the lines. (Each partner interviews half the class.)

Model questionnaire

POPULARITY QUESTIONNAIRE *Who/What is your favourite...?*					
names	categories				
	1 Pop song	2 Film	3 Musician	4 Comedian	5 TV show
us	Yesterday	Sound of Music	Bruce Springsteen	Woody Allen	Miami Vice
Maria	Bohemian Rhapsody	Home Alone II	Richard Clayderman	Eddie Murphy	Baywatch
Jan	Against all odds	Jagged Edge	Eric Clapton	Woody Allen	Star Trek

● When they have finished partners combine their results and work out the most popular choice in each category.
● Pairs present their results to the class.

Unit 18   The Art of Selling

Unit summary

Themes	Advertising; brand names; selling techniques
Structures	Participles in adverbial clauses, concessive clauses
Vocabulary	Buying and selling; the language of advertising (in Workbook); multi-word verbs with particle *on* (in Workbook)
Skills	*Reading*: finding evidence for an argument; skimming and matching *Listening*: listening to check information *Speaking*: false starts *Writing*: writing a discursive essay
Pronunciation	Linking sounds

Teaching notes

Introduction

1
- Ask the students to describe the photographs and use them to illustrate the idea that things which were luxuries in the past are now regarded as essential.
- Elicit further examples which illustrate the saying, for example washing machines, televisions and refrigerators.
- Divide the class into pairs to complete the first two columns of the chart.
- Ask pairs to compare their answers and think of a definition of luxury and necessity.

Suggested answers
luxury something that is nice to have but is not essential
necessity something that is essential

2
- Ask students how many of the names they recognise and elicit the descriptions of the products which the companies make.

Suggested answers
Kellogg's breakfast cereals
Nescafé instant coffee
BMW motor cars
Volvo cars
Philips electrical and electronic goods
Cadbury's chocolate
Levi Strauss & Co jeans

- Ask the students to explain why they recognise the names and know about the products. Elicit factors such as advertising.
- Elicit a list of reasons why people choose particular brands or makes of product and write a list on the board.
  You saw an advertisement.
  It was good value for money.
  You usually buy this brand.
  It was the cheapest.
  You tried it and it suits you.
- Now students complete the rest of the chart by interviewing their partners.
- When the charts have been completed, students compare their results in small groups, working out the most influential reasons for buying particular products amongst

their group.
- Groups report back their results to the class.

Listening skills

3   Listening to check information

A
- Read through the introduction and explain the task. Let the students read through the explanations before you play the tape but do not answer any questions about the vocabulary.
- Play section A of the recording.

Answers (corrections are in italics)

market research	finding out what people want	✔
focus groups	people on street corners with clipboards *people in rooms with specific aspects to them*	✘
empty nesters	children who have left home *parents whose children have left home*	✘
segmentation	establishing particular groups of people who want particular things	✔
niche	a defined segment of products *a defined segment of consumers*	✘
brand name	a badge or trademark	✔
brand	a brand name which has added value because it costs more *a brand name which has added intangible emotional or imaginary value caused by advertising*	✘
media planning and buying	establishing which media are read by, listened to or watched by minorities *establishing which media are read by, listened to or watched by sub groups of the population*	✘
position a product	find out how a product fits into people's lives and place it relative to other products they are already using	✔

Tapescript (Section A)
INTERVIEWER Hamish, what is the purpose of advertising?
HAMISH PRINGLE I think it's to sell things.
INTERVIEWER Just to sell things?
HAMISH PRINGLE I think it is really. There's a lot of chat about advertising by commentators, people in the business, which indicates that some of them may be a little bit embarrassed about the true nature of it; obviously I'm expressing a personal opinion but I think it is about selling things – I'm using 'selling things' in a fairly broad sense because obviously I could be selling a packet of these or I could be selling an idea, I could be selling a service. But I think we are in the business of trying to persuade people about things.
INTERVIEWER That word *persuade*, er trying to persuade people to buy things – are there any special techniques or methods that you can use to achieve that?

HAMISH PRINGLE   I think ... I think there are. I think if you ... if you accept that advertising is a form of salesmanship then I think that most of the techniques of advertising are essentially based on selling techniques. Um, often salesmanship is as much to do with finding out what people want and then presenting it to them as it is about just saying 'buy this!'

INTERVIEWER   Right. So how ... how do you go about finding out what people want?

HAMISH PRINGLE   Well there's a huge industry, a huge (*laughs*) invisible, or maybe not so invisible industry dedicated to doing exactly that – the market research industry: people on street corners with clipboards, people in rooms conducting group discussions or focus groups as they're called in the States. Er, where you would recruit eight individuals perhaps, with quite specific aspects to them in terms of age, class, perhaps occupation, perhaps buying behaviour ... um ... you know, young people who may be in the early stages of a home ... household formation are going to be very different sorts of people and are going to be wanting to buy very different sorts of things than older people who may ... who may be empty nesters, that's to say their children have left home and they are now thinking about going off on CarriBbean cruises, not about buying a fridge.

INTERVIEWER   So do you mean that advertising nowadays is very much aimed at a particular segment or group of people rather than at the population as a whole?

HAMISH PRINGLE   I think increasingly so. More and more of our work is ... is to do with segmentation – to do with establishing particular groups of people who want particular things. Trying to establish brands or services in niches where what the brand or the service is offering is in a way a reflection of the needs of that defined niche or segment of... of consumers.

INTERVIEWER   You just mentioned there *brands*, er this is a key word I think in ... in advertising and marketing. What is the purpose of a brand name?

HAMISH PRINGLE   A brand name, well, I think that there is a difference between brands and brand names. Um, lots of people have brand names but not necessarily do they all have brands. Er, brand names are clearly trade marks or dis ... or yes ... trademarks or badges for a particular product or service, they can be very valuable and very powerful. Um, so you ... anybody can have a brand name, um, I've got ... there's a brand name sitting here, isn't there – Abbey Well mineral water. Now have you ever heard of an ... Abbey Well before?

INTERVIEWER   No.

HAMISH PRINGLE   Well, nor have I. So I think although they have a brand name they don't have a brand and I think a brand is probably the difference between the product facts/the product reality and added values, almost emotional or imaginary values which have somehow been added to a brand by advertising and other promotional devices. So it's the kind of intangible value that's on something which will make you pay more for a bottle of Perrier than an exactly similar bottle of Abbey Well.

INTERVIEWER   How do you reach a particular group of consumers?

HAMISH PRINGLE   Well, assuming for the moment that we've established who they are, and where they are then that's another whole industry which is called media planning and buying, where, er, people are, er, devoting huge efforts and energies to establishing which media are actually read by, listened to or watched by particular sub-groups of the population – the sort of people that might watch in this country Channel 4, which is a minority commercial television station, the sort of people who are going to watch American football at 11 o'clock at night having come back from the pub, are clearly very different from the sort of people who might be watching *Neighbours* in the afternoon.

INTERVIEWER   Right, so presuming now that you've, um, found the group of people that you want to appeal to and the product that you think they want. Now how are you actually going to persuade them to buy that product or service?

HAMISH PRINGLE   I think again most of our effort goes into trying to establish how this product might fit into their lives, what role can it play in their lives, are theY already buying things in this product category, are there any lacks or a ... advantages in what they're already buying vis-a-vis the product that we are trying to sell them? And then we are trying ... we will then try and position our product in that context. Does the product they're using, er, ...is it ineffective in some way – and that might be functionally ineffective or it might be aesthetically ineffective – can we suggest that our product is superior in some respect vis-a-vis those other products?

B   • Discuss the pre-question and ask the students to match the adjectives with the countries.

C   • Students listen to section B of the recording and check their predictions.

Answers
1   Germany: *rational, facts-based, shiny, glossy, aggressive*
2   France: *whimsical, poetic, surrealistic*
3   Italy: *chic, elegant*
4   England: *humorous, jokey, irreverent*

• Elicit reactions to the interviewer's observations and ask students to give further examples.

Tapescript (Section B)
INTERVIEWER   Could you say something about how advertising varies between different countries?

HAMISH PRINGLE   Well the ... the example I ... I could use best is ... is of a car account I used to work on where we used to travel quite a lot within Europe, particularly having syndicate meetings of the various advertising agencies who worked for this car manufacturer – it was Renault in fact – and, um, campaigns would be being presented by different agencies from different markets for the same model. Now cars are remarkably similar across borders because they're made in one place and sent out around the world. So you would get a particular Renault model being advertised by all these different agencies and I have to say that more often than not the advertising produced fell into the kind of national cultural sterotype. So, advertising from Germany tends to be very rational, er, strongly facts-based. They're very keen on showing the car looking really shiny, really glossy, slightly aggressive perhaps. Er, in France they've got a much more whimsical attitude, much more poetic if you like. They tend to use a lot of surrealistic images, er, they're not afraid of showing the car almost in a cartoon style. Um, in Italy, er, they're much more chic and elegant. They tend to show the car as if it was a piece of sculpture or a... a... an object in that way. In England, um, they ... they play the sterotype back on us, we are often more humorous, more jokey, more irreverent about the product.

Further practice: Workbook Unit 18, Exercise 4.

Speaking skills

4   False starts

A   • Play the tape and ask the students to complete the gaps in the transcript. They should write down exactly what they hear, even if it isn't a complete or correct word.

Answers and tapescript

1 ... Er, brand names are clearly trade marks *or dis...* or yes ... trademarks or *badges* for a particular product or service.
2 ... Anybody can have a brand name, um, *I've got* ... there's a brand name sitting here, isn't there – Abbey Well mineral water.
3 ... Does the product they're using ... *is it ineffective* in some way?

B • Students underline the place where Hamish changes what he is saying and discuss the questions in pairs.
   • When students have finished discussing the questions elicit the answers.

Answers

1 ... Er, brand names are clearly trade marks or <u>dis... or yes ...</u> trademarks or badges for a particular product or service.
2 ... Anybody can have a brand name, um, I've <u>got ... there's</u> a brand name sitting here isn't there – Abbey Well mineral water.
3 ... Does the product they're <u>using... is it</u> ineffective in some way?

Suggested answers

1 Reasons why Hamish changed what he was saying:
   extract 1 c   extract 2 a   extract 3 b
2 Yes.
   You realise that what you are about to say may be offensive or inappropriate in the context.
   You realise that you've forgotten a word you were planning to use.
   You suddenly remember a better way of expressing what you mean.
   You are not sure of the answer/what to say, so your thoughts develop and change as you speak.
3 Native speakers don't mind making false starts, so there is no reason why foreign learners should try to avoid them.
4 Knowing about false starts can make you speak more fluently, because it gives you the confidence to know that, if you start to make a mistake etc., you can change what you are saying and it won't sound unnatural.

Pronunciation

5 Linking sounds

A • Say the sounds /j/, /w/ and /r/ aloud so that the students recognise them.
   • Explain the task and play the tape, stopping after each extract if necessary.

Answers

1 /r/
2 /r/ /r/
3 /j/ /j/
4 /j/
5 /w/
6 /w/

   • Ask the students to discuss questions a, b and c in pairs.

Answers

a The /r/ is pronounced even if it is usually silent.
b The sound /j/ is used to glide from the first vowel to the next.
c The sound /w/ is used to glide from the first vowel to the next.

B • Explain the task: students must listen and decide whether the sound /j/ or /w/ is used in the examples on the tape.

Answers

1 b   2 c   3 b   4 b

C Students should be able to apply the answers from sections A and B above to work out the linking sounds in the sentences.

   • When they have decided on their answers play the sentences on tape for them to check.
   • Ask the students to repeat the sentences to practise the linking sounds.

Answers

1 My mother /r/ and I took the car /r/ over the channel.
2 Did I tell you /w/ about the bird that flew /w/ away?
3 The /j/ other boy /j/ organised the trip.
4 Please go /w/ in and turn the radio /w/ on.
5 Don't say /j/ anything about the /j/ evening we spent together.
6 Is there /r/ anyone more /r/ efficient than my secretary?

Reading skills

6 Finding evidence for an argument

   • Explain that the four extracts come from four different books and represent different views on advertising and marketing.
   • Pre-teach that *Madison Avenue* is a street in Manhattan, New York, in which most of the leading American advertising agencies have offices. The term is often used as shorthand for *the American advertising industry*.
   • Ask the students to read the ten points before they read the extracts and complete the matching task.

Answers

1   D   critical
2   B   critical
3   C   supportive
4   A   supportive
5   B   critical
6   A   supportive
7   C   supportive
8   D   critical
9   A   supportive
10 D   critical

   • As a follow-up to the matching task, ask the students to tick those points with which they personally agree and use this to generate a class discussion on the merits and drawbacks of advertising.

7 • Students work individually to complete the chart.
   • When the chart has been completed check the answers and deal with any other vocabulary problems from the extracts.

Answers

EXTRACT	VERB	NOUN	ADJECTIVE
A	dramatise	drama	*dramatic
	deprive	*deprivations	deprived
B	dominate	*dominance	dominant
	*dictate	dictator	dictatorial
	persuade	*persuasion	persuasive
	*transform	transformation	transformed
C	*respond	response	responsive
	*imply	implication	implied
	choose	*choice	chosen
D	publicise	*publicity	public(ised)
	*propose	proposal	proposed

Language work

8 Participles in adverbial clauses

A ● Ask the students to re-write the two extracts without using the present participle forms *having* and *contributing*.

Answers
If you have nothing you will be nothing.
Advertising contributes little. Advertising's primary objective is to reap the financial rewards of the public purchasing it induces.

 ● Let students discuss the two questions in pairs for a few minutes and then elicit the answers.

Answers
a Participles used as adverbial clauses allow us to combine two ideas or sentences in order to give a reason or result.
b The subject of the main verb and the participle must be the same.

 ● Elicit further examples which illustrate these features and write them on the board.
   If we lose advertising, we will lose freedom of choice.
   → Losing advertising, we lose freedom of choice.
   She passed her driving test, then got a job as a chauffeur.
   → Having passed her driving test, she got a job as a chauffeur.
   If it is used correctly, this drug will cure most headaches.
   → Used correctly, this drug will cure most headaches.

 ● You may wish to refer students back to the work on participle clauses in Unit 15, Exercise 4 (page 113).

B ● Read through the examples with the class before students begin the transformation exercise.

Answers
1 Exploiting weaknesses, advertisers take advantage of certain people.
2 Losing advertising, we lose freedom of choice.
3 Suggesting things can be better, advertisers make us dissatisfied with our lives.
4 Containing intangible value, brands tend to cost more than exactly similar products.
5 Establishing segments of consumers, advertisers are able to market their products more effectively.
6 Competing with each other, companies are forced to be more efficient.
7 Spending a lot of money, advertisers can virtually dictate the products we buy.
8 Loving elegance, Italians tend to show cars as pieces of sculpture.

Writing skills

9 Writing a discursive essay

A **Note:** This is the third formal or academic essay type in *Distinction*. The introduction to this type of writing is in Unit 14. (See the teaching notes on pages 93 – 4.)

 ● Ask the students to explain what they understand by a discursive essay and elicit the following:
   A discursive essay is one in which a topic is discussed critically, opinions or contrasting viewpoints are expressed and a conclusion is reached.
 ● Elicit that this type of essay usually has a title beginning *Do you agree...* or *Discuss....*
 ● Students read the essay and answer questions 1 – 3.

Answers
1 Three parts: Introduction, main body, conclusion.
2 *Exercise 6*
   Television companies rely on income from advertising to pay for programmes.
   Advertisements increase our knowledge of different products and this enables us to make better choices as consumers.
   TV advertising increases competition between manufacturers who each try to produce the best quality products at the cheapest prices.
   New points
   If TV relied on government subsidies, it could lead to political control over news and current affairs programmes.
   Countries which do not allow advertising produce goods which are expensive and of poor quality.
3 Use of markers: *firstly, secondly, finally.*
   Lack of colloquial language.
   Full forms rather than contractions: *do not.*
   Use of formal vocabulary: *increased dramatically, of poor quality.*
   Use of formal cause and effect linkers: *as a result, therefore.*

B ● You may wish to set the writing task as homework. Alternatively, follow the group writing techniques outlined in the introduction or ask the students to prepare an outline in class, compare with a partner and then write it up at home.

Further practice: Workbook Unit 18, Exercise 8.

10 Assessing advertisements

 ● Focus students' attention on the three advertisements and ask them to describe them and suggest where they come from and what their purpose is. They are all advertisements from newspaper colour supplements and are trying to persuade people to take holidays in their country.
 ● Students work in pairs to complete the chart.

Suggested answers (Students should be allowed to disagree.)

SPECIAL FEATURES	JAMAICA	EGYPT	CYPRUS
climate	✔		
natural beauty	✔	✔	✔
wildlife	✔		
local culture	✔	✔	✔
special atmosphere	✔	✔	✔
sports	✔		
accommodation			✔

- Pairs should combine into groups of four to compare their charts and discuss the follow-up questions.
- Ask groups to report back their conclusions and reasons to the class.

Reading skills

11 Skimming and matching

A
- Use the questions to elicit students' experiences of sales people. Encourage them to recount their personal and anecdotal knowledge of selling techniques.

B
- Read through the introduction and check that students understand the meaning of *the close*.
- Explain the matching task and allow the students a few minutes only to complete the activity.

Answers
1 C   2 B   3 F   4 A   5 E   6 D

12
- Allow students to read the paragraphs more carefully and ask them to describe any personal experiences of these techniques.
- Students put the six techniques into rank order of effectiveness and compare their rankings in pairs.
- With the same partner students match the techniques with the five people listed.

Suggested answers
1 assuming the sale/the step-by-step technique
2 the inflation close
3 give the customer the product
4 assuming the sale
5 the planned pause

- Pairs compare their answers and then report back to class, giving the reasons for their choices.

Vocabulary

13 Buying and selling
- Elicit that a potential customer is known as a *prospect*.
- Students find the words in their contexts and work out their meaning.
- Elicit their answers and put some of the students' definitions on the board.

Definitions
A *I didn't mean to push* I didn't intend to put pressure on you
B *ploy* trick or device
  take something for granted assume or not question
C *tempted to* have a desire to

bring oneself (to do something) persuade oneself
last chance final opportunity
D *easy credit terms* a loan to enable purchase
  transaction deal/exchange of goods for payment
  try out use for a temporary period/use experimentally
E *clinch a deal* succeed in completing a deal
F *make the next move* carry out the next action
  evasive in a manner which avoids answering
  to think something over consider carefully before making a decision

- Students choose the most appropriate of the words to complete the gaps in the sentences.

Answers
1 evasive   2 last chance   3 bring myself
4 take good health for granted   5 try it out
6 clinch a deal   7 ploy   8 think it over

Language work

14 Concessive clauses

A
- Students study the sentence and identify the two facts. Write them on the board.
  1 The prospect may be very tempted to buy.
  2 He can't quite bring himself to agree to buy.
- Ask the students to explain the relationship between the two facts and elicit that they contrast with each other. (In other words, the second fact is surprising in view of the first one.)
- Ask the students to suggest the purpose of a concessive clause. Elicit that it allows us to combine two contrasting ideas when the idea in the main clause is surprising in view of the information in the concessive clause.
- Ask the students to think of further examples and put some of these on the board, for example:
  Mary is very wealthy. She never gives money to charity.
  → Though wealthy, Mary never gives money to charity.
- Students study the examples. Elicit that the construction which emphasises the degree of contrast most strongly is *No matter how...* .
- * Ask the students which of the examples carries the idea of a condition and elicit *Even if...* .
- Put the following summary on the board.
  Simple contrast: *although..., though..., even though...*
  Strong contrast: *in spite of..., despite..., notwithstanding...*
  Contrast with a condition: *even if...*
  Contrast which is true in a variety of situations:
  whatever..., wherever..., whoever..., whenever..., however..., no matter/it doesn't matter how/what/where/who...

B
- Read through the example and ask students to complete the exercise.

Suggested answers
1 Although paid to talk about their products, salesmen spend most of their time talking about themselves.
2 However unwilling to spend a lot of money, people will spend it if they think they are getting a bargain.
3 Although they say they never watch commercials, TV viewers can always remember the names of the most heavily advertised brands.
4 No matter how unpopular they are, pushy shop assistants always sell more than their colleagues.
5 Even if dissatisfied, British people rarely complain about the products they buy.
6 Although unlikely, people who know when to keep quiet often make successful salesmen.

7   Despite being unreliable, high-technology products are always more expensive than less sophisticated items.

8   Although expensive, advertising helps to make products cheaper by stimulating competition between manufacturers.

Further practice: Workbook Unit 18, Exercise 6.

Final task

15   Writing an advertisement

A   • Refer the students to the incomplete advertisement on page 140 and ask them to tell you anything they know about Thailand.

   • Read through the introduction with the class and explain the first task.

   • Ask the students to work individually. They should read the Holidays in Thailand information sheet on page 162 and decide on the most important features of the country. Having done this, they should think up a headline and prepare the words (or *copy*) to go with the incomplete advertisement on a piece of paper.

Note: If students find the task difficult, they can refer back to the advertisements in Exercise 10 for ideas and inspiration.

B   • Students compare their 'copy' in pairs. They should discuss their versions and together write out a joint final version. This can be either a combination of the best features of each version or a new version. If students are unable to agree with their partners allow them to use their own versions for the next stage.

   • Students write the final version into the space in the advertisement.

C   • Divide the class into groups of 4 – 6. The members of each group should exchange advertisements with another group so that nobody is looking at their own advertisement.

   • Explain the task to the groups and emphasise that they must go through the four points in the checklist before deciding on their preferred advertisement.

   • When groups have completed the task they should read out their chosen advertisement to the class, explaining why they have chosen it.

Further practice: Workbook Unit 18, Exercise 9.

Unit 19 Personal Space

 ## Unit summary

Themes	Architectural styles and issues; concepts of privacy
Structures	*Would rather/sooner; as if/though* + unreal past; *wish* + *would*/past simple/past perfect
Vocabulary	Architectural styles, matching and expanding, multi-word verbs with particle *out* (Workbook)
Skills	*Reading*: finding evidence, identifying bias *Listening*: identifying speakers *Speaking*: expressing annoyance and regrets / complaining *Writing*: expressing attitude indirectly

 ## Teaching notes

Introduction

1
- Go through the questions and elicit a brief discussion on the building in which the class is being held.
- Divide the class into pairs and nominate A and B in each pair.

Note: In a small class this can be a whole class activity with the teacher taking the role of Student B.

- When pairs have finished, encourage them to discuss the results and comment on people's awareness of and response to their surroundings.

Vocabulary

2 Architectural styles

A
- Students may work in pairs or small groups to complete the matching task and answer the questions.

Answers
A Post Modernist (The Galleries, Broadmead, Bristol, UK, 1992)
B Gothic (St. Mary Redcliffe, Bristol, UK, 15th century)
C Classical (Marble Hill House, Richmond, London, 18th century)
D Modernist (Robinson Building, Bristol, UK, 1960s)
E Baroque (Midland Bank, the old city, Bristol, UK, 1900s)

B is the oldest, A is the newest building.

- Using the photographs, ask students to describe the main features of each style.
- Ask the students which buildings they prefer and how architectural style influences them.

B
- Ask the students to match the buildings with countries and elicit information on the typical architectural styles of their countries.

Answers
1 Japan   2 Turkey   3 Switzerland (or any Western European country)

Reading skills

3 Finding evidence

A
- Read through the introduction and explain the meaning of

carbuncle – an unattractive red swelling under the skin caused by a local infection.
- Ask the students to read the article and explain the meaning of the title.

Answer
The Prince refers to the Prince of Wales, who described the designs for the extension to the National Gallery, the famous art gallery in central London, as *a carbuncle*. Critics accused the architect, Terry Farrell, of acting as if he was living in *Disneyland* when designing his plans for the area north of St Paul's Cathedral. Hence the reference to *Disneyland*.

B
- Students must find the phrases or sections of the text which prove or disprove the statements.

Answers
1 TRUE. *The modern movement with its unornamented facades, its rigorous simplicity and its love of concrete and steel had never been a big hit with the British public.*
2 TRUE. *the Prince declared the proposed building 'a monstrous carbuncle ...'; ... his words struck a chord with the public ...*
3 FALSE. *the British profession has split into two camps: those who cling to the modernist philosophy ..., and those who seek to give the people what they want ...*
4 FALSE. *Developers seek to pull down the surrounding post-war office blocks and recreate the cathedral's original surroundings ...*
5 FALSE. *Critics ... say ... Terry Farrell, is acting as though he were living in Disneyland.*

C
- Ask the students to choose between the schemes and give their reasons.

Vocabulary

4 Matching and expanding

A
- Students find and underline the words and phrases in the text and study the contexts.
- Students use these to replace the phrases in italics in the text.

Answers
1 anachronistic   2 renounced   3 outmoded
4 unprecedented   5 undercurrent   6 rigorous
7 ferocity   8 strike a chord with

B
- Student may work on the lists in pairs.

Suggested answers

ARCHITECTURAL STYLES	BUILDING MATERIALS	BUILDING ELEMENTS
classical	concrete	wall
gothic	brick	window
modernist	stone	door
post modernist	steel	floor
Romanesque	wood	ceiling
Rococo	glass	roof
Baroque	plaster	foundations

- Elicit students' answers and write up the lists on the board.

Reading skills

5 Identifying bias

A
- Ask the students to explain the meaning of *bias*: a prejudice or predisposition either in favour of or against something.
- Read through the introduction and the first example in the chart, explaining how the use of negative vocabulary (*choked, overloaded, motley*) indicates the writer's negative bias towards London.
- Students study the text more carefully and complete the chart.

Answers

SUBJECT	ATTITUDE			EXAMPLES
	POS	NEG	NEUT	
London		✓		once- elegant choked streets, over-loaded subways a motley collection
New buildings in London		✓		decaying products faceless new buildings
The British architectural profession		✓		outmoded beliefs
St Paul's Cathedral	✓			Britain's greatest architect baroque masterpiece
Terry Farrell's scheme			✓	critics have called the scheme anachronistic ... Disneyland. good design is good design
The existing buildings around St Paul's		✓		dwarfed by steel skyscrapers, steel and glass

- Ask students if they can find any other examples of bias in the text. They may be able to detect that the writer has a slightly negative attitude towards what she sees as the reluctance of British people to *speak out* on issues such as architecture.

B
- Ask students to study the sentences carefully and complete the matching exercise. Students may find a dictionary helpful.

Answers
1 2b;   2 1b;   3 1a;   4 2a

- Explain that *cling on* and *denigrates* express a negative attitude whereas *maintain* and *criticises* are neutral.

Writing skills

6 Expressing attitude indirectly

Note: Exercise 5 should be completed before this exercise is undertaken.

A
- Students may find it helpful to use a dictionary for this and the following sections.

Answers

POSITIVE/NEUTRAL	NEGATIVE
generous	spendthrift
a popular uprising	a riot
sophisticated	affected
the people	the masses
slim	skinny
a freedom fighter	a terrorist
to compliment	to flatter
respectful	subservient
an opponent	an enemy
to debate	to argue

B
- Read through the examples and explain the task. Students should work in pairs and compare their answers.

Suggested answers
2 a He's a terrorist!
  b He's a freedom fighter!
3 a He's always complimenting her.
  b He's always flattering her.
4 a She's really affected.
  b She's rather sophisticated.
5 a He's really subservient.
  b He's very respectful.

C
- Divide the class into three equal sized groups.
- Explain the task. Students can write their five sentences on any subject they choose.
- If students are not clear about the task go through the first set of words as an example and put these sentences on the board.
  A (negative) Lazy students often *plagiarise* text books.
  B (positive) Salvador Dali sometimes *emulated* the techniques of the old masters.
  C (neutral) Shakespeare often *copied* the plots of earlier writers.
- When the groups have finished, they should split up and form new groups consisting of at least one A, one B and one C in order to compare their sentences and check they have used the correct words.
- Elicit this chart from the class and write it on the board.

	NEUTRAL	POSITIVE	NEGATIVE
1	copy	emulate	plagiarise
2	teach	enlighten	brainwash
3	interested	fascinated	obsessed
4	enthusiastic	committed	fanatical
5	influence	inspire	overawe

- Ask students to read out their sentences.

Further practice: Workbook Unit 19, Exercise 11.

Language work

7 Would rather/sooner, as if/though + unreal past

A
- Let the students study the extracts and discuss the questions in pairs or small groups then elicit the answers:

Answers
1 No.   2 *as though ...*   3 *would rather ...*

- Elicit the following explanations and write them on the board.
WOULD RATHER/SOONER + UNREAL PAST
Structure used to introduce an alternative action or one the speaker wishes somebody else would do. It is a polite form of *wish + would*.
They would rather stick to subjects they know something

about.
They would rather the prince stuck to subjects he knew something about.

AS IF/AS THOUGH + UNREAL PAST
Structure used to make a hypothetical comparison which may or may not be possible.
Terry Farrell is acting as though he were living in Disneyland.

- Now ask the students to look at sentences **a** and **b** and answer the questions below.

Answers
something you know is not possible: b
something which may or may not be possible: a

- Explain that, in this construction, the present perfect (or present perfect continuous) indicates something which may or may not be possible, whereas the past perfect (or past simple or past/past perfect continuous) is only used for something which is definitely impossible.

B   • Students complete the sentence transformation exercise.

Answers
1 He would rather/sooner architects studied the classical style.
2 Most people would rather/sooner St Paul's were surrounded by traditional-style buildings.
3 Some architects act as if/though they were dictators.
4 I'd rather/sooner members of the royal family didn't get involved in architectural debates.
5 He is acting as if/though he has seen the plans.
6 She talks as if/though she had lived in a palace.
7 These drawings look as if/though they've been done by an architect.
8 She would rather/sooner the British weren't so obsessed by old-fashioned styles.

- Students complete the unfinished sentences with an appropriate construction.
- Students can compare and check their answers in pairs or small groups.
- Elicit one or two answers to check the grammar.

Further practice: Workbook Unit 19, Exercise 9.

Listening skills

8   Identifying speakers

A   • Students should have no difficulty naming the six types of building. Elicit the answers and write them on the board:

Answers
A   semi-detached houses   B   terraced houses
C   a cottage   D   a block of flats   E   a bungalow
F   a detached two-storey house

Note: In American English, B are *row houses* and D is *an apartment building.*

- Now play the tape and ask the students to match the speakers with the buildings. (One of the buildings cannot be matched.)

Answers
Speaker 1   photo C
Speaker 2   photo D
Speaker 3   photo E
Speaker 4   photo A
Speaker 5   photo B

B   • Explain the task and allow students to read through the questions before playing the tape again.

Answers
1 Speaker 2
2 Speakers 2 and 5 (the problem of neighbours)
3 Speaker 4 (American)
4 Speaker 3 (because he couldn't get up the stairs in his previous home)
5 Speaker 4 (surprised how well this British type of housing works)

C   • Use the questions to generate a brief discussion on the problems of neighbours and the design of residential buildings.

Tapescript
SPEAKER 1   Well, of course it's lovely living out here, but you know we do have problems. I mean it's a mile to the nearest shops and the school's right on the other side of Stoke Burges. I sometimes wish I lived in a town, you know, right next to the shops and everything. But I suppose I'd soon get fed up with all the noise and the pollution. No, I think we're better off here – there's nothing like waking up to the birds and looking out over the fields in the morning..
SPEAKER 2   Actually it's a nightmare. Like, the lifts – they're always on the blink. And the noise, you never get any privacy – you can hear everything in the next flat – the phone ringing, the kids screaming, even the alarm clock! And when they have rows it's like being in the same room, you get every word! No, no privacy at all. You know we call this place Colditz 'cos it's just like a prison camp, all concrete. Some architect's paradise I suppose, but then they don't have to live here, do they? You know I wish we'd never moved here but we couldn't afford anything else at the time, and now Joe's lost his job it looks like we're stuck here ...
SPEAKER 3   Well it was the stairs. Hopeless. You know I never thought I'd get to the stage where I couldn't get up to my own bedroom! But I did. Oh, it was my daughter's idea to buy this place. I suppose it is practical ... and I like the garden – that's my hobby actually, although it's not so easy to get around with the stick. I can do the pruning but I can't get down to the weeds. One of those volunteers comes and does that for me. Trouble is, it's all old people around here ...
SPEAKER 4   Yeah, I love it – it's so British. Back home we don't have anything like this. I mean you're either crammed in apartments or surrounded by acres of space. This half-way idea is kind of weird but it works real well. When we arrived I thought I'd, well, I grew up in a pretty big place, I thought I'd feel claustrophobic.. but we don't get any noise through the shared wall, and it's only the one neighbour to worry about anyway. I mean people mind themselves, they don't get in your way, but they're there if you need them ...
SPEAKER 5   Yeah, there's a real community spirit. Well, it's a sort of tradition in these streets, you know, everyone gets together for special occasions. You remember the Queen's jubilee? Yeah, we had a brilliant street party for that, er bunting, loads of drinks, really nice. Mind you, there are some disadvantages, um, with houses sort of on both sides you do get a bit fed up with all the gossip. You can't really get away with much! We've got a retired couple in the house opposite and all they ever do is stare through the net curtains trying to see what's going on. I must say I often wish they'd mind their own business but then that's the price you pay isn't it? I guess nosiness and community spirit are sort of two sides of the same coin, if you know what I mean ...

Language work

9 Wish + would / past simple / past perfect

A **Note:** In addition to the sentence transformation practice in this exercise, there is oral practice of the structures in Exercise 10.

- Students study the extracts and match with the descriptions.

Answers

1 b   2 c   3 a

- Discuss the questions and elicit these answers.

Answers

c expresses annoyance.
Wish + would can only refer to an action or situation outside the control of the speaker.

- Elicit the following grammar summary from the students and ask students to think of their own example sentences for each.

WISH + WOULD
Expresses a desire for something to change when the situation is outside the control of the speaker. Often used to express annoyance. Example: a.

WISH + SIMPLE PAST/PAST CONTINUOUS
Expresses dissatisfaction or personal regret about a present situation. Example: b.
(Point out to the students that *were* can be used instead of *was* in this construction, especially in more formal English: *I wish I were taller.*)

WISH + PAST PERFECT
Expresses regret for an action in the past. Example: c.

B **Answers**

1 I wish I hadn't bought such an expensive house.
2 I wish I lived in a house with a garden.
3 I wish people wouldn't complain about modern design all the time.
4 My sister wishes she had never studied architecture.
5 I wish my neighbours wouldn't keep interfering in my private life.

Further practice: Workbook Unit 19, Exercises 8 and 10.

Speaking skills

10 Expressing annoyance and regrets/complaining

A
- Focus the students' attention on the photo of Grimethorpe House and elicit a description of it and its surroundings. Tell the students that they must imagine they live in this building.
- Divide the class into groups of three to discuss the questions. Encourage the students to use their imagination and think of as many responses as they can.
- Monitor the groups and check that students have thought of at least five or six responses to each of the questions.

B
- Read through the instructions and remind students to use the structures previously studied when they are talking.
- When the groups have finished, ask one or two to repeat their conversations for the whole class. Check that they have used the correct constructions.

Model answers

Student A: I wish we hadn't been evicted from our previous home. I wish we had paid the rent on time in our last place. I wish I hadn't lost my job.
Student B: I wish the flats were larger. I wish we didn't have such thin walls. I wish we had a car park. I wish it wasn't so noisy.
Student C: I wish the landlords would install damp-proofing. I wish they'd plant some trees. I wish somebody would repair the lifts.

C
- Students describe their feelings about their own homes. In a small class, this can be a whole class activity. If students are reluctant to talk about their own homes, start them off by talking about your home – the things which annoy you and things you would like to change.

11
- Ask students if they remember how the people on the tape in Exercise 8 regarded privacy. Elicit that they didn't like *nosy neighbours* and preferred people to *mind their own business*.
- Ask students if they have the same or different attitudes.
- Read through the introduction. Ask the students to read the text and answer questions 1 – 4.

Answers

1 The stories illustrate the different concept of privacy in China: the Chinese seem to have no embarrassment about looking at other people's mail.
2 They have a rather drab and monotonous life, they are naturally nosy and they have a genuine concern for the welfare of the Westerners.
3 She tells the story to illustrate how the Chinese view a discussion between a teacher and student as something public rather than private.
4 The writer seeks to give examples of the ways in which the Chinese have a different concept of privacy from Westerners.

12
- Students work in pairs to find the phrases in the text and write descriptions.
- Pairs get together to compare their ideas.

Suggested answers

a an enthusiastic collector of postage stamps
b an innate desire to find out about the personal lives of others
c everday life which is boring, repetitive and lacking in excitement and variety.
d thought of as something everyone is entitled to know about.
e interference which cannot be justified

13
The organisation of this activity will depend on whether your class is monolingual or multilingual. In a monolingual class, the questions can be used as a basis for a whole class discussion or students can work in small groups. In a multilingual class, students from the same country should first work together to discuss the questions and then report back to the whole class. An additional phase of comparing cultural differences can then be added to the activity.

Final task

14 Decision making

This type of exercise involving financial decisions may be unfamiliar to some students. If so, explain to them that the figures are just as important as the items and that they should be prepared to do some simple mathematics as part of the process of reaching a decision.

- Divide the class into groups of 4 to 6 and read through the instructions.
- Set a time limit for their discussions (ten minutes is usually adequate) and remind them that they will have to present their proposals to the class at the end. Point out that the budget of £500, 000 is fixed and must not be exceeded, and that the cost of individual items is also fixed.
- When the time limit is up. ask each group in turn to present their proposal to the class. (Ask a numerate student to check the figures!) Take a class vote on which proposal is the best.

Unit 20   A Changing Language

 Unit summary

Themes	Language awareness unit covering the story of English; language development and change; new languages
Structures	Generic nouns and pronouns; text reference
Vocabulary	Formal and informal verbs: review of multi-word verbs (in WB)
Skills	*Reading:* finding specific information; scanning for specific words
	Listening: identifying speakers and opinions; understanding arguments
	Speaking: giving a formal speech
	Writing: writing a chronological summary, using text reference
Pronunciation	Sound-spelling correspondences (2)
Language awareness	Words with similar meanings; homonyms, homographs and homophones

 Teaching notes

Introduction

1 This introductory exercise encourages students to think about the position of English in the world today and the different types of status that it holds.

- Read through the instructions with the students.
- If necessary, explain the difference between the three *categories of language*: mother tongue (spoken as the native language, i.e. the first language of most people), second or official language (learnt in primary or secondary school, as the language is necessary in certain spheres of life in the country, such as higher education, government and the media), and foreign language (learnt in school as an academic subject, the language playing no official role in the country).
- Students work in pairs or small groups to complete the chart and the key on the map. They use the colour coding on the map to help them make their choices.
- Make sure that students are aware that this is only a warm-up exercise and that it doesn't matter if they get some of the answers wrong.
- Some of the answers are given in the reading passage, so it is better to leave the checking until after the passage has been read.

Answers

COUNTRY	M/S/F	MAP REF.	COUNTRY	M/S/F	MAP REF.
Australia	M	26	Kenya	S	16
Burma	S	22	Madagascar	F	19
Cameroon	S	13	Mexico	F	3
Canada	M	1	Morocco	F	6
Denmark	F	12	New Zealand	M	30
Ghana	S	11	Pakistan	S	20
Guyana	M	5	Philippines	S	28
Hong Kong	S	27	Saudi Arabia	F	18
Iceland	F	7	Singapore	S	24
India	S	21	Spain	F	8
Indonesia	F	25	South Africa	S	14
Ireland	M	9	Thailand	F	23
Israel	F	17	United Kingdom	M	10
Jamaica	M	4	United States	M	2
Japan	F	29	Zimbabwe	S	15

Key: red = mother tongue; yellow = second language; green = foreign language

Reading skills

2 Finding specific information

A
- Students scan the text very quickly to check some of the answers from Exercise 1. Make sure they realise that they should look through just for the names of the countries to find out what is said about them.
- Check which answers they have found in the text.

Answers
The status of English in the following countries is mentioned: Australia (M), New Zealand (M), United States/Canada (M), Ghana (S), Singapore (S), South Africa (S), India (S).

- Now check the completed chart around the class.

B
- Tell students to go back to the beginning of the passage and read through it again in order to complete the key for Exercise 2 on the map. They can work in pairs to complete the key once they have read the passage independently.

Answers
1 Irish to New England, USA, 1720s
2 English (Pilgrim Fathers) to Massachusetts, USA, 1620
3 English (James Cook) to Queensland, Australia, 1770; first immigrants 1788
4 Irish to Australia, late 18th and 19th centuries
5 English to South Africa, 1700s
6 Irish US immigrants south to Pennsylvania and west, after 1720s
7 Vikings to north of England, 750–1050 AD

8 Germanic tribes, including the Angles, to England, 449 AD
9 Normans to England, 1066
10 English to India, 1600

C
- Ask students how the text treats the spread of English around the world, i.e. how the paragraphs are organised. Make sure they understand that it is treated by area of the world. Explain that the other way to organise a historical account of this nature would be chronologically.
- Tell students to go back through the text and to make a list of the events in chronological order, following the model in their books. Tell them also that they will not be able to order the events precisely, as many dates are vague, and that they may not be able to find a result for every event.
- Check that students' lists are in the correct order.

Answers

date	event	result
449 AD	British Isles invaded by tribes from Denmark and Germany	Language of the Angles became vernacular
750–1050 AD	Vikings from Norway colonised the north of England	Norse had an effect on the language
1066	Norman invasion of England	Language changed because of the influence of French and Latin
1600	Settlements were established in India by the East India Company	Eventual control of commercial life in India by an English company
1620	The Pilgrim Fathers left England and settled in Massachusetts	Start of colonisation of North America
1720s	Northern Irish immigrants arrived in America	Most of the North American continent was colonised
1700s	Pioneers established a colony in southern Africa	English became the dominant language in South Africa
1770	James Cook sailed *The Endeavour* into Queensland	Discovery of Australia
1788	The first group of immigrants from England arrived in Australia	–
18th century	Most of the commercial life in India was controlled by the East India Company	–
late 18th and 19th centuries	A large number of Irish emigrated to America	–
early 19th century	East India Company was dissolved	India was the keystone of the British Empire; English became the widespread language
late 19th century	Boer War in South Africa	Afrikaans established as the dominant language in South Africa

Note: This information will be used later in the unit, so make sure students keep their lists.

Vocabulary

3 Scanning a text for specific words

The first part of this scanning exercise is a task that students will be used to, but the second may not be. It is a more general searching exercise which encourages readers to look for types of word, rather than for specific words.

A
- Students use the section references to help them find the synonyms.
- If you want to speed this exercise up, divide the class into A, B and C students. Student As look for words 1–4, Bs for words 5–8 and Cs for words 9–12. The class then divides into groups, each of which has at least one A, one B and one C, to discuss the words.

Answers
1 lives on   2 warlike   3 vernacular   4 at their disposal   5 nuances   6 hybrid   7 seaboard   8 rough-and-ready   9 convicts   10 indigenous   11 keystone   12 new order

- Check that students understand all the words from the passage. Explain any other unfamiliar words at this point, though this exercise should have dealt with most of them.

B
- Read through the four things that students have to search for and check that they understand.
- Students work individually to search and then check their answers in pairs.

Answers
1 It is the language of shipping, aviation, science, technology and commerce.
2 English, Gaelic, Welsh, Norse, Norman French, Latin, French, Afrikaans, Hindi.
3 *founded* (line 47), *set up* (lines 61–2), *established* (line 64).
4 Other examples are ... *the language that was to become English* (lines 21–2), ... *the area now known as England* (line 24), ... *what is now called Queensland, Australia* (lines 59–60).

Note: This exercise could be done as a speed-reading competition, with the first group to find all the items winning.

Language awareness

4 Similarities in words

A   Words with similar meanings
This exercise builds on the mention in section 1 of the passage about the nuances of English, and the fact that it has the largest vocabulary of all languages.

- Ask students to go back to section 1 of the text and to find the examples it gives of words with similar meanings. (They are given in the instructions.) Remind students of Exercise 8 from Unit 5, which dealt with words which have multiple meanings. This exercise looks at the opposite aspect of English.
- Check that students have found the correct words. In groups, they can use dictionaries to find out the differences between the words given, and write their own definitions. Make sure that they realise they should be looking for the similar meanings of the words.

Suggested answers
time general term to refer to the concept of the passage of existence; one point/period in this passage of exisitence

age period of history marked by some special characteristic(s); the length of time a person or thing has been in existence
epoch a long, distinct historical period marked by social change at its beginning and end
The last word here is much more specific and is likely to be used in an academic (i.e. related to history) context.

rise to go up (intransitive verb)
mount to get up on something (transitive), e.g. a horse
ascend to move up (transitive), e.g. ascend a ladder/hill, to rise to a higher point (intransitive); (unlikely to be used in everyday conversation)

Extension
- Students write examples to show the use of the words.
- Divide the class into groups of four.
- Each group looks at the twelve words, divides them into the meaning groups and decides which students will take which group.
- Students write their definitions individually.
- Each students one or more others which have defined the same group of words. They compare their definitions.

Answers
Meaning groups
animals, beast, creature animate beings
chase, hunt, pursue following something
effective, influential, powerful adjective concerning effect
journeys, tours, travels moving around

Definitions (These may vary but the following distinctions should be made.)
animals living, non-human creatures
beast wild, dangerous animal (sometimes used of humans)
creature non-human, possibly outside our comprehension
chase run behind a person or animal
hunt chase; with intention to kill
pursue chase, also used of ideas and intangible concepts
effective getting the desired result, reaching the objective
influential having a certain effect on, able to change of affect another's action or ideas
powerful having a great effect on
journeys movements from one place to another
tours trips, visiting several places on the way
travels rarely used, similar to *journeys*, but sounds quite literary

- Students can try to make up meaning groups of their own for other students to define.

B Homonyms, homographs and homophones.

Explanations are given in the Students' Book.

- Read through the introduction with the students and check that they are clear about the differences between these three concepts.
- Explain exactly what they have to do with the list of words they will look at. Read the instructions with them.
- Students work in pairs. They work out their own words then compare them with a partner. They will find that their partners have the other spelling of each homophone. They will also find that some of the words fit in more than one category.

Answers
STUDENT A
homonyms:
arms upper limbs/weapons
coach bus/teach
fare money payable for a journey/food

plain simple/large, flat area
suit fit, match/jacket and trousers/skirt
homographs:
read (/riːd/ – present tense, /red/ – past tense)
refuse (/rɪˈfjuːz/ – not to accept, /ˈrefjuːs/ – rubbish)
sow (/səʊ/ – scatter seeds on the ground, /saʊ/ – female pig)
homophones:
fare fair
flower flour
pair pear/pare
plain plane
pour poor
road rowed
sow sew, so

STUDENT B
homonyms:
address street and town/speak to
fair blonde/funfair
ground floor/past of grind, e.g. ground coffee
plane aeroplane/type of tree/type of tool
pound unit of money/unit of weight/to beat someone or something/pen, e.g. dog pound
homographs:
desert (/ˈdezət/ – dry wasteland, /dɪˈzɜːt/ – to abandon)
lead (/liːd/ – to go before, /led/ – past of lead, type of metal)
wind (/wɪnd/ – movement of air, /waɪnd/ – circular movement, e.g. of a watch)

homophones:
fair fare
flour flower
pear pair, pare
plane plain
poor pour
rowed road

C
- Students complete the text, choosing the correct gaps by using the information from this exercise.

Answers
1	b	(*tongue* is archaic, *vernacular* is local only)
2	b	(homophones)
3	a or c	(*power* is too strong)
4	c	(*emissions* sounds too technical, *outputs* suggests computers, production etc.)
5	a	(*infiltrating* suggests devious ways of entering)
6	b	(homophones)
7	a	(*dialect* refers to grammar as well as pronunciation, *stress* refers to placement of emphasis only)
8	c	(*necessary* implies obligation, not intended here; *unavoidable* implies one wishes to avoid it, not the suggestion here)
9	b	(*dependant* is a person, not an adjective)
10	b	(homophones)

Further practice: Workbook Unit 20, Exercises 3 and 4.

Listening skills

5 Understanding arguments

This exercise encourages students to look at some of the problems in English with gender-based pronouns. This is an awareness-raising exercise and as such is not trying to persuade students of any political stance.

A
- Ask students to read through the riddle and explain it if possible. You may find that some students are unable to perceive it as a riddle; if so, explain that the word *mayor* in

English is usually taken to refer to a man, though that is not necessarily the case.

B
- Play the first part of the panel discussion for students to check their answer. (Play as far as ... *we need only one word for the function – mayor*.)
- Discuss the riddle with the students and make sure they understand it. Discuss whether the same riddle would work in their language, and if not, why not? Is it because of the language or because people's perceptions are different?

C
- Students read the four statements.
- Play the whole discussion. Students work out whose opinion each statement summarises. This should not be difficult as each speaker is clearly introduced.

Answers
1 Rachel Macmillan
2 Melvyn Winchester
3 Geoff Graham
4 Arlene Simmonds

Tapescript
INTERVIEWER Good afternoon, ladies and gentlemen, and welcome to *Friday Live*. I'm Andrew Ansell and I'm here today with my guests to talk about the subject of language. And my guests are The Right Honourable Melvyn Winchester, Conservative MP for Dorking South.

MELVYN Good afternoon.

INTERVIEWER Arlene Simmonds, author of the controversial bestseller, *Dinner at Midnight*.

ARLENE Hi.

INTERVIEWER Geoff Graham, editor of *Public Ear*, the current affairs radio programme.

GEOFF Hello.

INTERVIEWER And, last but not least, Rachel Macmillan, model and star of the new television soap, *Our Street*.

RACHEL Hello everyone.

ANDREW Now, before this programme began each of our panellists was given the riddle that you received before the news. Let's see what they made of it. Did any of you work it out?

ARLENE Yes, well, it's rather old now, isn't it? And it probably doesn't work any more in today's society. I assume we all understood it?

MELVYN Erm, well, no, actually.

GEOFF It's obvious; the mayor is the mother of the child. It's an old riddle playing on sexist use of language.

MELVYN The mother? Well, then why not say so? In that case she'd be a mayoress, wouldn't she, not a mayor?

ARLENE That's the whole point. A mayor is a public function, like a minister, or a councillor. There's no reason at all why we should point out that a particular mayor is a woman, so we need only one word for the function – mayor.

MELVYN That's ridiculous! The language has developed for perfectly good reasons and it's wrong of us to change it just because it suits a lunatic fringe in society!

ARLENE A rather large lunatic fringe, I think.

MELVYN I suppose you'll be saying next that we should change words like chairman to chairperson, and postmen to postpeople?

ARLENE Well, that depends, doesn't it? If a woman is in the chair, then it's not only incorrect, but also rather insulting for her to be called a chairman, why not just chair? And if the plural is kept as postmen, for example, then women are excluded from that group of people by definition ...

MELVYN I've never heard such twaddle in all my life. Everyone knows that chairman can refer to both a man and a woman and ...

ANDREW Let's move on a bit. Rachel, what's your opinion of all this?

RACHEL Well, I think it's all a bit overrated, personally. In fact, I'm not really interested in it at all. I don't care if people call me an actor, an actress, a star, whatever. I think there are far more important things to worry about these days. I think people do go on about relatively trivial things.

ANDREW Mmm. Right. Yes, Geoff.

GEOFF I think I fall somewhere between the extremes here. I agree with Rachel that it can be exaggerated, but, on the other hand, I know that there have been university studies which have shown that children can't make out the exclusion of women in certain phrases, for example, the man on the street, the working man, and so on. In fact, they believe that these phrases refer only to men. I can understand how these phrases came about originally, when society was really run by men, but I do think we ought to be changing language somewhat now to reflect reality.

RACHEL But don't you feel that it will change in time, that language changes gradually anyway, and that we shouldn't force the change?

MELVYN But surely language shouldn't change? We have an old, traditional language which is perfectly adequate to express all our needs, so why change it? I find it appalling the way young people speak these days, using less instead of fewer, and double negatives ...

ARLENE I think you're getting just a little off the point here, don't you? I mean, we're not talking about grammar; we're talking about words that offend a certain section of our society ...

MELVYN Ah! But you are talking about grammar, my dear. I can't believe you agree with the pronoun *he*?

ARLENE What do you mean?

GEOFF You know, things like 'Anyone who says that needs his head examined.'

ARLENE Oh, yes. Of course I don't agree with it.

MELVYN So how would you rephrase that sentence?

ARLENE Something like 'Anyone who says that needs their head examined,' I think.

MELVYN There you are. You are proposing that we change the grammar then? You're suggesting that we use a plural pronoun with a singular noun, surely that's not right?

ARLENE Maybe it's not right but you have to agree that it's the grammar that Shakespeare used. I can quote you ...

ANDREW Er, thank you Arlene, but I don't think that will be necessary. Perhaps we could move on now to the influence of American English on the language ... (*fade*)

- Students can discuss what in the discussion shows us the opinions.

D
- Apply the discussion to the students' language(s).

Language work

6 Reference within a text

A
- Read the introduction with the students. Does the same apply in their country/countries?
- Students discuss the examples in pairs or small groups.

Answers
1 makes a special case for a woman (the *-ess* ending, which is a diminutive) when it is not strictly necessary; the alternative is just *mayor*
2 excludes the possibility of the chair being a woman; alternatives are *chair/chairperson*
3 excludes women; alternative is *the average person*
4 excludes women from the working environment; alternatives are *workers* (can have left-wing political connotations) or *working people*

5 pronoun *his* refers to a non-gender-specific subject (*anyone*); alternative is *their*

6 grammatical mismatch of singular subject (*anyone*) and plural pronoun (*their*); alternative is to use plural, e.g. *If people say that, they need their heads examined.*

B This section of the exercise looks at general text reference.

● Students look back to the text to find what the pronouns refer to.

Answers
1 English
2 the British Empire
3 its history in the Empire and position as first foreign language
4 the Celts'
5 Gaelic
6 Welsh
7 bringing Norman French and Latin to England
8 this hybrid language
9 Irish farmers
10 the immigration of groups to America
11 the southern lands of Africa
12 refers to things in order, in this case the three races

● Discuss the two further questions with the students.

Answers
Its (item 8) refers to something which comes later in the text. This is a cataphoric reference. Cataphoric references refer forward rather than back and are generally only used as literary devices, creating suspense, e.g. *She came into the room, looked disdainfully around her, sat with her back to the rest of us and went to sleep. She was a very haughty cat.*

The former empire (item 2) assumes that the reader knows which empire is being referred to. This is an example of exophoric reference – referring to something outside the text.

Note: These two forms of reference are described in the language summary, but there is no exercise work on them as students do not need to use them actively, only to understand their function in terms of reference and be able to understand them.

C ● Students read through the text and rewrite it in better English. Remind students of the use of *it/this/that* as reference items, and if you think it necessary, discuss ways of rewriting sentences constructed around the *he* pronoun, e.g. using *he or she*, making them passive, making them plural.

Model answer
Someone – I don't know who – once wrote something very interesting about language. This person wrote that men's language and women's language were actually quite different because the former reflects the world of the worker while the latter reflects the world of the home. The idea that the two should be different may have been true some years ago when many professions were very male-dominated and men only mixed with each other, but these professions, for example, the fire service, the police force and bartenders, are now rather more mixed, and can be joined by anyone who so desires. Whatever else can be said about language, I think that it is human beings' use of language that makes us different from animals in that it is unique. Use of language is essential to live life as a full human being – just imagine deaf and dumb people; they are treated like idiots. But whatever language a person speaks, however he or she speaks it, that person is accepted into society.

Further practice: Workbook Unit 20, Exercise 5.

7 Formal and informal verbs

A ● Read the introduction to the exercise with the students. Tell them that this is looking at some more formal equivalents to multi-word verbs.
● Students complete the exercise in pairs. If you do not wish to replay the tape, photocopy and distribute the tapescript on the previous page.

Answers
1 lives on/survives   2 set up/establish
3 work it out/solve   4 point out/specify
5 go on/talk excessively   6 make out/understand
7 came about/originate   8 move on/progress

● Students can reformulate the sentences, using the more formal verbs. Make sure they make any necessary changes, e.g. to remove the word *originally* in item 7.

B ● Students enter the words in their chart.

Further practice: There is a final round-up exercise on multi-word verbs in the Workbook, Unit 20, Exercise 6 a – d . This may be a good opportunity to have a general discussion about the students' charts, to check what meanings of participles they have found, and to find out if there are problems with any verbs.

Pronunciation

8 Sound-spelling correspondences (2)

This exercise is similar to the one in Unit 15, Exercise 11, but it deals with the diphthongs in English.

A ● Remind students of the exercise in Unit 15.
● Students read through the list of words, and practise the diphthongs after the tape. (Ensure that students understand that a diphthong is two vowel sounds together, as reflected in the phonetic symbol.)
● If there are any distinctions which your students find particularly difficult, practise as necessary.

B ● Students work in pairs to say each of the words and decide which diphthong each contains. They then complete their chart.

Answers
/eɪ/   bay: break, eight, gauge, gaol, late, they, train
/aɪ/   by: aisle, dye, either, high, lie, time
/ɔɪ/   boy: noise
/əʊ/   bow: brooch, home, mauve, road, sew, though, toe
/aʊ/   bough: cow, out
/ɪə/   beer: fear, here, idea, weird, year
/eə/   bare: pair, pear
/ʊə/   boor: during, fewer, dour, sure *
* Often pronounced /ɔː/ .

● Play the tape for students to check their answers and to practise the pronunciation. Remind them that they now have the most common spellings of all the English diphthongs.

C ● Students work in pairs to complete their charts.
● Monitor as they are doing this, and do any practise necessary if students are having problems with particular diphthongs.
● Make sure students check each other's charts to ensure they have completed them correctly. See the notes on page 100 of this book (Unit 15, Exercise 11) for more information on this exercise type.

Writing skills

9 Using textual references

This exercise helps students forward from understanding of a number of textual references to using them in a piece of writing.

A Discuss the first part of the exercise with the students. They then go through the text underlining the references.

Answers
line 6   *It* (Krio)
line 11   *they* (the captured tribes people)
line 14   *the latter two languages* (French and Portuguese)
line 18   *that time* (the 18th century)
line 20   *This* (the abolition of the slave trade)
line 22   *they* (slaves returning to Sierra Leone)
line 22   *their* (the slaves)
line 23   *them* (the slaves)
line 23   *it* (their language)
line 24   *Its* (the language's)
line 26   *that* (position)

- Students read through and match the phrases in italics with their functions.

Answers
a *originally, initially*
b *subsequently, the next stage, its final influence*
c *as a direct result of, consequently, this meant that*
d *over hundreds of years*
e *the current position*

B
- Students go back to their charts in Exercise 2C and write a chronological summary of the development of English, starting with the words given. They should use the expressions from the text, and think carefully about their use of textual reference.
- This could be done individually for homework, or in groups in the class.

Model summary
The language originally spoken in the British Isles was that of the Celts, but the islands were invaded in 449 AD by tribes from what is now Denmark and Germany, and consequently, the language of one of these tribes – the Angles – became the vernacular.

The language was further changed during the 8th, 9th and 10th centuries with the Viking invasions of England. Then in the 11th century the Norman invasion of 1066 introduced Norman French and Latin to the country, as a direct result of which English now has such a large vocabulary.

The first move out of the British Isles was to South Asia, when the East India Company started trading on the Indian sub-continent. Subsequently, from 1620, groups of emigrants from England and Ireland settled in North America, taking the language with them. This resulted in the development of what has become the most influential variety of English – American English.

The next stage in the spread of English was its introduction to Australia and South Africa in the 18th century. it quickly became established in both countries. Also, over the two centuries from 1600 to the early 1800s English was firmly established as the common official language in India, where consequently it still remains an official language.

The current position of English is that it is the most widely spoken language in the world (though Chinese has a greater number of speakers), spoken as a mother tongue by several countries developed world and as a second language by a substantial proportion of the developing world. It is also widely learnt as a foreign language across the world and is considered the international language of fields such as aviation and commerce.

Further practice: Workbook Unit 20, Exercise 7.

Speaking skills

10 Giving a formal speech

A
- Familiarise the students with the tape by asking them to listen and make notes of the position of each of the speakers.
- Play the tape again and ask students to pick out features that are the same as in the written summary, i.e. those words in italic in the Krio text.

Answers
Geoff: *consequently* (result)
Melvyn: none
Rachel: *as a result* (result)
Arlene: none

- Students listen again or look at the tapescript on page 183 and write down phrases expressing sequence, result or conclusion.

Answers
1 sequencing: *my first/second/final point* (Melvyn), *first/second* (Arlene)
2 result: *consequently, then* (Geoff), *as a result* (Rachel)
3 conclusion: *in essence* (Melvyn), *in conclusion* (Arlene)

Tapescript
See page 183 of the Students' Book.

B
- Students check their answers in pairs.
- In the same pairs, they choose two of the topics given (or others connected with the theme of language/language change if they wish), and discuss them. Make sure they make notes, or they will find it difficult to write a speech.
- Students follow the procedure to write a short talk, using the expressions from above.
- Students give their talks to the class. They should not be more than one minute each.

Note: In a weak class, or to save time, divide the class into four groups and allocate one topic per group. The group prepares the speech together and chooses one person to deliver it.
Alternatively, treat the topic as a debate (see Unit 6, Exercise 19), or allow students to choose topics they are interested in to talk about, using the procedure and expressions given in this exercise.

Final task

11 Different styles of writing

This exercise is a brief look at stylistics, but is handled on a very simple level. It is not intended to be taken very seriously.

A
- Discuss the concept with the students of the way that we change our language according to the person we speak to. (In most European languages this will be a familiar concept, because of the use of formal and informal forms of *you*. Likewise, Oriental languages have even more pronounced distinctions.)
- Students discuss the two questions in groups, relating them to their own languages. Discuss as a class, either to ensure that the whole class agrees (in a monolingual class) or comparing languages (in a multilingual class).
- Transfer the discussion to English: how can levels of

formality be put across in English? (Discuss multi-word verbs, adjectives, contractions in writing etc.) Remind students of exercises throughout the book where levels of formality have been addressed, e.g. spoken/written reviews in Unit 11, writing formal/informal letters (Units 4 and 9), comparing multi-word and Latinate verbs (this unit, Exercise 7), the style of writing used in children's books (Unit 15), literary style (Unit 16) etc.

B ● Explain the jigsaw reading activity to the students. They work in groups of three and each read a different text.
   ● As they read, they make notes as directed about the narrator, the events and the style of language. They should note the following:
   STUDENT A: external narrator (we don't know who); the style is quite literary (use of dramatic adjectives, adverbs such as *Suddenly* etc, use of metaphor *fifty sheep followed the newspaper*, foreign words *frisson*, etc)
   STUDENT B: written by a policeman; the style is that of a report (factual use of times etc, no adjectives etc. and to the point)
   STUDENT C: informal letter style, written by the tour guide to a friend (contractions, fillers such as *well* and *anyway*, rhetorical questions, indefinite times and descriptions, e.g. *one-ish*, informal vocabulary such as *pinched* [stolen], *bloke* [man])

C ● Students use the information they have got to reconstruct the story, and to describe the characters involved.
   ● As a group, students choose a character and write an account of the incident according to that character. The most obvious characters are: the thief, the second police officer, the victim, another tourist from the bus.
   ● Students should decide what type of account to write, e.g. it could be the thief's statement (factual, probably denying the incident), the victim's statement (factual) or a letter to a friend (informal). Alternatively, it could be a newspaper report by a journalist in the crowd. Discuss the style with students if necessary before they write the account.

Further practice: Workbook Unit 20, Exercise 9.